Around Cape Horn

*A Maritime Artist / Historian's
Account of His 1892 Voyage*

by Charles G. Davis

Edited and Introduced by Captain Neal Parker

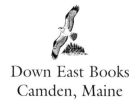

Down East Books
Camden, Maine

ISBN: 0-89272-646-6

Printed and bound at Versa Press, Inc. East Peoria, Illinois

3   2   1

Down East Books
Camden, Maine
Book Orders: 800-685-7962
www.downeastbooks.com
a division of Down East Enterprise,
publishers of Down East magazine

Library of Congress Control Number:2004106343

To all the ship modelers
who toil in their shops,
keeping the tradition alive.

Thanks to Jerry Davis for trusting me with the brig *Lexington* and this manuscript; Art Herrick for documenting much of Charles Davis's life; Richard O'Shea, who many years ago introduced me to the world of ship models; and Mary Riley Edwards for her candid input and support.

The Sailor's Resolve

A sailor on the topsail yard,
    While reefing softly sings,
"I'd rather pick some cherries here
    Than pull on these 'ere strings.

"I'd sooner of a kicking mule
    Be the undisputed boss,
Than haul this weather ear-ring out
    On this 'ere Flemish hoss.

"I'd rather steer my Betsy Jane
    Up to the alter rail,
Than be aloft on this 'ere night,
    A reefin' this 'ere sail.

"I swear that when I get ashore
    I'll splice that lovely lass,
Buy that aforesaid mule as kicks,
    And peddle garden sass."

Portrait of Charles G. Davis taken several years after his 1892 voyage aboard the *James A. Wright*.

Preface

Several years ago I received a call from a gentleman in Portland who was interested in having me restore a ship model his grandfather built. He explained that his grandfather, Charles G. Davis, had been a model builder of some renown. Never was there a greater understatement.

Charles Gerard Davis was one of the world's leading model builders. During the first half of the 20th century, he was acclaimed as a naval architect, artist, historian, and author. His model ships are not readily found outside museums.

In my youth, Charles Davis unwittingly encouraged my interest in the romantic days of seafaring. His writings on the subject are countless. Though his books were an inspiration, they tended to be technical in nature, revealing little about the man other than his love for old sailing vessels. The model I had the pleasure of restoring was of a brig named *Lexington*. Photographs of the model were used to illustrate his 1933 book *The Built Up Ship Model*. When I completed the restoration and returned the model, Charles Davis's grandson brought an old manuscript to my attention. It was handwritten, fragile, and had never been read.

Introduction

A tired old man peered through his window into a bleak winter night. From inside he could hear the hiss of the wind-swept snow. His life spanned two centuries and now, at the age of eighty-eight, he didn't much care for the world he saw. Almost destitute and resigned to leave this earth, his attention was drawn back to a blank scrap of paper before him. He searched his long memory but nothing stood out from his eventful life. Just then the window shook with the full fury of the winter gale outside. His eyes widened as a small grin crept across his face. He was back on the deck of the bark *James A. Wright* as she rounded Cape Horn in the winter of 1893. He laughed quietly to himself, recalling the wonderful foolishness of his youth. Then he began to draw. They were a few pencil lines from a trembling old hand, but anyone who might see the scrap of paper he used as his canvas, would be transported with him back to the storm-tossed sea.

Charles G. Davis was born in Poughkeepsie, New York, in 1870. Growing up on the Hudson River inspired his early romance with the sea. When his family moved to Brooklyn, young Davis took to roving along the docks. One day, at the age of twelve, he was granted permission to board a merchant bark. His visit to the heavily laden vessel stirred him to build his first ship model.

After years of yachting adventures with his father and brother, Davis, still a teenager, became an apprentice draftsman for the famous yacht designer William Gardner. By then Davis was an accomplished artist, never without pencil and paper, ready to capture in simple line a moment, a person, a place.

During three years as a draftsman, Davis's eyesight became strained. His doctor conveniently recommended Davis go to sea, surmising that focusing on distant horizons would effect a cure. Davis eagerly took his doctor's advice. At twenty-two he joined the burdensome three-master *James A. Wright*. She was bound around Cape Horn with a cargo of general merchandise for ports on the west coast of South America.

During his voyage from August 1892 to May 1893, Davis kept a journal of his adventure and illustrated the voyage on whatever scraps of paper he could find.

Charles Davis's account is a well-told tale of a young man's yearning to go to sea. He narrates his story in a manner that reveals his boyish wonder as he enters the harsh reality of life as a sailor. From the moment he signed aboard the *James A. Wright*, Davis had second thoughts about the wisdom of his choice. When the bark finally set sail, leaving New York astern, the uncertain young man fantasized about falling overboard from the rigging on the off chance that some yacht would pick him up. A more honest account is hard to find.

Because Davis was an artist and a relative newcomer to shipboard life, he recorded details that other working seamen would have taken for granted. Unlike some authors of the period, he doesn't belabor the reader with jargon and long-winded descriptions. Instead, Davis paints with words a story that reads more like a letter home.

Davis's account is not just an another sea story. It fills an important historical gap in the popular writings about life at sea. The majority of seafaring lore was penned in the mid 1800s, during the Great Age of Sail, by authors such as Dana and Melville. The next writings leap to the last days of merchant sail in the 1920s and 1930s and include great firsthand accounts by Villiers and Newby. Davis's story breathes life into the last years when sail still ruled the world's oceans. In his first chapter he explains the changes in shipboard life:

"Richard Dana, in his book *Two Years Before the Mast*, has given the truest account of sailors' life ever written, but this was during the forties; things have changed considerably since then and where a ship used to carry thirty men in her forecastle she now carries ten…. and instead of a feeling of fellowship between one end of the ship and the other, the afterguard are now more like professional slavedrivers who make ten men do the work of thirty by the aid of bare fists, brass knuckles, and belaying pins." The life of a sailor would become harder still during the last days of sail. By the 1930s, sailing ships had quadrupled in size while the number of crew stayed the same.

To be sure, Davis's story holds much hardship and deprivation; and, though the captain of the *James A. Wright* seems to go unappreciated by Davis, we discover that Captain Freeman was not an exceptionally hard man. He showed a concern for his crew and gave them greater liberties than they might have expected from other shipmasters of the period. During one Cape Horn gale, the *Wright*'s decks were continually awash. The only dry place aboard was the traditionally forbidden quarterdeck and master's cabin. As Davis describes, "Things got so bad about noontime, the captain ordered all hands to stay aft where the decks were higher; and when our watch was up we went down into the captain's cabin and slept in our oilskins on the polished hardwood floor." That kind of concern by Captain Freeman of men who sailed before the mast was most unusual.

Also revealed through the story, which Davis may not have been aware of, is the relatively indulgent treatment he received from Captain Freeman. In all probability, Freeman recognized Davis was more than a common foremast hand. He certainly observed Davis's art, writing, and well-bred manners. From the time Davis first signed aboard, it was clear to others that Davis was not the experienced seaman he had claimed to be. They correctly suspected he was just an avid yachtsman off on a big ship adventure. However, Davis learned the ropes quickly and earned the respect of his fellow shipmates.

By the end of his voyage, Charles Davis swore he would never go to sea again. He was almost true to his word. Two years later however, Davis made another passage as a foremast hand aboard a three-masted schooner bound for the West Indies. After that he contented himself with yacht racing, for which he developed an excellent reputation.

Davis held many different jobs over the years. He excelled at whatever he put his hand to, but, for reasons unknown, he drifted from one career to another. Davis's work ranged from editor, author, modeler, and yacht designer to government ship inspector during the wars.

During the Great Depression, he and his wife moved to Cazenovia, New York. Davis, who was sixty-four years old, was given a model studio along with a modest stipend by Mr. Remington, heir to the Remington Arms Company. Davis's benefactor wished to learn ship modeling.

The following years were prolific for Davis, but in spite of his celebrity he never gained financial success. He continually undervalued his work and there was no end to the people willing to take advantage of his talents.

Eventually Davis shut out the world around him, cantankerous even to his closest friends. No longer was he the bright vivacious man that he had been in his youth. He sadly witnessed the end of a great era and never fully realized how much he had done to preserve it. Charles G. Davis passed away on January 25 1959.

The manuscript contained in this book was written by Davis from journals he kept during his ten-month passage. Davis revised the journals into a manuscript several years later which he titled *My First Voyage*. By then he was a well-known author and, beginning in 1908, the manuscript was published serially in *Forest and Stream* magazine. This book is predominately from that manuscript. Because a number of pages were missing, passages from the original journals were used to fill in the gaps. Those journals are now part of the Davis Collection at Mystic Seaport

Museum. I have left the text as original as possible. Changes were made if a sentence or paragraph was so unclear as to give the reader pause.

As in most books about the sea, there are numerous references to race, creed, and color. Some of the epithets and comments may seem unkind, but must be viewed in context of time and place. Merchant sailing ships were mostly comprised of multi-national crews. They were, in fact, the best example of a racial melting pot. The heritage of a shipmate was a novelty if you liked the fellow, but an object of derision if you did not. My own sense of propriety called for abbreviating the most offensive references and leaving the reader to fill in the blank.

All of the artwork in this volume is by Charles G. Davis. Some of the drawings were scattered through his early publications and used to illustrate life at sea. Others were made during his voyage all those years ago.

Captain Neal Parker
Rockland, Maine
January, 2004

FACING PAGE: (c. 1877) Newly launched from the Jackson and Sharp shipyard in Wilmington Delaware, the 880-ton bark *James A. Wright* awaits completion. Her basic rigging is set up but her running gear is not rove off. All the *Wright*'s ironwork is freshly galvanised and unpainted. The galley stack protruding from the deckhouse is still unused. In another month it will be black with soot. Missing from the deckhouse are the chocks and boats that the *Wright* eventually carried. Not even her davits, used for launching the jolly boat, are rigged yet with their falls.

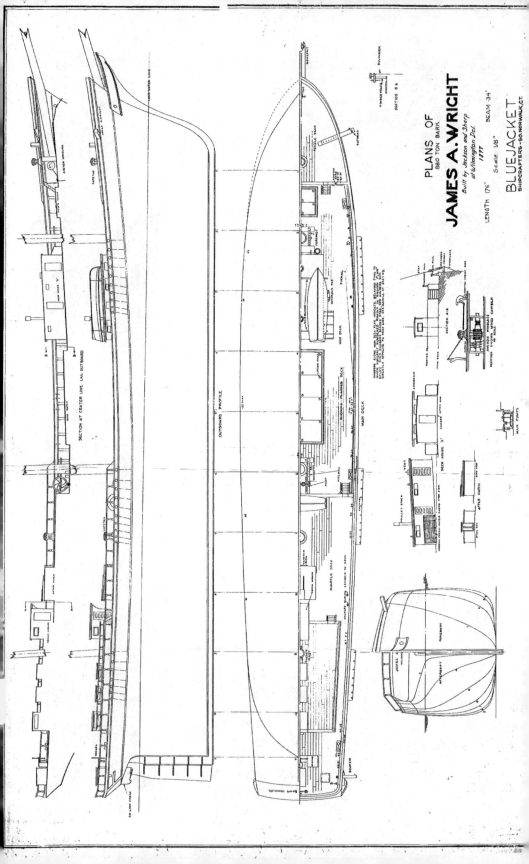

PLANS OF
JAMES A. WRIGHT
380 TON BARK
Built by Jackson and Sharp
at Wilmington Del.
1877
LENGTH 176'   Scale 1/8"   BEAM 34'

BLUEJACKET
SHIPCRAFTERS—SO.NORWALK,CT.

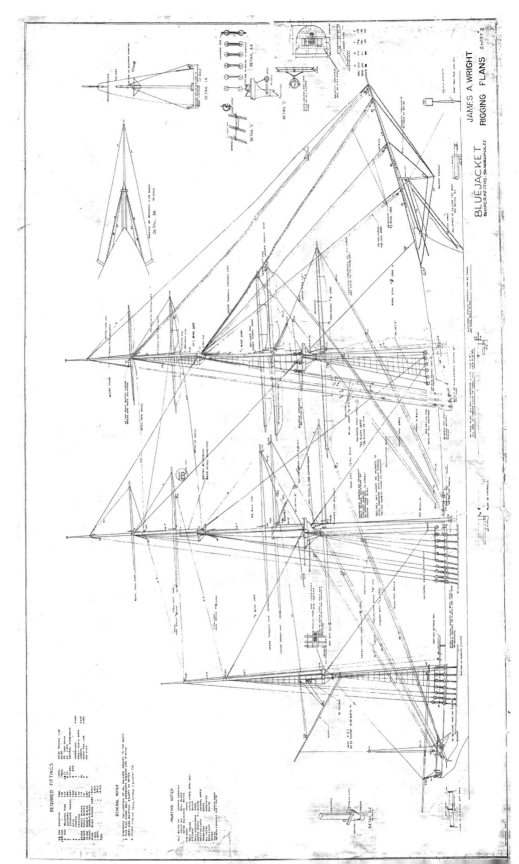

JAMES A. WRIGHT
RIGGING PLANS   SHEET 2

BLUEJACKET
SHIPCRAFTERS · 50 · NORTHAMPT

PRECEDING PAGES: The deck and sail plans of the *James A. Wright* were graciously provided by Blue Jacket Shipcrafters, Inc. and reproduced by permission. Copies of the plans are available for sale. For further information, or to purchase a set of the plans, contact Blue Jacket directly:

Blue Jacket Shipcrafters, Inc.
160 E. Main St.
Searsport, ME 04974
Ph. 800-448-5567
Fax 207-548-9974
E-mail: info@bluejacketinc.com
Web site: www.bluejacketinc.com

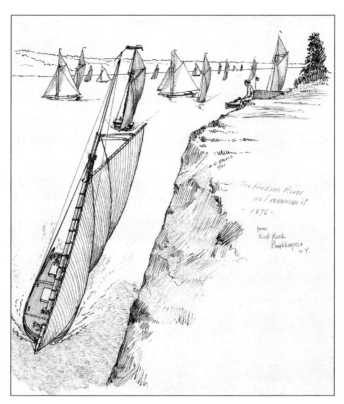

Chapter 1

The little green bark—I decide to go to sea—
My arguments—How I came to go to sea.

W hen but a mere child I used to fairly worship anything relating to the sea. Stories of adventure told by those who had seen the ocean and sailed on it filled me with awe. For hours at a time I used to sit on the town dock at Poughkeepsie, with the broad waters of the Hudson flowing past, and listen to the tales told by the congregation of boatmen who lounged about the freight house waiting for the day boat. The clumsy river sloops and schooners passing up or down the river became full-rigged ships in my imagination, and whenever one of them beating down with the tide happened to stand in toward where I sat on the dock, I'd rehearse all the expressions I had heard the boatmen use. "Porret yer hellum," "Vast ye lubber," or "Hard down yer hellum" were expressions I'd rip out in childish mimicry and when, to prevent wrecking his craft against the pier, the helmsman threw the heavily loaded craft into the wind and she shot past, her bluff bows slapping the wake, forereaching into the wind with her grimy, patched sails giving out cannon-like reports as the canvas slapped in the wind and the sloop filled away on the other tack, to sidle down the river and dwindle to a toy under the high west bank, I'd score a victory over one more bloody pirate and tramp home covered with glory and long to be a man that I might go to sea.

It is the unexpected that always happens and so at the age of twenty-two it came to pass that I went to sea on a bark bound around Cape Horn to Chile, making the round voyage.

The way I came to go was this. Close application to the drafting board in a naval architect's office had broken down my eyesight, compelling a suspension of that kind of work, and it was while idling away my time that the old longing for the sea again attacked me.

Yachting I had had in plenty, both cruising and racing, and had become an adept at small boat handling and sailing. Outdoor living of this kind had browned me to the color of a mulatto and I was a fairly strong young man, yet not accustomed to any real hard work. And so when idleness became a burden to me, I decided to change the monotony for a life I knew nothing at all about. My first move, naturally, was to find a ship and, with this end in view, I spent nearly a week traveling about the piers along South Street, New York.

My usual dress—for I never cared for society—was a blue serge suit, blue flannel shirt, low shoes, and a black felt hat. So my dress was rather in harmony with my surroundings, but the shrewd eyes of the shipping men probably detected something in my looks that told them I was not very salty.

Old Captain Curtis of the San Francisco clipper *State of Maine*, when I gained admittance to him in his cabin, spoke very kindly but advised me to stay ashore and refused to take me, saying he only carried experienced seamen and but few of them.

My reception was the same on all of them and I wondered how it was any sailor got a job. I was standing on a corner after an unsuccessful sally aboard a ship when I saw something that showed me there was another side to a sailor's life and one which I knew nothing of. A truck loaded with bags and chests and a crowd of seamen sitting atop of them drove down on the pier to a bark that was ready to sail. How was it these men got their job and how was it they all came along at once in one load? That was something I pondered over that night and next day, the first day of August 1892, I found out. My chum Bob accompanied me that day and when we came to pier nine we saw a bark on either bow of which in white letters was painted the name *James A. Wright* and under this on her elliptical stern was an American shield worked in colors—as I well remember for it was I who repainted it as the ship lay anchored off the Chilean shore—and the name Boston U.S.A.

Her foremast was decorated with various festoons of sails that had been sent up like so many bags slung in the middle on gauntlines by the gang of riggers who were just then lined out along the fore yard hauling out and bending on the fore-sail as one of their number on deck slacked the gauntline on which that sail was sus-pended.

With many a "Yo! Ho! Heave 'em!" The heavy, many-patched, and many-col-ored canvas was stretched along the yard and its upper edge secured with rovering to the iron rod called the jack stay that was secured by eyes along the top of each yard.

After watching these men and admiring the freedom with which they worked high up in the air on slender footropes, I turned my attention to the bark's deck.

She was what is known as a half-decked vessel; that is, she had a raised deck level with the top of her bulwarks that extended from the stern to amidships, end-ing just abaft the mainmast in the waist, as the middle of a vessel is called. Here a ladder on either side led down to the main deck, some four feet below, which ex-tended forward to within about twenty feet of the bow, where there was another raised deck called the forecastle head. The half-deck aft was designated as the poop. Just abaft the foremast was a long white deckhouse with the galley in the after end of it and the forecastle (fo'c'sle) or sailors' quarters in the forward end, with a nar-row compartment between the two called the carpenter shop, where all the tools were kept. On top of this house and turned upside down on skids were two large white boats, while aft across the front of the poop was a smaller boat lashed upside down on deck. The rest of the after part of the ship was given up to a raised hatch cover, called the booby hatch, set over the after hatch, the raised cabin trunk from just abaft the booby hatch to within about fifteen feet of the stern, with its little square coach house forming the doorway in the forward end, a square skylight aft of the mizzen mast that went through the deck or roof of this after house, a raised cuddy on the port side to cover the after companionway stairs. Wheelbox and steer-ing wheel occupied the after deck.

A motley-looking group of men were assembled around the main hatch down on the main deck watching the stevedores cramming and jamming in the last of her cargo.

"Ask for the mate," said Bob as I left him and swung myself into her channels and so over her rail onto the deck. Clerks, stevedores, and boarding-house runners mostly composed the crowd on the *Wright*'s deck.

Stepping to the open galley door, I asked the darkey cook within if the mate was around.

"Yas! Dat's 'im over dere," indicating a man of medium build who was just coming down the poop ladder. An old battered straw hat, yellow from exposure to the weather, covered the head of this individual, whose bristling, stubby beard, square jaw, and cruel, restless black eyes indicated a nature both energetic and bullying. A cotton shirt, baggy-kneed, threadbare trousers, and red leather slippers completed the make up of the man I met on his way forward and asked if he had his crew shipped yet.

"Don't know! Don't know nawthing 'bout 'em!" was the curt reply as he passed on without even pausing to see what else I wanted. A man standing near heard my question and told me to go see Johnnie Walker at the Sailors' Home, that he was going to put the crew aboard; and so I found the key of the way to go to sea. How long I might have wandered about the docks trying to get a position is doubtful, but had I known more about it at the start, I could have gone directly to any sailors' boarding house, of which there are only too many, and told them I wanted to go to sea. They would have found me a ship quickly enough.

Bob said he knew where the Sailors' Home was, it was on Cherry Street; but, we walked several blocks before we found it at number 190. The atmosphere, the quaint-looking signs, and the character of the people we met in our walk down "Cherry Avenue"—as I afterward learned the seamen called this street—put me in mind of Dickens's writings more than any place I was ever in. Yellow birds, cockatoos, and parrots, occasionally a black bird in a large wicker cage, the immensely fat dames, and bleary-eyed, rum-soaked males were the living images of those characters Dickens peopled his stories with—even the dingy windowpanes, rickety furniture, and the hollows worn in the stone thresholds were suggestive of that greatest of all character-writer's works.

Once we saw the name Sailors' Home painted over the doorway of a dirty little basement hovel, but no sooner did I descend the steps and see the gin mill into which I had stepped than I knew that was not the home I was looking for. A fat dame fathoms in circumference sat puffing a short black claypipe and she referred me, in answer to my inquiries, to a card near the door, on which was printed a list of all the union boarding houses. Here I saw the address, number 190, of the home I was in search of. I knew it a block away by a large white sign painted on the side of the building, which towered several stories above its neighbors. So bidding Bob wait at the corner, I went on, up the broad stone steps between granite columns, four of which supported the face of the building to the height of the second story, and enquired of several sailors who sat tilted back in their chairs on the veranda, smoking, for Johnnie Walker. They told me to go on in, he was in the office. So there I found him and applied for a position as able seaman on the *James A. Wright*.

"Where are you stopping?" asked Johnnie.

"With some friends over in Brooklyn," I answered. And then told a lie by adding, "I've just come on from Philadelphia."

He sized me up for a second and then said, "Bring your bag over, she sails in a day or two."

"All right," said I, "I'll have it here this afternoon." And tickled to think I was at last shipped, I rejoined Bob in a highly delighted state of mind.

He went out to South Brooklyn with me and helped me select from the assortment I had, such things as we thought a common foremast hand would be likely to possess. The bag, in which all these were then stuffed, was one Bob's father, Captain Edward Johnson, had used several years in his voyages to and from the West Indies in the old sugar bark *Rebecca Carusuo*; so the bag bore every indication of having been to sea even if I did not.

I bid farewell to my sister and, riding the front platform of the trolley car into Brooklyn, I realized just what a serious move I was making. When I reached the ferry I had to pocket my pride, shoulder my bag, and enter through the ferry house, where the horses go. Perhaps I was making such a jackass of myself as to warrant this but, having come thus far, I was not to be stopped by a trifle.

It was three in the afternoon when I tossed my clothes bag onto the floor of the office at the Sailors' Home, signed my name in a book, got a key to room number twenty-one, and saw Johnnie Walker lock my bag up in a room that was piled nearly full of chests, bags, and old battered trunks lashed with rope.

I looked about the Home, went into the library where periodicals of all kinds lay on the tables and cribbage, chess, and backgammon boards stood in every corner. Sailors of all nationalities sat or stood about in groups, smoking and spinning yarns. I sauntered about the hallways and sitting rooms and then went out to walk until dark.

I got my supper at a restaurant and on my way to the Home to turn in for the night I bought a little standard diary for the year 1892. That night in my room I made my first entry in it and did so every day for two hundred and ninety-one days thereafter, or until we were paid off at Wilmington, Delaware, at the end of the voyage. And it is from this log, as I called it, this yarn has been written with no attempt at embellishment or exaggeration. There are enough stories of fiction already printed for those who want to read exciting yarns. The object of this narrative is to give the man of the present day some idea of just what a sailor's life was in 1892.

Richard Dana, in his book *Two Years Before the Mast,* has given the truest account of sailors' life ever written, but this was during the forties; things have changed considerably since then and where a ship used to carry thirty men in her forecastle she now carries ten, single topsails have been divided into double topsails and, instead of a feeling of fellowship between one end of the ship and the other, the afterguard are now more like professional slavedrivers who make ten men do the work of thirty by the aid of bare fists, brass knuckles, and belaying pins.

August 2, 1892. My next entry was made in Dennett's Lunchroom on Park Row, where I had gone to eat and kill time until one P.M., when I was to meet my brother and bid him goodbye, my parents being away at the seashore at that time.

I had arisen at six, had my breakfast in the large dining room of the Home, and then Johnnie Walker told two other men and me to go to the U.S. Shipping Commissioner's office, which I found to my surprise was at the corner of White-hall and Pearl streets, within a block of the office where, for several years, I had been working.

We found five other men with the runners from the boarding houses where they had been staying. They were waiting at the door, and as soon as the commis-sioner appeared we all followed to a large room on the second floor and stood out-side a railing behind which many clerks were busy at desks.

As our names were called, we stepped up to the railing and gave our ages, birthplaces, etc. When it was my turn, the clerk put down my height: five-feet-eight, color of my eyes: blue, hair: black, and general complexion as dark. Then I signed my name to the ship's articles, where I noticed the crew numbered only eight. With captain, two mates, cook, and cabin boy that made just thirteen souls in all to man the _James A. Wright_ of 880 registered tons burden for a voyage, not to exceed two years, to such ports on the coast of Chile as the captain might direct and back to a port in the U.S., wages eighteen dollars a month. Then I signed a note—called an advance note—which Johnnie Walker took and which was good for two months of my pay, or thirty-five dollars. From this my expenses at the home would be deducted, along with the cost of whatever articles I might buy at the store in the basement of the home.

Standing apart and scanning the men who would be his crew, his subjects over which he was to be king for two years, stood Captain C. H. Freeman, a Cape Cod man whose ancestors for several generations had been sea captains. He stood over six feet tall and was gigantic in every proportion. His face was a stern, yet pleasing one, showing a perfect profile with blue eyes and a broad high forehead that con-trasted strongly with the unshaven, cruel-looking dark face of Mr. Humphill (but we called him Hill for brevity), the mate, who stood smirking beside him.

When all were signed and Johnnie had four notes of thirty-five dollars each tucked away in his pocket, he told us to clear out and the crowd shuffled noisily down the stairs to the street.

I had a long talk with Will when I met him at one o'clock and then, although it was raining hard, I went over to Brooklyn and bade Bob goodbye, feeling very much like an animal going back into its cage when I returned to the Home that night.

The entry made on August 3, 1892 was a rather confused one, but it well illustrated my feelings. Here was I, a gentleman's son, who had always had a good home and loving parents, leaving all the luxuries I was used to and selling myself into modern slavery for what?—for the fun of it.

I found very little fun but got training in good hard work and endurance such as I would not have tolerated for a day ashore. I had signed on as one of a crew of eight; six of whom were not over twenty-two years of age, the other two being over fifty, who were to work a vessel that required all hands to one topsail. And I had signed on as an able seaman. I became one, before I got back, but at that time I had a great deal to learn. I knew the names of all the spars, sails, and standing rigging; but of the running rigging, the gear, I knew nothing.

After breakfast we three *Wright* men went into the store in the basement of the Home and completed our equipment. Following Johnnie's suggestions, I found there was a great deal I needed: a straw mattress, a pair of rubber boots, a suit of oilskins and a sou'wester, mittens and six pairs of woolen socks, soap and tobacco, and shirts and hats were some of the many articles I took from the Home.

At about nine o'clock, when all was ready, the horse was hitched to the truck that stood at the curb and into which we put all our belongings. Then, with a farewell to everybody and a crack of the whip, we started for the dock and sea with Johnnie Walker driving and Alexanders, the manager of the Home, on the seat beside him.

Chapter 2

The bark James A. Wright — The Sailor's Home — We sign the articles — Leaving the dock — Setting sail — Our pilot — The tug leaves us.

I cannot begin to describe my feelings during that ride. One minute I felt as happy as could be and the next I was half tempted to jump off the truck and run. Then as we passed Wall Street Ferry and met the crowd of businessmen coming out of the ferryhouse, my heart went into my shoes. What would my friends think if they should see me perched up among the bags and chests like a common Swede along with three other sailors, one of whom was decidedly drunk. Surely their good opinion of me would not be strengthened any. But to my relief I didn't see a face I knew in all the crowd. I didn't want my new companions to think I was any better than they, by having some gentleman come up and speak to me. If they did, I would have had a harder time.

As is always the case when a ship is outward bound, there were idlers on the dock to see her off. They closed around us as we drove alongside the bark and tossed our bags over the rail. They wanted to see "the crowd," as a crew is called, and make comments on us.

As soon as our feet struck the deck, the first and second mates told us to clear out the fo'c'sle and change our clothes.

At the time, I didn't even know where the fo'c'sle was; but I soon found out. It was piled full of hawsers, old rope, wood, and barrels of coal. The other four men, making the rest of our crew, were there, having come from different boarding homes. We piled all the duffel on the fore hatch, threw our bags into the bunks, and, of course, the bunk a man's bag went into was that man's for the voyage. The fo'c'sle was in the forward end of the deck house that was built just abaft the foremast and was a dark little box entered by two doors on each side, with a double row of bunks that looked more like stalls than bedplaces. There were bunks for ten. I put my clothes bag into the lower fore and aft bunk on the port side as the upper one was already taken by Joe, a young Hollander my own age, who turned out to be in the same watch with me. I changed my serge suit for a suit of dungarees with the breeches about six inches too long in the legs.

We didn't have long to change our clothes before the mates came to the fo'c'sle door to get us to turn to, but in the short time we did have I was watching the rest of the crew. They all seemed cheerful enough and were all but one quite young; the one exception was Jim, an old codger whose nationality no one could determine, but whose age was close on to sixty. He, by the aid of his whisky bottle, was fast getting drunk. Then there was a powerful young Swiss who went by the name of Fred and was kind of a queer character; he also came from the Home along with Bill, a Norwegian with a long pointed beard, and me. The others were Kaiser, a little bit of a short German just up to my shoulder; Peter, a Spaniard; and Charlie, a Prussian who turned out to be the strongest man on the ship. These were the men who would be my companions for close on to a year and it was but natural we should make ourselves acquainted.

When we stepped on deck we were put at once to work passing the towing hawser, a great big twelve-strand rope as big around as your legs. We fisted it aft onto the poop deck and down to the tug lying close under our stern, waiting to pull us out into the river. I had been aboard several ships before this, but never as I now found myself and I cast my eyes about to see what sort of a craft it was that was to be my home.

The mizzen mast pierced the afterhouse just abaft the companionway. This part of the ship was sacred to the use of the officers alone. No foremast hand ever thought of intruding there unless ordered to do something aft. But now, with the decks all littered with people from the shore and dunnage—such as loose boards, firewood, barrels of coal, etc.—the crew went everywhere and was kept busy from one end of the ship to the other by the mates. While we were passing the hawser aft outside the rigging to the tug for a towing line, Johnnie Walker came up to me to give me what money was due me before we sailed. Our advance money was thirty-five dollars, two months pay; out of this was deducted my board at the Home, such clothes, boots, bedding, etc. as I had bought there and I was surprised to see five dollars was charged for the "chance." It footed up so that nine dollars was due me but I was so anxious to get to sea at any price that I said, "All right give me nine dollars then." But no, Johnnie wanted something more for himself, and in a wheedling begging tone kept hinting until, to get rid of him, I took the five-dollar bill he kept offering me and left him, for I had no time to argue then and he knew it.

When all was ready, those who were not going on the voyage jumped ashore. The tug started to puff and slowly, very slowly, the bark began to back along the pier. The crowd on the dock threw our mooring lines off and followed us out to the end of the dock, some to shout farewell, others simply drawn by curiosity. We on the bark had our hands full pulling in wet and dripping hawsers, and getting the heavy fenders on deck. But I managed to find time to glance ashore just as we were leaving the dock and there, standing a full head above the crowd was Bob, looking rather dubious but still bravely waving a farewell to me.

And now there was no retreating. So, pulling my thoughts together, I made up my mind to go on to the end. It was a beautiful clear day, the East River was alive with ferry boats, tugboats, smacks, and schooners; while down the bay was a fleet of outward-bounders. To make the most of the westerly wind and save towing, the schooners were all under sail, but the square riggers, like ourselves, all had a tug ahead. The atmosphere was so clear the red houses on the Bayonne shore back of the Statue of Liberty seemed closer than usual, while Bay Ridge, with its fleet of yachts, looked strange and unfamiliar.

I had never viewed the shores from so high a platform as I was now on and perhaps that was the reason. We braced round the main yards, and in doing so the topsail brace parted; and Bill and I went up to get hold of it and splice it. From here, as we sat on the main yard, I could see the streets opening up along South Brooklyn as we passed them; and I could trace out my home on 47th Street and even see the row of houses it was in, the brick school house on the corner, and the little church spire beyond. On deck the heat was intense and all hands were hard at work. All the fenders were put down the fore hatch, the barrels of coal were rolled under the fo'c'sle head, and all the spare lumber was lashed and re-lashed across the main hatch. Then sheets and tacks were got out and bent on and the anchors hove up on the bow and lashed.

I never had done any really hard work before, but now I was working like a stevedore; my pride would not let me hang back. I'd do as much as the rest or drop, and when an order was given I jumped to obey, although many of the orders were Greek to me and I had to wait until someone else took hold first. But I showed I was willing, and this alone was probably what saved me from abuse for my ignorance. Then, although I was half dead already, we were ordered aloft to loose everything. I climbed up the main rigging with some, while others went up and loosed the sails on the foremast. I never knew how the sails were kept on the yards until I lay out on the topsail yard and, imitating the others, began to cast off the gaskets.

Then, when all hands had come down on deck, we cleated home the lower topsails and then started to hoist the fore topsails. But Jim had snuck into the fo'c'sle as soon as he came down from aloft and was not missed until we tallied on to the fall. Then the mate saw he was missing and, while the second mate and the rest of us slowly hoisted the heavy yard in time to a "chantey" sung by the second mate, he went forward to hunt up Jim. The next thing I knew I heard some swearing and there was the mate dragging him by one leg aft to the main hatch. Jim was dead drunk and limp as a rag. The combined kicks of the captain and mate had no effect on him, so they left him alone after sousing him from head to foot with a couple of buckets of salt water to sober him up. I noticed as he lay there on his side that one ear was full of water and so it stayed until the sun drank it up and his coarse red skin was turned to a bright scarlet by the sun.

Sail after sail was mast-headed and sheeted home while I did my best to remember where the different ropes led. The gear was old and worn, and our crew none too large; very few vessels have large crews nowadays, so when we came to the heavy main topsail, the captain, cook, and all hands tallied on.

Going through the Narrows, we were boarded by a pilot, although our captain refused to take him, saying he had waited over an hour for his pilot at the dock and didn't want one now. There was just enough wind in the lower bay to keep full what sail we had set. My strength was well nigh exhausted and I was just beginning to think I could get a minute's rest when the mate came forward with a blue flag on his arm and a couple of rope yarns and told me to secure the flag on the fore royal backstay. So I started up and got halfway up the top mast rigging when my strength nearly failed me. I hung close to the ratlines for a minute, waiting for my head to stop spinning, and then slowly crawled up the to'gallant rigging. More than once I thought I would pitch backward and go overboard. I was completely exhausted and began to feel really indifferent as to whether I fell or not. How I wished then that I had never undertaken such a step. Oh, how I wished some yacht would come near enough to pick me up if I fell overboard. For there were several yachts in sight that I knew and had sailed on more than once. I would gladly have dropped over and taken my chances of being picked up. Would the tugboat captain take me back? No! I knew he would not; and so my thoughts ran.

I reached the royal rigging, secured the flag, and noticed as it blew out that it was the blue peter, the pilot flag. Looking ahead as I made my way slowly down, I saw the flag was a signal, for there lay a pilot boat at anchor just ahead of us; her large blue flag flying from a long pole at the main topmast. As I watched, a boat put off from her side and pulled off to intercept us. Our tug then slowed down, the heavy hawser sagging and dipping into the water, but still the bark forged ahead so it took some skill for the men in the pilot's yawl to hook on to our main chains. But they knew their business and made no effort to catch the line hove to them by our mate. They caught the main chains with their boat hook while the pilot, disdaining the use of the side ladder our captain had thrown over for him, dropped into the boat from the channels, and boat and all were soon far astern.

Off to the eastward a breeze was showing on the water and a fleet of vessels that had come out of New York ahead of us was close hauled slowly crawling out to sea. Our tug held on until the lightships were out of sight astern, and by that time we were well up with the tail of the fleet and I counted eight ships or barks besides ourselves. We all tallied on to haul the heavy hawser aboard and then the tug, after coming up alongside our counter for his pay, wished us "Happy Voyage" and soon dwindled to a dot of steam astern.

Chapter 3

Picking the watches—Supper—On look out—Calling the watch—My first trick at the wheel—Coffee and washing down—Overhauling the bark's gear—Mates go fishing—Harpooning a porpoise—The effect of the moon on meat.

With the tug went our last connection with New York. Nothing was in sight now astern. The horizon ran a clear unbroken sweep all around, save ahead where the outward-bound ships were beginning to scatter and disappear, some bound south and some east.

The sun was sinking in the west when the mate told all hands to "knock off" the job we were then on (clearing up decks, coiling down, etc.) and come aft on the half deck.

I had partly recovered my wind by that time and Kaiser and I were sweeping off the poop. So, dropping our brooms, we assembled with the rest of the crew to leeward. Captain Freeman stood aft near the wheel and one man, Bill I think it was, was there steering. The first mate, Mr. Hill, first chose one man, then Mr. Stevens, the second mate, picked one and so on until we were divided into two watches. I was in the port or first mate's watch with Joe, Bill, and Peter. We were to have the first watch from eight o'clock until midnight, so we went forward to get our supper.

Among the things I had bought at the Home were a tin quart measure called a "pot" for my tea or coffee, and a shallow, round tin disk that went by the name of "panniken." These I pulled out of my clothes bag along with my blankets, for I would need them that night, and while thus engaged, one of the others went to the galley and brought in the supper. To tell the truth, I messed about putting my bunk in order because I didn't know where the supper was to be got or the manner of eating it, so I waited until someone else went and got it.

I was not left long in doubt as to the way it was to be eaten, for all three pitched in and helped themselves from the food that was in dishpans on the floor. There was a black pan, like my mother used to cook meat in at home, full of what the others called "cracker-hash." Peter cut this into four divisions with his sheath knife and it made us each a good portion, as much as we wanted then to eat. Another pan, an old dishpan with several holes in the bottom, too leaky to hold pea soup any longer, contained four slices of bread per man. The tea was in a large teapot and held enough to give each man his quart "pot" full. But it was black tea, no milk or sugar as I was used to at home, but acceptable even at that to men as tired and hungry as we were then.

Dark and barren as the fo'c'sle was, it was better than the deck. An old cracked lantern swung from a beam in the middle of the room and threw unsteady shadows as the bark rolled. We had a couple of sail-maker's benches at the foot of the bunks; on one of these sat Peter and Joe, while I sat on the edge of my bunk and opposite me was Bill, seated on his chest and smoking his pipe, his long beard smeared with tea drippings.

Thus we sat and talked for some time after supper was over, and were not called until eight bells were struck on the small bell aft and echoed on the heavy ship's bell on the fo'c'sle head, indicating eight o'clock.

I felt very much better when we went on deck; the rest and food had done me good. The night was dark in spite of the multitude of stars overhead. A gentle breeze kept the canvas quiet and, after the other watch had settled down in the fo'c'sle, there was nothing to break the silence but the slight rippling of water at the stern, the wash passing slowly along the sides, and the faint, soft humming of the breeze in the sails and numberless ropes. I had gone on lookout, not caring to trust myself at the wheel yet, and had not been there long before the mate appeared at the ladder and gave me some instructions. He said the bell would be struck aft every half hour and I was to answer it on the bell in the bow and also was to hail the poop and sing out whether the sidelights, which were swung out from each quarter aft, were burning all right or not. Then he left me and I began my lonely beat. Back and forth I walked from one side of the deck to the other, a distance of about eight or ten steps, and never knew time to move so slowly as it did that night. It seemed nearly an hour before I heard the tinkle of the bell aft, and jumping forward I struck one heavy stroke. To see the sidelights I had to lean out on the catheads; they were both burning brightly, green and red, so I shouted aft, "All's well! Sir."

I had two hours on the fo'c'sle head and then was relieved by Peter while Joe relieved Bill at the wheel. Bill, my watch mate, was a Norwegian, a queer kind of a fellow who seldom spoke and, even when obliged to, always made his answers as short as possible. Peter and Joe, both young fellows about my own age, the former a Spaniard, the latter a Hollander, were more talkative and had picked each other as mates on that account. This arrangement suited me to a dot. I did not want to talk and Bill was in the same mood. Back and forth we walked from the galley, which was in the after end of the same house as the fo'c'sle, to the break of the poop or half deck, along the weather side of which the mate was trotting up and down almost on a run, he took such short, quick steps. One minute his figure showed black as ink in the shadows and then white as a ghost when he came out into the clear light of the moon, which had risen shortly after our watch had come on deck and was now well overhead. The shadows of all the square sails lay in patches of ink on the white deck, and came and went as the bark gently rolled them against the moon, making the scene full of life and motion. Ropes swung in and out and their shadows wiggled and squirmed in black lines across the planks and hatches.

Many were the thoughts that came into my head that night as back and forth I walked, one leg slightly bent, the other stretched its full length to meet the incline of the deck, and my whole body swaying to meet the lift and fall of the bow as the bark rose and fell over the long and easy ocean swells, her hull slightly heeling under the full spread of sail.

Seven bells (half past eleven) had been struck and I was waiting every minute to hear the welcome sound of eight bells, when suddenly one short stroke rang out sharp and clear. I did not know what that meant, so I looked over to see what Bill was going to do. He disappeared forward and in another minute I heard his voice giving that peculiar call that penetrates a sleepy sailor's dreams:

"Hay-yah, ya, a, a, a, a, a!, there, you sleepers, turn out!"

Then, when eight bells were finally struck, there came a straggling, sleepy crowd of dark figures from forward. The second mate was now on deck and stood at the break of the poop with the mate.

"The watch is aft, Sir!" one of the other watch then called out and was answered by the second mate to "Relieve the wheel and lookout!"

This was a signal for us to go below, and was promptly obeyed. I pulled off my outer clothes, took off my shoes, and tumbled into my bunk before Joe arrived from the wheel. I thought he was coming down on top of me as he rolled into the bunk above me, the bunk boards creaked so.

My hands burned from the blisters that had raised in my palms from pulling ropes. Few words were spoken that night, for all were tired and I soon fell asleep wondering what made my bed jump and slide so.

It seemed as if I had just fallen asleep when I was wakened by a gruff voice in the doorway bawling, "Turn out now, you sleepers." I didn't want to. I wasn't half slept out yet, my muscles ached and the warm nest under my blankets was so comfortable. The lantern had burned out and it was still night outside. I heard the other fellows drop out onto the floor and grope about, half asleep, looking for their clothes. So out I jumped and got into my clothes, which I had put carefully away in the foot of my bunk when I took them off. I was going to go out as soon as I was dressed but Joe called me back. He sat calmly smoking his pipe and I wondered why we didn't go on deck; but I was green then and had yet to learn the ways of the sea. It is all such little customs as these that make a beginner's life embarrassing. I never thought of these points when I decided to go to sea. I knew I would have to learn the names of the ropes and gear, but never imagined there were so many little customs in the everyday life of a sailor; this you will see a little later when I was at the wheel.

August fourth, we turned out at eight bells, four A.M., and relieved the other watch. It was my turn at the wheel, so aft I went along the lee side. As I took the wheel from Fred, he gave me the compass course we were steering: east-southeast. I noticed he was standing to windward of the wheel, so I did the same. The compass was in a wooden box on the after end of the cabin and could be easily seen from the wheel. A little lantern threw light enough on the face of the compass to make the marks discernable and I watched it sharp to see that the black mark, called the lubber's mark, did not move any. But it did and I put the wheel over to see if it was the right way to bring the bark back to her course, but she fell off more and more. So then I put the wheel over the other way, put it hard over, and was getting scared. I thought she would never come back to her course. The only craft I had ever steered before with a wheel was a yacht and she always minded her helm promptly, so I could not account for the bark's slowness and began to think I was going to make a failure of this part of my undertaking, when suddenly I noticed she was swinging around to her course at an alarming rate. So back went the wheel the other way and I had just got her to within half a point of east-southeast when a dark figure came around the cabin and the mate stuck his face close to the compass to see if she was on her course. And I knew by the way he shoved his face close to mine to see who was steering, that he had noticed the bark's yawing. If it had been bright starlight he would have noticed it in a moment, but it was just that hour of the morning that is neither daylight nor darkness, just at dawn when faint streaks of yellow mark the eastern horizon and everything about the bark appeared hazy and indistinct.

After standing for a moment watching the compass card he said, "Keep her on her course," and went forward again. He had hardly left me when the bark got away from me again and I had another wrestle with the wheel. It was my first "trick" and I had not yet got used to her steering.

At half past four, by the little cheap clock hanging over the compass, I struck one bell and the echo on the heavy bell forward sounded miles away, coming as the sound did under the arching foot of the broad fore and main courses out of which the wind poured, fanning the decks below. I could see a flame through the now-open galley door and knew the cook must be astir.

Soon after I struck two bells, Joe came and took the wheel, telling me to go get my coffee. I stopped at the galley door and the cook, seeing me waiting, asked me if I had my "pot." "No," I answered and ran and got it from my bunk. He then filled it with black coffee and gave me one hardtack to eat with it. Bill was smoking when I came into the fo'c'sle, having finished his coffee, and he didn't go on lookout until I had finished mine. It was getting light enough by this time to see clearly about the decks. The mate was taking off his shoes and stockings and rolling up his breeches when I again took the wheel, and he called Bill down from the lookout and all three came aft with their buckets and brooms and commenced washing down the poop deck. One man drew up water from over the side with a draw bucket and kept filling a barrel standing inside the rail by the main rigging. Another carried two deck bucketsful back and forth to the mate, who threw them about the decks while the other man scrubbed with a broom.

They had cleaned all the deck aft around the cabin when I struck four bells and went forward to take Joe's place carrying water while he took the wheel. It looked easy, when I was steering, to see how Joe carried the buckets, but when I had rolled up my breeches and started aft with two buckets of water, I found it was not as easy as it looked, for me at least, to keep my balance on the wet decks as the bark rolled and lifted to the sea. But I managed to do my part to the mate's satisfaction and all was going on nicely when the mate, returning from a look at the compass aft, stubbed his foot against an eyebolt at the forward end of the cabin on the deck and struck it so his big toe went squarely through the hole. Such a yell he gave! He nearly broke his big toe and for several minutes hopped about trying to hug this injured toe, cursing eyebolts from A to Z. Such swearing as he indulged in can only proceed from the mouth of a deepwater mate; they are the past professors of this art. Old Bill nearly fell off the rail he laughed so, and I could not hold it in and yet was afraid any moment the mate might turn on me for laughing. He hurt his toe pretty severely and soon stopped us washing down and set us next to work with canvas and water scrubbing the white paintwork.

We had a good breakfast when the other watch came on deck and relieved us, and then we turned in and slept all morning. After a dinner, where both watches ate together, all hands were kept at work throughout the afternoon, sending down the main course and bending on a new one. Then all the sails in the sail locker were passed on deck, opened, re-tagged, and stowed away again.

In this way the days and weeks soon slipped along until the bark had been given a thorough overhauling. One day we cast loose every sail on the ship and rebent them; the mate not being satisfied with the way the riggers had done their work, said, "The first breeze of wind we meet will strip every stitch off her."

Some of the sails were indeed a foot or so to one side on the yards.

I was soon familiar with the names and uses of the various ropes and became used to laying out the yards and handling the sails. Then for several days we were kept dangling aloft in the rigging unreeving gear and sending down the blocks so the mate could put new pins or sheaves in them, as the case required. How some of those blocks ever held the strain put upon them was a mystery, for in some the pins were worn through so there was not a quarter-inch of good metal left.

By the time we had been out two weeks, the bark had been put in thorough order and we fell into the regular routine of watch and watch and the work became comparatively easy. We were no longer driven, but after the mate gave us a job he went and talked with the cook at the galley door or else walked about on the poop, sometimes varying the monotony by fishing.

One day the second mate caught several bonito by fishing off the end of the jibboom. He had a gunnysack seized onto the rigging and when he had two big fish in it, he sung out for me to come out to him. I could climb about like a cat now, and soon ran out on the foot ropes. The second mate was a young man with a peculiarly small, wrinkled, and impish face. Stevens was his name, and he often talked to me, so as I got out to him I said, "What luck are you having?"

"Oh! I got two. Do you think you can carry them in?" he asked.

I never saw a bonito and didn't know how big a fish it was, so I said, "Yes, of course I can." But when I got hold of the sack and tried to lift it, I found out my mistake. He was grinning all over and, looking inboard, I saw a broad grin on the cook's black face at the corner of the galley. With the help of the second mate, I got the sack, with its kicking, wiggling fish, balanced across the jibboom and managed to shove it in as far as the cap of the bowsprit. Here it was easier work, as I could stand on the spar instead of the swinging foot rope and get hold of the jib stay to steady myself. But even then I found it took all my strength to lift the sack and swing it around the stays and onto the bowsprit. If I fell I would fall, sack and all, under the bow of the bark, which was cutting through the green seas, sometimes throwing her forefoot out to expose the clear, yellow-copper sheathing and then again plunging until her hawse pipes came down into the roll of white froth she was turning off. Just under the surface of the water I could see several bonito close to the bow, in front of which went a-skipping the mate's hook with a piece of white muslin tied on it.

I took the fish aft to the cook and went to work again sawing the old main yard into kindling wood. It was one of the four spars that were stowed close under the rail along the main deck and on which many a night we lay stretched out sleeping in our watch on deck.

But once more came a cry from forward and the cook came running aft, calling to Joe and me to lay forward and help the mate. We found him hanging over the bow, struggling with a dolphin that he had harpooned and which nearly pulled him overboard. It took all of us, including the cook and second mate, to get the fish over the bow. Then aft we dragged it with such a bump when it came off the fo'c'sle head that you would have thought it was going through the deck.

We dragged it aft as far as the scuppers but once there, it made such a fuss jumping and slapping its tail about that no one cared to get too close to it. I had often read of the beautiful colors this fish turns as it is dying, but either I was color-blind or else this fish was an exception, for I saw nothing beautiful or remarkable. There was a slight tinsel sheen to be seen with some red, green, blue, and yellow casts in it, such as you see in oil floating on the water, but it was not what I had anticipated.

Joe finally killed it by cutting its backbone with an axe and I let him take my clasp-knife to cut it up with. That was on a Saturday afternoon and that night for supper we had fried dolphin's liver, but I didn't care to eat much. Joe hung the meat he had cut off the dolphin under the fo'c'sle head and in the evening, as we sat in the fo'c'sle spinning coppers while the other watch had the deck, Old Jim came in to light his pipe. After he had it lit, he said to Joe, "Ef ye don't want that meat ye got hung up for'd to rot, ye'd better hang it whar the moon won't shine on't."

"Ye?" asked Joe in his broad Holland accent.

"Why?" echoed Jim, with just a touch of scorn in his voice. "Anybody knows 'twill make it maggoty." And for over an hour after he went back on deck all hands in our watch carried on a lively discussion, amid clouds of tobacco smoke, as to whether the moon's rays could make meat rot or not. Some of the men cited instances where the moon had blinded men who slept in its light over night and so affected them that as soon as the sun set they were unable to see.

Chapter 4

Sunday, our wash day—Scraping pitch—Hunger and a scant supper—
My watch mates—How the starboard watch was run—Trouble in our
watch—Peter wants to fight—Painting the fo'c'sle—A flying fish wakes up
Old Jim—Rats—I sit down at the wheel—I didn't know there were foxes
on a ship—Steering by a jury-gear—Squally weather—The slop chest—
Heavy showers—A halyard breaks.

The next day was Sunday and was nearly calm all day, so there was nothing to do after we had washed the decks and swabbed the paintwork but keep one hand at the wheel.

The rest of us got out our accumulation of dirty clothes and proceeded to wash or mend them. Every Sunday we were allowed two deck buckets of fresh water for each watch to wash with; other days we were limited to one bucket of drinking water a day and consequently had none left for washing. When we got our Sunday allowance, we first all stripped and washed ourselves on the fore hatch and then each man—with the same half-bucket of water—washed his clothes. This was not much water to wash a week's dirtying of clothes in; we arranged it so first one man would take all the water and wash, then when he had finished, another washed his clothes and so on until the fourth man.

As a rule, by the time the fourth man went to do his washing, he found a tub full of water that was about as thick as pea soup and black as ink. Sometimes, in fact, it was too thick to soak into his clothes; then he either had to let them trail under the bow overnight on the end of a jib downhaul, or wait and pray for rain.

We had several empty beef barrels that we sawed into halves and made into washtubs; they were, of course, rancid with the smell of beef brine, but far better than nothing.

On this Sunday, I had washed my clothes the night before and hung them up on top of the fo'c'sle to dry. So I spent Sunday morning sewing and making some sketches. I had laid in a stock of drawing paper and pencils before I left and also had a box of watercolors with me. After doing all my sewing, I sat on the spare spars opposite the fo'c'sle door and made a sketch of the bark's decks looking aft, and this is one of the few sketches I managed to save as I sent it home from Valparaiso in my first letter.

During the following week, we were kept on our knees most of the time, scraping the pitch in the seams of the deck. It was no joke to get down on your knees for four hours at a stretch, and then the pitch all stuck and melted on our hands and arms. When we knocked off at suppertime it took about ten minutes to clean the stuff off; and the only thing that could take it off was slush wiped off with a piece of old sailcloth or a handful of rope yarns taken from the shakings barrel that always stood under the fo'c'sle head by the windlass.

Our meals were daily growing smaller and smaller in quantity. The first few days we had more food than we could eat, but that was before the liquor had been worked out of the crew. When they had sweat for several days, those who at first had had no appetites soon became ravenous. When the supper was brought in from the galley and the pans laid on the floor, all four of our watch would be grabbing for bread at once. Several times blows came near to being struck over the way the man who'd cut the cracker-hash had helped himself. Men who had worked and joked all day shoulder to shoulder would squabble and curse over a spoonful more or less of food; and I was as bad as the rest. Hunger made us act more like animals than men, and many a time after I had eaten my pot full of tea, into which I soaked my three slices of bread, I felt as hungry as when I began and became decidedly ugly in temper to think that I could not even satisfy my appetite. While at home, probably at that very moment, my father, mother, brother, and sister were sitting down to supper at the neatly laid-out supper table with china and glassware sparkling in the gaslight and Bridget with her clean apron waiting upon the table. There were no silver knives for me at my supper and my mouth watered when I thought of the large plate of scrambled eggs that used to be my favorite dish at home. Here I was sitting, unwashed and uncombed, with a Norwegian, a Spaniard, and a Dutchman in a smoky, unventilated little box of a fo'c'sle.

Joe, the Dutchman, was the cleanest of the lot and usually sat next to me. Peter, the Spaniard, was disgusting in his talk and as hoggish in his manners. Bill, who always sat on his own chest, would, after each meal, shave off some plug to-bacco, roll it in his hands and, after wetting it, stuff it into his pipe and then sit silent and grimy; his long tangled beard still smeared with grease and tea drippings, he'd puff out clouds of smoke and expectorate all over the floor.

In the other watch it was different. Jim, the old fellow who was drunk when we came aboard, was the tyrant of that watch and made Kaiser—the little Dutch-man—and Fred—a Swiss—wait on him, hand him food at suppertime, and always helped himself first. The other man in that watch was a Prussian, Charlie, as strong as a giant, but as good-natured as a lamb. The cook used to give him all the food that came back from the cabin and he was the only man the cook would allow in his galley except, of course, the mates.

More than once when we were down in bad weather, I have seen Kaiser so hungry he was crying like a child. Several times I tried to console him and that was how I came to find out how the other watch was run. He told me Jim made him wait on him; he said he even had to get out of his bunk some nights to light Jim's pipe. I argued with him and tried to get him to stand up and revolt. But it was no use, he was a Dutchman at heart and was afraid to stand up for himself.

I came near getting myself into trouble by siding with Kaiser. Several times af-terward when I would enter the fo'c'sle during the dogwatches—when both watches were about, smoking and talking—I found Jim in earnest conversation with Peter and Joe, and the result of his yarning soon made itself apparent.

It was one Sunday morning in our watch below, and happened to be Peter's turn to wash the fo'c'sle floor, for we took turn and turn about in our watch, each doing equal work. I noticed Peter looking my way more than usual. We had eaten our breakfast, and all through the meal both Peter and Joe had kept telling how they had to wait on the rest of the watch when they first went to sea; how they had to clean the other men's pans and do all the waiting on the crew, and Peter finally said to me, "Davis, you got to wash out the fo'c'sle after this and bring the grub from the galley."

I expected this and knew Old Jim had put them up to it, so I told Peter to go to a place where the climate is supposed to be warm.

"As long as I work watch and watch with you fellows, I'll do my share and no more," I said as I rolled into my bunk for my morning's sleep.

Peter flared up in a moment and, jumping out on deck, he flourished his fists and shouted, "Come out on deck and show yourself a man."

"You come in here and stop acting like a damn fool; there's enough bulldozing in the other watch without you trying to start any in this," I answered.

Peter continued to threaten to lick anybody or anything until Joe, seeing it was no use, told him to come in and stop his noise, and that was the last of that trouble.

They never tried to impose on anyone after that, but each man did his share and the work went on smoothly in our watch.

We were now getting down pretty close to the line and had run nearly through the north-east trades when one day the mate made us take everything out of the fo'c'sle and paint and varnish it inside from one end to the other. Most of the crew put their blankets, mattresses, and clothes under the fo'c'sle head, but Old Jim and I put ours on top of the house.

It was a cool, airy bunk up there and as yet there was no danger of a wetting from showers; although a week or so later we ran into the smooth, calm belt called the doldrums, and then nearly every day it rained hard enough to wash bed and all clean off the house had we left them there.

One night Old Jim lay peacefully sleeping on his mattress under the long boat on top of the fo'c'sle and I was standing by the carpenter-shop door just beneath him. It was about nine o'clock and our watch had the deck. The bark was sweeping along with her deck at a slight angle and all sail set to a favorable slant of wind. The cook had not yet closed his galley, but was mixing his dough for the next day's bread and a bright bar of light shone out of the galley window onto the lee rail and off over the water to leeward. I was standing close to the house to keep out of the wind when I heard Jim let out a fearful curse. Stepping out so I could look up at him, I saw him feeling about for something. When he found it, he flung it down on deck, saying, "There, Davis, there's another one of your damned flying fish." It had sailed up toward the galley light and hit Jim squarely in the face, waking him up.

Nearly every morning when we washed down the decks, we found three or four flying fish lying about. I had taken two of the largest I could find and cut their wings off and dried them. One pair I had opened, and held so by putting them into a split stick, and hung them way up under the fo'c'sle head on the heel of the bowsprit to dry. The next day when I went to look at them, I found nothing but the stick there. When I examined this out in the light I saw where the wings had gone. The rats had gnawed them off as close to the stick as it could have been cut with a knife, so I never hung any more up there. I managed to save one pair that measured from tip to tip on the fish about fourteen inches and preserved them by giving them a good coat of varnish.

One morning when it was my trick at the wheel, and we had only been out of port a few days, I was standing alongside of it on the gratings, giving it a lazy turn once in a while to keep the bark on her course for she was just creeping along at about two knots an hour. I was watching the flying fish shoot like showers of silver darts away from the side of the bark or the little pink Portuguese man-of-wars (little jellylike masses with two uplifted arms and on each a pinkish, gauzelike circular fan acting as sails), going slowly floating past. But getting tired after a while, I did just what I always did when I was steering a yacht: I sat down.

The watch was busy on some job up forward, and the captain had come up on deck and gone forward with the mate to see about something, leaving me in sole possession of the poop deck. I made myself comfortable on the wheel box and just cast a glance once in a while at the compass to see she kept on her course. Any thoughts were back home in Brooklyn then, and I was living over again in imagination some of the good days I used to have there. I was just thinking to myself as I looked over the rail at the smooth expanse of ocean how the *Freyja,* my father's yacht, would walk ahead of the bark in this breeze. And I saw her in my imagination, all her light canvas set, wrinkling the water as she cut through it. All of a sudden, the captain and mate, who had come aft unobserved by me, turned the corner of the house and looked at me in amazement.

My daydreams vanished like smoke and I realized I was not doing right.

As soon as Captain Freeman recovered from his surprise he exclaimed, "Well! By God! You get down off of there "PDQ" (pretty damn quick) before I help you down, and don't you ever let me catch you in that position again."

I knew he was not as mad as he tried to appear and Mr. Hill, the mate, was nearly choking with laughter behind him. "You stand on both feet," he added. "And don't you take your hands off that wheel. Where do you think you are, off yachting?"

I didn't dare open my mouth while he was looking at me, but as soon as he went down into his cabin, the mate went below by the cabin stairway and I could hear them both roaring with laughter. They liked a little amusement once in a while and more than once they got it at my expense.

One morning the captain stuck his head up the after companionway to take a look at the weather and seeing me standing at the wheel, sleepy and tired after a squally night's work clewing up royals and to'gansels, he made a wry face at me and, imitating a seasick person, said, "Oh! Don't I wish I was home with some of my mother's hot pies." Then smacking his lips, he went below again, leaving me to meditate on the memories his words brought up.

Another time, when we were only a few days out and the second mate was allotting us each some job to keep us busy, he left me until the last and then said, "Davis, you go make foxes."

"Make foxes," I thought, "what the Dickens are foxes doing on a ship?" I had never heard of such a thing.

He noticed me standing looking at him and asked, "What's the matter? Why don't you go make foxes?"

"What do you mean by foxes?" I asked.

"What!" he exclaimed. "You mean to say you don't know what foxes are, and here you shipped as an able seaman? Well, you are a beauty." So he showed me how to unstrand an old rope, take out the good heart strands, and twist them up three at a time with something that looked like what we used to call a "cricket" when I was a boy, only it made no noise. He hooked the rope yarns into a bent nail in this affair that was called a "fox reel," then whirled it 'round and 'round and so twisted the three strands into a small stout cord. This was then rubbed down hard with a piece of old canvas and rolled up into a ball to be used about the rigging for lashings or servings.

One morning at eight o'clock when the watches changed, the second mate called all hands forward and we carried an old topgallant yard aft and laid it across the rail just aft of the wheel. Then our watch went below to get our breakfast and turn in. When we all turned out again at noon and I went aft to the wheel, I found they had rigged up a jury steering gear. A tackle was rove off on each quarter from the ends of the yard to the after side of the rudder. This was taken to the barrel of the wheel, and so we steered the bark for three days. The mate did this because the iron tiller in the rudder head, by which the helm was worked, had come loose. When he tried to unscrew the nuts that held the tiller in place, he found them all rusted fast. He tried every means he could think of to loosen them, from burning oil to shrink them, to applying brute force with all hands and a watch tackle, but it was all no use.

The captain said he would give five dollars for every nut that any man could get off. The helm had to be fixed if we ever expected to round Cape Horn. Finally the cook, a Barbados nigger of considerable intelligence, came aft with a hammer and a cold chisel and got off every nut that was necessary to remove the tiller. They found the tiller had chafed in the rudder head until it had more than half an inch of play and caused the helm to kick severely. But we soon had it wedged up good and solid, fit to round half a dozen Cape Horns, as far as that part of the ship was concerned. But I'd guess the cook's whistling yet for his reward.

Day by day the bark slowly crawled toward the equator. We had been steering nearly east for a couple of weeks and then gradually headed away to the south'ard so as to cross the line far enough to the eastward as to enable us to fetch across the Equatorial Current clear of the Brazil coast. For if a vessel fell short, she would have a hard time beating eastward against the current and strong southeast trade winds far enough to clear the land.

Our bark was taken far enough to the eastward anyway. Some of the fellows said jokingly that if we held on much longer we would see Africa.

Then we ran into squally, showery weather and knew we had left the northeast trades astern. Nearly every night we had to clew up our light sails for some squall that would come up black and threatening enough to make me stand in awe of what was coming. Once or twice we had to up helm and run before it; but as a rule it was clew up royals and haul down the light staysails, then we'd get a drowning downpour of rain and up went the sails again. Yards were boxed about continually; sometimes when we were hauling the main yards for a new slant of wind, it would shift again before we had the braces belayed.

It was hot work running back and forth under such a sun as was now shining down on us each day, heating the deck planks so hot we could not stand on them with our bare feet and causing the pitch to run and lay in soft pools like molasses.

All I wore in such weather was a low-necked undershirt, dungaree breeches, and low shoes. For a head covering, we had each bought a wide-brimmed straw hat from the slop chest, as the supply carried by the ship is called.

I put on my hat one day when it was my turn to relieve Peter at the wheel, and started aft. Just as I cleared the galley, the current of wind sweeping down out of the large mainsail picked my hat off my head and gently set it down on the water to leeward. I followed it as far as the rail and saw it floating astern with an inquisitive seagull having a novel ride on its broad brim. The captain had seen my mishap and as I passed him he asked, "Did you mark the rail where it went over so you can find it again?"

"Oh! No!" I answered. "There's plenty more in the slop chest."

But there was not, and after that I had to stand in the sun wearing only a small cap.

Every American ship is compelled by law to carry what is called a "slop chest," which contains clothes, boots, blankets, oilskins, and such other things as a sailor needs. The law is also supposed to regulate the prices that shall be charged for such articles. Sometimes the captain supplies the slop chest as his own investment, but the crew likes it better when the owners of the ship supply it, for sometimes the captains will work their crew hard so as to wear out clothes and so sell out their "slops" and realize something by the time the voyage is over.

Where we were now, we needed as little clothing as possible, but oilskins were often in demand. Nearly every day we had rain, and some days it would pour all day long. I had never seen such rain before. It did not seem to come down in drops, but fell in sheets and spouted in streams out of all the scuppers. By this time, we had used nearly all the water out of one of the casks stowed alongside the galley, and what little was left was thick with iron rust.

Mr. Hill broached this cask and let the dirty water run off and then we filled it up with rainwater that we caught in barrels. It took us a couple of days carrying water in buckets back and forth to fill it again. Two days of dripping wetness; sails, ropes, clothes, everything was running with water. And yet it was so warm it was not very disagreeable; we just put our oilskins on over our underclothes and went splattering about barefooted.

One blessing of this weather was the drinking water we got. The first shower came when our watch was below and woke us up with its roar as it smote the decks and top of the house. I went to the fo'c'sle door and looked out. Aft, by the poop, the other watch was busy catching the water in barrels and I heard the mate sing out, "Get that funnel out of the carpenter shop, Fred." And saw they were preparing to fill the water cask. Forward the water was pouring off the fo'c'sle head in small waterfalls and for once I got a good drink by putting my mouth to one of the streams.

That noon, when our watch went on deck, we all took our blankets out of our bunks and spread them out to be rained on. We plugged up the scuppers on the main deck and soon had about a foot of water from the galley to the break of the poop, and whenever the mate left us we would spend the time trampling on our blankets to wash them. That night, all hands stripped and went out and had a shower bath and a good scouring with soap, but that was the only thorough washing we had the whole voyage.

It was a curious sight, during the day, to see the showers moving about across the calm ocean. When at the wheel, as there was not much steering to do, I used to watch the showers coming along with the wind. Each one was indicated by a bank of clouds underneath which, like a black veil, hung the water that was falling, some trailing one way, some another as the wind blew it in different directions.

I would see a small cloud on the weather bow, that, in an incredibly short time, mounted in the heavens until nearly over the bark, while under it came what looked like a fog bank rushing along straight for us. By the time it hit I would have my oilskins on and could see not a thing forward but the cabin in front of me, and that was a mass of seething, splattering, white spray.

Sometimes these showers would be accompanied by fierce squalls of wind, so every time the rain came driving along toward us, the mate, who proved a thorough old sea dog, was ready for it. Running up onto the poop so he could command a better view, he would sing out, "Stand by royal halyards!" One man would run to the fore and one to the main and get some of the turns off the pins, ready to let the royals come down on the run should there be wind enough in the squall to require it. How the mate could tell when there was wind in a squall and when there was not, was more than I could see. But he never made a mistake and when he sung out to "Let go!" there was sure to be a squall that justified the order.

Once, we had let go royals and topgallant staysails and were hoisting the main topgallant staysail after the squall had blown over, when something jammed aloft. The three of us could not start it up an inch more, so the mate ran forward and cleared the downhaul. "Now, hoist away," he shouted. "Pull! Pull!" and was working himself into a passion over it. But pull our hardest, we couldn't budge it; so aft he came on a run, took the half-deck ladder in two jumps, and gave a fearful yank on the halyards. "Get hold here!" he ordered. So all of us prepared for a mighty pull. We gave it, but were somewhat startled by the result; for the seats of four pairs of trousers struck the deck with a thump that made us think the mast had come over on top of us, and the fifth man went sprawling off the poop onto the main deck. When the mate painfully picked himself up off the deck, he never stopped to look aloft, but walked aft and muttered, "Go up and splice that." So Joe and I took the parted rope aloft and spliced it together up at the crosstrees, where we found the other end.

Chapter 5

Stealing drinking water at night—Our watch goes aft and kicks for more grub—Fair winds—Crossing the line—I get shaved by Neptune's barber— A close shave—We speak to a blue-noser homeward bound.

There were many hot days when not a drop of rain fell, and how we suffered for lack of drinking water no one knows, unless they have been deprived of it as we were. Every morning after we had washed down the decks, two men got the water for the cook, one on top of the cask pumping and the other carrying the six or seven buckets into the galley. Then, with the cook watching to see we took no more than our allowance, we pumped one bucketful up to the mark the captain had cut in the bucket and this had to last us eight men all day and night. But it never did. Before noontime the bucket would be dry and not another drop could we get until next morning.

But we found a remedy. I took four or five sheets of paper off my drawing pad and rolled them into a long tube. Then when it came our watch on deck at night, I would take this tube with me and pretend to lean over the water cask and doze. It was too dark for the mate to see anything more than that one of the watch was leaning on the cask, asleep. He never suspected I had the bung out and was sucking my fill of water, for every night he drove the bung in hard with a hammer.

But our thirst made us equal to that difficulty and after repeated yanks, first one way then the other, it came out.

When I had satisfied my thirst I would put the bung in and pretend to just wake up, stretching and yawning so the mate could see me, and then Bill would edge around to the cask and get a drink. They were doing the same in the other watch, only instead of sucking it up, Charlie had a small canvas bag just small enough to go through the bunghole; when he hauled that up full, it was enough to give quite a drink.

In this way we satisfied our thirst, but the matter of food we were unable to improve, and the "whack" gradually grew less and less. Many an angry debate was held by our watch after supper as to what should be done. We knew we were not being treated right; the question was "How are we going to get more grub?" We were all determined to do something and so sounded the other watch and proposed all hands go aft and complain. If we had all been of one nationality, all hands would have stuck together; but as it was there were no two who came from the same country.

Old Jim, in the other watch, said, "Wait till we get down in bad weather, if we don't get more then we'll all go aft." Charlie would not do anything, he was getting fed secretly by the cook every night. And poor little Kaiser, as we called him, didn't dare do anything unless Jim did it too. And so matters ran on for several days, until the night of September tenth; we were then five degrees north of the line and all day long had been working hard, bracing the yards about and doing the usual Saturday jobs such as sluicing down the topmasts and the mizzen, and cleaning up generally. The dinner had been poor enough; each man received only about one heaping spoonful of potato hash, a very small whack of pea soup, and two half-slices of bread. However, we comforted ourselves all the afternoon by thinking we would receive a good supper to make up for the dinner. But when I went to the galley that night, the cook only handed me the teapot, bread pan, and some beef and boiled potatoes about the size of eggs, one for each man.

When I set the pans on the fo'c'sle floor, the other three looked at me.

"Fere ish de rest of it?" asked Joe.

"That's all there is," I answered.

"It can't be," said Peter. "The other watch had their cracker-hash."

"Go ask de cook, you must have left some," Joe said.

"Well! I'll go see," I replied for I could hardly believe myself that that was all we were to get. I could easily have eaten all that myself and still had none too much.

The cook got angry when I asked him for more, and said that was all we'd get.

When I told this in the fo'c'sle, there was some cursing, you can bet.

"Who'll go aft?" asked Peter, kicking the pans aside.

"I will," said Joe.

"I'll go," I declared, although I didn't think anything would be accomplished, yet I was going to stick with my mates.

Bill, as usual, said nothing, but rose with the rest and we all four marched aft onto the poop deck with Joe carrying our supper in the pans. The cook looked surprised as we passed the galley and Mr. Stevens, the second mate, looked over at us from the other side of the poop, where some of his watch were busy, and asked, "What are you men doing aft?"

"We want to see the captain," I answered.

Lawrence, the cabin boy, came along just then on his way to the cabin with the clean dishes, and the cook called to him to tell the captain we were waiting to see him.

There was some nervous shifting from one foot to the other while we waited for Captain Freeman to appear. We were out of our element when aft on the poop deck and never felt as comfortable as when on our own, the main deck. But there was no backing out now. When the captain stepped out of the cuddy and confronted us, he had a very stern look on his face and in a harsh voice demanded, "Well! What does this mean? What do you men want here?"

One man looked at another, for we had not chosen a spokesman and each man was waiting for another to speak. Finally, Joe said, "Ve vant more food, sir."

"You do hey! What's the matter with your food?"

"Ve don't get enough, sir. Dot's all ve get for supper," and Joe held out the pan of beef and potatoes. All the other watch had stopped their work to look at us and I noticed Charlie had a sneering kind of a grin on his face. The cook had come aft as far as the break of the poop to hear what might be said of his cooking. Captain Freeman never even looked at the food, but puffed out with anger and exclaimed, "That's all is it? Well, you had better be damned thankful you get that much." And then he added, "What do you want, your whack?"

Our "whack," as it is called, is the allowance of food laid down by law as the sailors' just amount and regulates the bread to so many ounces per day, beef so much, water so much, and so on. But I would like to see the man who made out that scale of allowance fed on it himself for a while. He would not get fat on it, I'll bet.

"No sir, we don't vant our vack, ve vant enough to eat," Joe answered.

"Well, clear out of here now, the lot of you," he ordered. And as we marched forward again he said, "I'll see about your grub in the morning."

We ate what we had for supper. All I had was two small slices of thin bread so full of holes you could shoot the sun through them, a piece of beef as big as my two fingers, and one small potato the size of a silver dollar; this with a pint of black tea was all we had. I was as hungry after I had eaten it as I was before I commenced.

Our kicking did some good, however, for after that day our food was a little better for a while. Next morning the cook asked each one of us as we came to the galley if we wanted our whack or would take what was given us, and, as we didn't want to starve, we took the latter.

We were fast nearing the line now. One day we caught a shift of wind from the westward and the way the bark swept foaming along through the cross seas, formed by the sudden shift of wind, was a grand sight to see.

I happened to have the wheel when it came and so could see how the bark behaved. We had the wind over the starboard quarter, the mainsail hanging in the buntlines, and the fore royal stowed, but she had all the sail she could carry and for the first time I saw her heel over so she shipped water over her rail. On she rushed at a glorious rate, sometimes plunging her bow so that a green sea came over the fo'c'sle head at the cathead and poured aft a rushing torrent all along the lee scuppers, washing the pork barrel box and all aft against the poop, making kindling wood of it and sprinkling the decks with chunks of salt pork and the rock salt in which it was pickled. Then as the stern settled with that peculiar lurch a flying vessel takes as it settles over a sea, her whole lee side would disappear in the suds to leeward; the rigging and stanchion tearing through it in showers of spray wetting the poop deck for about five feet in from the rail.

A couple of days of such wind as this brought us at last to the line and on September sixteenth we crossed it, just forty-four days since leaving New York.

When I was at the wheel that afternoon, the captain told me to keep a good lookout forward as Old Neptune would be coming aboard soon. I was prepared for him, for all that afternoon the mate was busy on the main hatch making something that looked like a wooden razor about three feet long, and I noticed Jim in the carpenter shop combing out a piece of new rope he had unlaid.

I had read in novels how Neptune came aboard and shaved all the green hands on ships when crossing the equator, but I did not know the practice was still kept up. I was expecting something all day, but nothing happened and when I went on lookout on the fo'c'sle head at six o'clock that evening, I had come to the conclusion that nothing was going to happen.

It was a very dark night with no moon or stars in sight. Soon after I had struck six bells, someone came up on the fo'c'sle head.

"Who's that?" I asked and shoved my face close up to Joe's before I could make out who it was.

"It's me, Joe. I'm a policeman sent to bring you aft."

"You're a devil of a looking policeman," I answered, not realizing that the fun had commenced. When he told me Neptune was coming aboard and that he had been sent forward to lead me aft, I realized there was to be some skylarking after all and submitted to whatever he wanted to do. He tied a handkerchief over my eyes and led me aft.

When we got to the main hatch, we halted and for several minutes all was still. I knew there were others standing near us, but as I was blindfolded I could not see who they were.

Then there came a hail from forward and I recognized Old Jim's disguised voice.

"Hallo! What bark is that?"

"The *James A. Wright* of Boston," sung out the mate who was on the poop above us.

"Have you got any of my sons aboard?" again hailed the voice.

"Yes," answered the mate.

"Well stand by, I'm coming aboard of ye!" And then I heard several figures drop off the fo'c'sle head and come marching aft in the darkness.

When near us they halted and Father Neptune said, "Well, where are my noble sons?"

"Here's one, sir," said Joe, shoving me in front of him a step.

"Oh! Ho! So you want to become a son of Neptune, do ye? You want to make seagoing your profession do ye?"

"Yes sir," I answered.

"Very well then, take him along policeman," said Neptune, and I was shuffled along, still blindfolded, down to what I knew were the lee scuppers. Here I was made to sit on a capstan bar laid over a large deck tub filled with salt water, although I didn't know at the time what it was. "You see," continued Neptune, "to become a sailor you must first go through a few little things. Are you willing to do this?"

"Let her go!" I answered.

"Very well then, barber, give him a shave; he'll make a good son of Neptune." And then I got a swab across the jaw, under my chin, up my nose, and an attempt to get some into my mouth as I answered the questions Neptune kept asking me. But I kept my lips closed and mumbled out my answers.

"Open your mouth when you answer," said Neptune. But I knew better than to do so. My face was beautifully smeared with a mixture of tar and slush. Then it was scraped off, none too gently, with a large wooden razor, which I now knew was what I had seen the mate making.

"You'll have to excuse him," went on Neptune, "as my regular barber I had to leave on a stock fisherman astern here. Shave him well, barber." And after that operation was over he asked me, "Are you still willing to go on?"

I mumbled out, "Yes," taking care to keep my mouth closed and thereby avoided getting it full of the tar and slush lather that was aimed at it.

"Well, go on then attendants," ordered Neptune.

And the next minute the bar was yanked from under me and down I sat in the tub, up to my neck in water. At the first shock I tried to get up, but was forced down. The water by that time had lost its chill, so rubbing my clothes I said, "If you'll give me some soap now, I'll go on and take a bath."

That ended my christening. I was released and saw Lawrence, the darky cabin boy, put through the same process. Only as they yanked the bar from under him, the mate and second mate each dumped a bucket of water off the poop deck onto his head. He was a half-drowned coon when they let him go.

Old Jim was Neptune and had on all his oilskins and a long flowing beard of combed rope yarns that reached to his knees.

This ended the fun and the watch turned in to spin yarns of how they had crossed the line in other ships on other voyages, smoke their pipes, and then fall asleep.

One night we had a close shave, but spared all hands from going to the bottom. It was a fierce, windy night, so black you could not see half the length of the bark. That day we had run by the log two hundred and forty miles and were still doing the same. I was on lookout and about midnight I saw a faint green light dead ahead.

"Light ahead, Sir!" I shouted aft with all my might, but got no answer. So I started aft, shouting to the mate. "Ship ahead, Sir! Light dead ahead, Sir!"

Before I got to the main mast there was a rushing, roaring sound and a large full-rigged ship swept past us, so close it seemed as if her yards would surely lock with ours. She had skysails set and I saw the glimmer of her binnacle lamp. It was all over in a second and the ship was out of sight astern. But I tell you it sent cold chills over me when I thought of what might have happened, and it was a long time before I could close my eyes in sleep when our watch turned in that night.

When it was all over, the mate ran forward, cursing at me, and swore I had never sung out about the ship. But Joe, who was at the wheel at the time, told me afterward the mate was leaning with his elbows on the booby hatch and had not moved for more than half an hour. Joe had heard me sing out clear enough, so I concluded the mate must have been asleep.

Several ships passed us the next day, but most of them were several miles off. One little bark came near enough to speak to us. It was early in the morning and Joe and I were swabbing off the white paintwork around the after cabin. When the bark was a short distance ahead, the mate called below to the captain and he came up on deck. "Make our number, Mr. Hill," he told the mate. So we knocked off swabbing and got out the code signals that made our number and I hoisted them up on the signal halyard to the mizzen topmast head while Joe ran the American flag up to the peak.

On came the other bark, a wooden vessel of about our own size and rig, but with a decided "Blue Nose" look and so she proved to be; a Nova Scotian with the British ensign floating away from her gaff end. She had a fair wind and her gaff topsail was hauled down on the cap so the string of signal flags could be seen by us.

When both numbers had been made out, though it took a good deal of squinting through the glasses by both captain and mate before they could do so, the signals were hauled down, the ensigns dipped three times and then left flying as the other bark disappeared astern.

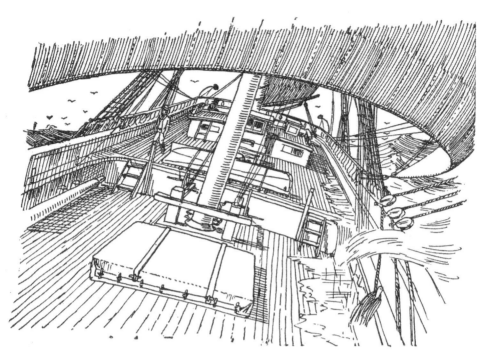

Chapter 6

Colder weather—A Pampero at night—Fishing for seagulls—
A sea library—Peter's strong teeth—Joe's yarn—Sea cuts—A cabin
mess spoiled—The fog horn—Using the dipsy lead—Heavy winds—
Reefing topsails—I think of home.

Day by day the weather grew colder, for each day we made long reaches southward under the influence of the strong, steady southeast trades. On September 29 we were opposite the River Platte and all day had carried a fair wind, with every stitch of canvas bent. Our watch turned in at eight o'clock to sleep until midnight. The nights were quite cool now, so I had put both my blankets into my bunk and was having an elegant sleep. Once I was dreaming of home and was just walking up Forty-seventh Street when something woke me with a start. It was the mate yelling like a fiend in the fo'c'sle door for us to tumble out on deck. The minute I came to a realization of where I was, I knew something was wrong. The fo'c'sle floor was nearly on end; none of us stopped to dress, we were needed on deck and knew it by the actions of the ship and the loud excited orders the captain and mates were shouting at the tops of their lungs. I jumped out on deck as I was, with nothing on but my underclothes, and scrambled aft as fast as I could in the darkness. I can't remember a night blacker than that one. The bark lay on her beam ends and a gale of wind shrieked with such a roar aloft it drowned out all other sounds and whiffed a shout away almost before it was heard. Aft we four scrambled with the mate, stumbling over unseen coils of gear until we reached the mainmast. What followed beggars description from my pen, but I hope I shall never experience another such night of excitement. We had been struck by a "pampero," one of those sudden gales that form on the Pampas, as the prairies of South America are called, and rush out to sea after sunset, dismasting many a stately ship. When we arrived in Valparaiso I heard that a ship I had come near sailing on, the *State of Maine,* had been totally dismasted just a short time before by one of these very squalls, and been forced to put in to Rio.

Everything aboard the bark had been let go by the other watch, and the sails were slapping and booming up aloft. Not a thing could I see as I looked up to check what state the bark was in. Above the roar of the wind on deck, I could just make out the faint, faraway sound of slapping sails. We manned the clewlines and buntlines and hauled up the large mainsail to relieve the pressure of its mighty surface off the ship. We didn't stop to do it neatly either, but clewed up the topgallants and royal while the second mate with his watch took sail off the foremast. Then we clewed up the gaff topsail and ran aloft to furl the sails we had clewed up before they blew away. The captain and another man had hold of the wheel and had got the bark before the wind, which somewhat eased her. While running about and hauling the ropes on deck we were warm enough, but when we got up aloft, with only our underclothes on, it was decidedly chilly. Everything was jammed, but no matter how loudly we yelled, it was impossible for the mate on deck to hear us, so we had to stow the sails the best we could. It took us more than half an hour to get the canvas off, and then it was past eight bells and time for our watch on deck. So as soon as we had put our clothes on we relieved the other watch.

We were now getting down into the region of hard winds and the mate lost no time in bending on the storm canvas. Every sail that the bark had on was sent down one at a time and new, stronger ones sent up in their places, both watches being kept on deck one day to finish the job.

For several days after the squall we had fine weather and cape pigeons, gulls, and molly-hawks were getting numerous, sometimes as many as a couple of hundred of them were following the ship's wake.

It was my chief amusement at the wheel to watch their quarreling and fighting over the slops the cook sometimes threw over the side.

Mr. Stevens, our second mate, spent several hours of his watch below on deck, fishing for them. He caught them by tying a piece of salt pork on a triangular piece of copper. I asked him once why he didn't use a fishhook. He told me the insides of their bills were all hard bone and a fishhook would not catch, while the copper jammed crossways in their bill. His way was certainly a good one, for he caught sometimes as many as three or four in one watch.

Some of the men began to grumble about the captain's allowing him to catch them. According to superstition, it would surely bring bad luck upon the ship. Some of the pigeons measured about seven feet from wingtip to wingtip and were beautiful white birds with pretty pink feet and bills. Graceful as they were when sailing about the ship, sometimes for days at a time, they were the most ungainly looking birds you ever saw when placed on deck, and were totally incapable of escaping. Their legs were so far aft on their bodies that they were unable to stand, much less fly, and toppled over on their breasts.

One day we ran into a school of whales. They were the first I had ever seen and I watched their long, black snouts spouting a thin stream of water into the air. The spouts blew away to leeward like a puff of steam, and I wished they would come near enough so I could get a good look at them. Finally, one of them, a small black fellow that we judged to be about thirty feet long, came head on for us, throwing his big, bulky body along with the sea until we thought he was going to ram us head on, but he didn't. About a hundred feet away he threw his immense tail in the air and sounded. We never saw him again, but next day we saw a white whale, which Joe told me was a rare occurrence.

One Sunday, the captain called us aft and opened a chest full of books and let us take whichever ones we wanted to read. There were books printed in English, French, Spanish, and German that had been put aboard the bark at New York by the American Seamen's Friend Society for the sailors' use.

The books pleased me immensely. I had devoured everything readable in the fo'c'sle by this time, from the tables of weights and measures, rates of postage, and list of presidents of the United States printed in the front of my diary, to the advertisements and news that I found on old newspapers some of the fellows had brought aboard. I took two books and, as it was our watch on deck, sat in the carpenter-shop doorway reading them.

That afternoon, when all hands were awake in the first dogwatch, Peter, the young Spaniard in our watch, got telling us what he could do with his teeth; he said he could chew glass and nearly broke his jaw trying to prove his assertion that he could make a dent in Joe's sheath knife. He made a mark in it, then lifted Charlie, a man weighing two hundred and ten pounds, off the deck by pulling a rope, made fast around Charlie's waist, with his teeth. None of us had believed him when he said he could do it, but seeing is believing. Then we all fell to yarning, sitting on the spars near the bulwarks. Joe was telling us about his experiences on the last voyage in an English bark. He ran away from her at a place called Caleta Buena, Chile; he and a Swede and neither of them could understand what the other said. Aboard the bark he said there were four Swedes in one watch and four Germans in the other, and neither watch could understand what the other said.

Joe and his mate, according to Joe's yarn, climbed the mountains to a city at the top and then started to walk to Iquique, a city some thirty miles to the south'ard. Joe had some buns and a flask of whisky and his mate had some buns and two bottles of wine. The country he described as a sandy desert with not a tree, blade of grass, or a drop of water anywhere; all they had to drink was the stuff they carried in bottles.

Joe, in the course of their walk, fell over the edge of the mountain and the Swede followed, losing his buns and breaking the wine bottles. They hunted for water or someplace to get some food, but could find none. When night overtook them, they were afraid to lie down it was so cold, and they didn't dare walk along the shore for fear of wild animals. For three days and nights they climbed about the mountains without food. Joe finally fell exhausted and the Swede climbed a mountain to see if he could see a town or a ship. He saw a ship at anchor in a bay a short distance ahead, just at the bottom of the steep mountain he was on.

They were so exhausted they were unable to walk and rolled and slid down the mountain. At the shore they met an American working as a stevedore. He gave them some bread and wine and tried to get them to go to work in the saltpeter mines, but they wouldn't. So they started walking again, and again got lost. All along the footpath they had been traveling were dead horses and mules standing up as if alive, but the minute they touched them they would fall over, all dead and dried up for want of water.

I thought this was a pretty steep yarn, but a sailor doesn't like to be questioned as to the truth of his remarks and, since no one else objected, I settled back again and listened to the rest of his yarn.

He said they came to one place where a railroad had broken down and the valley at the base of the mountain was a mass of skeletons, thirty of them, men, women, and children.

When he and his mate were nearly dead after tramping for several days, they heard a dog barking. It was at night and they had some difficulty in finding the house where the dog belonged. The Chilean that lived there gave them plenty to eat and drink, and put them up for the night. In the morning he drove them in to the nearest town, which, to their dismay, was Caleta Buena, the place they had left.

They got board at a house there and when the proprietor found out who they were he was going to turn them over to their captain, as the bark was still at anchor in the bay. "We told him," said Joe, "that we wouldn't stay on the bloody vessel, that we would jump over the side, so he said if we'd give him four pounds he'd ship us on another vessel." This Joe and his mate agreed to and were shipped aboard a vessel bound for England.

The weather continued to grow colder and each day was accompanied by squalls or shifts of wind. We had some time of it before we ran out of the trade winds. My hands were black with dirt and cracked, with the saltwater pickling they had been subjected to, into what are called sea cuts. At the middle joint of all my fingers, the skin had become so hard and callous that the bending of my fingers had cracked the skin on the inside. This, combined with a blister in the palm at the base of each finger gave me no end of pain. Some nights as I lay in my barren bunk, I could not sleep, I could feel my pulse throbbing at each sore where the air touched the raw flesh. If you want to know how it felt, wait until you get a cut on your hand and then sprinkle salt in it and you will have a taste, but only a taste of what I suffered. I had a pair of kid gloves with me, and to save my hands I cut the fingers off the left one and wore it, as that hand was the most painful one. It pained me so when I squeezed a rope to haul and the fibers of the rope touched the raw skin, I had to wear it. One day the mate saw me with this glove on and threatened to heave it overboard if he ever got hold of it; but he never did. I never gave him the chance, but kept it on until it was worn out.

We no longer washed down the decks in the mornings now, they were getting washed enough and we were glad to see them dry once in a while. When it was not raining, the bark was romping along with spray running off the decks in streams.

One evening a sea came aboard just as Lawrence, the cabin boy, was on his way aft with the cabin mess in his basket, and it knocked his feet clean from under him. Down he went, dishes and all, and picked himself up in the lee scuppers with a spoiled mess and a basket of broken china.

"Good job, that," said Joe, speaking of it afterward. "Let them see how it feels to get a spoiled mess."

"No fear," says Jim, "we'll get that mess ourselves and they'll get the best of ours."

October 9 we struck a heavy fog and the mate brought a foghorn on deck that looked like a hand organ. Placing it on the booby hatch, he called me up on the poop to work it. He tried it himself first, but could not get a sound out of it; then the captain ground and ground away until red in the face, but beyond making it give a faint little grunt, not a sound came from it. So the mate took it apart and fixed it. Then he told me to blow two blasts every few minutes.

I turned and turned, but couldn't make it blow until I got up on top of it to hold it steady and then turned the crank as hard as I could. Once, I was grinding away when the bark gave a roll and the horn and I thumped down onto the main deck, with me on top. I nearly wrecked the machine and was glad to hear eight bells struck and turn the horn over to the other watch.

That night in our watch from twelve to four A.M. we got up the deep-sea lead from the lazaret to get a sounding. Bending on the heaviest lead aboard, the line was carried forward outside the rigging, with a man in each channel holding it clear. Joe, on the fo'c'sle head, swung it well forward of the bow and sang out, "Watch ho! Watch!" Then Bill, in the fore rigging, sang out "Watch ho! Watch!" as he let it go there.

"Watch ho! Watch!" I repeated as the line tightened in my hand and I let it drop. Then climbing on deck, we all scrambled aft to find the captain and mate watching the line run out, but the lead had not yet reached the bottom. The bark was going too fast; so slipping the line into a small snatch block seized onto the royal backstay, we hauled it aboard again. It was a long haul and the line was so small it cut into our hands.

Then we backed the main yards and tried two more casts before we got one that satisfied the captain, and the depth proved to be fifty fathoms.

A couple of days more found the bark running south with a moderate-size gale piping out of the west. It started to blow up in our watch on deck, and I went up and stowed the main royal, while Bill furled the fore. Then our watch went below and turned in all standing, that is, with our clothes on. We just took off our oilskins and sea boots and fell asleep, glad enough for a watch below. But we had not been in our bunks fifteen minutes when there came a cry in the fo'c'sle door that woke all hands, "All hands reef topsails!"

We pulled on our cold, clammy oilskins and turned out a swearing, disappointed watch. The two to'gansels were clewed up first, then the fore upper topsail was hauled down and all hands went up and reefed it. From there, some of us were sent up to furl both to'gansels while the others lowered the main upper topsail. I was one of those who went up to furl the main to'gansel, and when we came down, the others were coming up the main rigging, so all hands lay along the topsail yard and put a reef in the sail. Then we clewed up the mainsail and furled it. By the way the bark was plunging and drowning herself in showers of spray, it looked as if more sail would soon have to come in. But at six bells, three o'clock in the morning, we were sent below and had just forty-five minutes more in our bunks until it was our watch on deck again.

I did some tall thinking of home that watch, and wished I was back in Brooklyn, where I could sleep in a warm bed all night; I realized then what a good thing a home is. By the time our watch was up at eight the next morning the breeze had moderated a little, and we had to stay up until the reefs we had put in during the night were shaken out and the yards hoisted.

Chapter 7

"Land ho!"—Off Patagonia—A heavy squall in the Straits of Le Mair—
Something carries away—We sight the Horn—Reefing down for a
so'wester—A full-fledged gale—Hove to—Nearly washed overboard—Two
hands at the wheel—I go over the wheel—Aloft in the gale—Pumping ship
off the Horn—The gale breaks—Sleeping aft—We wear ship.

S
unday October 16 (1892) was a windy, cloudy day and that night we caught another squall that gave us a foretaste of what was in store for us off the Horn. We lost our watch below and instead of crawling into our bunks and steaming up with the heat of our bodies, we had to go aloft with the other watch and reef both topsails and the mainsail besides furling all the other sails. Our watch worked like fiends and in just one hour had reefed the two topsails and mainsail, which was not bad work for a short-handed crew like ours.

The first thing I heard Monday morning was "Ho! Sleepers, seven bells, turn out and get your breakfast, there's land in sight!"

"Land!" I shouted. "Land! Land! Where?" All our watch jumped out, teeth chattering from the cold, and hurriedly pulled on our wet clothes to go on deck and get a look at the welcome sight. "Real, solid ground," I thought as I feasted my eyes on the barren, brown hills of Patagonia looming up all along the starboard bow. Viewed from the sea, the land looked misty and I hardly knew whether to believe it was real land or some cloud effect conjured up to deceive us. But it was land and I could gradually make out small stunted bushes, brown like the ground, dotted all up the side of the high hills that rose in the background to high, broken ridges and peaked snow-capped mountains.

"Patagonia," I thought. "Tierra del Fuego, or the land of fire, as it is called." And I recalled a story I had once read about a shipwrecked crew that was cast away here among the natives and the hardships they endured at their hands.

We had to eat our breakfast, for eight bells would soon go and then we'd have to go on watch, so we fell to and ate our whack of hot cracker-hash and drank our pot of coffee.

All day long those barren snow-topped mountains were in sight. That night it fell a calm and we became anxious lest we should drift in to shore. Something seemed to attract the bark toward the land; she drifted so close in we could hear the roar of the surf on the shingley beach and we did some lively box hauling of yards to get her headed offshore.

About four o'clock in the morning we sighted a revolving light off the port beam and when I took the wheel at six o'clock the mate gave me the compass course east-southeast and said we were entering the Straits of Le Maire.

When the gray morning dawned, we could see land on both sides of us and all hands were called to make sail. Every stitch the bark carried was shaken out and hoisted. The captain himself had come on deck, as it was a passage not always accomplished by a sailing vessel, and he wanted to save some seventy-odd miles of sailing by this shortcut. There was very little wind, but with royals and all her light staysails set, the *Wright* was making good headway through the smooth water. I could hear the spasmodic whir of the log back of me as it spun around registering our speed and knew by the spin of the white suds past the counter that the bark was reeling off some six or seven knots. The other watch had gone forward and finished their breakfast and when I struck eight bells, Old Jim of that watch started aft to relieve me at the wheel.

Captain Freeman sang out for the mate to hold on with the watch for a moment. So Jim stopped where he was and the captain and both mates got up on top of the house and looked over toward Patagonia with the glasses. I had been looking, too, and saw trouble in store for us. All along under the land, the water was black with a squall of wind coming offshore and before it came a line of white water whipped into foam by the wind.

Then came the orders from the mates one after another.

"Let go royal and topgallant halyards!"

"Stand by your clewlines!"

"Haul down your outer jib!"

"Let go the staysail halyards!"

The captain and both mates were giving orders and letting go halyards and sheets while all hands, cook, and even cabin boy were clewing up sail after sail. But the squall hit us before the sail was half off her. The old man came running aft to watch the compass and see she held her course, for we could only go straight ahead or else turn back and run off clear of Staten Land, which was now abeam to leeward.

It was an old whistler when it struck. For a few minutes I could hear no sound but the screeching wind and seething foam as it struck the weather side of the bark and hove her over until her rail was buried to leeward. The crew was making desperate efforts to reduce sail for there was weight enough in the wind to blow things away. Fred, one of the other watch, was up furling the main topgallant sail when it struck, and the whole topsails on that mast proved too great a strain for it. There was a report as if a gun had been fired on board, and a tremor ran through the bark. From my place at the wheel, I could not tell what it was that had parted, but knew some stay had gone, for the whole towering height of the main mast jumped and buckled. The old man ran forward and yelled to Fred at the top of his lungs to "Lay down you fool! Lay down!"

All hands stopped work after a minute to watch the jumping mast and every man, as they said afterward, expected it to go over the side. The main topmast stay had parted, one of the main supports to the main topmast. It was a double-wire stay, as large around as your wrist.

Up where Fred was, the mast was whipping enough to throw him off the yard at every jump; and I noticed a scared look on his face as he turned and looked down at us on deck. He saw the captain motioning for him to come down, but thought he meant to hurry up and furl the to'gansel. It was a job fit for three men the way the sail was bellying out full of wind, but he was able to stow it and came down never knowing the danger he had been in.

It was just eleven o'clock when the captain told the mate to send our watch below. By that time we had got the bark under reefed topsails, storm spanker, and lower staysails, and were setting up a temporary stay to replace the one that was carried away. A heavy mooring hawser had been taken up, passed around the main topmast, and the two ends set up with the fish tackle and another heavy one to the fore bitts and hove taut with the capstan. They were putting the finishing touches on this job when I was relieved at the wheel and our watch went below.

We had not yet had our breakfast and the cook asked the captain if he should give us both our breakfast and dinner now. "Yes," answered he, "they have earned it, let them have it." That was one of the very few good meals we had the whole time at sea and we had no difficulty eating all that was given to us.

Our watch had lost so many watches below lately that the captain wouldn't let them call us until half past one. This gave us two hours below and we felt decidedly improved by it, and were not worked very hard during the afternoon. Maybe the captain suspected something else was coming and wanted to save our strength for it, but all we did was sit in the carpenter shop and scrape blocks with our sheath knives. But in the dogwatches reefs were shaken out of the topsails as the wind had moderated a little.

After he'd locked his galley about eight o'clock that night, the cook came over to the rail where Bill and I were leaning with our chins on our hands, watching the steep, rugged black rocks of Cape Horn and three other ships that were slowly creeping over the cold-looking sea ahead of us.

"If we have thirty-six more hours of weather like this, Davis," said the cook, "we will be around the Horn."

"Well, I guess we'll get it, won't we?" I asked.

"Oh! No!" he answered. "We'll have a gale before morning."

His words didn't bother me much when our watch was up. I turned into my bunk and was asleep as soon as I struck the mattress.

But when we turned out at midnight there was a change of affairs and the first order we heard as we stepped on deck was, "Lay aft and reef the main topsail." So the cook was right, we did get a gale and as I hung over the yard knotting the reef points I thought of him with envy, for he was sleeping soundly aft in his stateroom. One sail after another was clewed up and furled until all that remained set was the storm spanker and the fore topmast staysail. When daylight broke, the bark lay hove to, with her head pointing south by east.

When daylight showed us the height of the seas that were running, I was amazed. I thought I had seen some pretty big seas up north, but now with a Cape Horn so'wester blowing I saw such seas as I hope never to see again. And every one seemed to get larger and larger for the gale had only just begun, and the wind blew with such force it seemed to slide the bark bodily to leeward. How she ever rose to some of those walls of solid green, or rather dirty-gray water that seems to prevail down in those low latitudes where the sun never seems to shine, was a mystery to me. The one square sail that was set would heave her over on her beam ends until her lee rail was clean under water. Braces and all the running gear blew out in semicircles and had to be hauled taut. Every evening at the change of watches, the mate took us from one end of the bark to the other and made us put a watch tackle on all the braces and sheets and haul them tight as fiddle strings. He was a hard worker and a good seaman, and I believe it was due in a great measure to the mate's tireless energy that the bark came through that gale without parting a rope yarn, save one sail.

Once when we were "sweating up" the lee fore braces, the whole crew came near to being washed overboard. We were bending our backs on the fore brace when the bark went over on her beam ends and a solid green sea broke over the lee rail. It took every one of us clean off our feet and those who were near the leading block on the rail were held down so the sea broke fully two feet over their heads and buried them completely. I was about in the middle of the brace and hung on to it for dear life when the water hit me. We were all washed pretty near to the main hatch and then, as the water poured back again and over the rail as the bark rolled, we were nearly washed over with it.

I was blinded and choked by the water that was washing me about, but when my knees hit something hard I caught it with my feet as well as I could, and hung on. I was lucky I did so, for when the water drained off at the next weather roll I found myself on top of the rail and lost no time getting inboard. Some of the fellows had let go the brace and saved themselves by climbing up on top of the water casks.

By watching our chance, we hauled the braces tight and were heartily glad when we heard the last order, "Belay!"

It was getting dangerous now to go on the lee side at all. The wind had the bark on her beam ends every time she rose to the summit of a sea and filled her decks with water flush with the rails. When she toppled over the crest with a heavy roll to windward, the sea went washing across from rail to rail like a young waterfall. It was as wild a sight as you would want to see, and I could not help admiring the wild beauty of it. Of the thirty-odd boards that were lashed on top of the main hatch, not a one was left after the water began its mad race back and forth across the deck; one after another they snapped like straws and went over the rail.

When the water struck the lee bulwarks it spouted like a geyser, fully fifteen or twenty feet in the air, a blinding mass of white foam that sprayed off to leeward as rain.

Water was flying in every direction. Every scupper was running a stream, but instead of going down, the eddies of the gale carried them up until level with the rail and then sprayed the water off to leeward, or if it was the pipe that drained the top of the cabin, the water came up in a cold shower into our faces. Every way we turned we were blinded by flying spray and, although our oilskins were lashed to our boots and tied about our wrists and waists, the water found its way inside and kept us chilled to the bone all the time. Dry feet were unknown, for some such job as pulling braces or standing at the pumps would surely end in a soaking.

To make matters worse, the cook could not make a fire in his galley and our last comfort, the pot of hot tea or coffee, was cut off. My oilskins were so worn I got another pair from the captain during the afternoon and put them on that night when it was our watch. Bill and I went aft to relieve the wheel; it took two of us to hold it and keep the helm from wrecking itself.

There was no steering to be done as the bark wasn't going ahead a foot, she was sliding off to leeward with every sea. We found two of the other watch at the wheel with a heavy lifeline stretched from rail to rail in front of them. It was as black as a tar barrel, with only the compass visible in the bright ray of light its lamp threw in the binnacle box. Bill took the wheel to windward and I took hold to leeward. When the bark went over a sea and settled her stem, it was all the two of us could do to hold the wheel. We got along all right for about an hour and then I could tell by the way the bark lifted that an extra-heavy sea was coming, though we could not see five feet ahead of us. Bill let go of the wheel and hung on to the lifeline, but what happened to me and the wheel I didn't know for a minute. I thought I had hold of a mule's leg instead of a ship's wheel. Then I felt a sharp pain in my left elbow and the next thing I knew, my head struck the deck behind Bill and my feet were up in the air on the wheel box. I was standing on my head, but soon scrambled to my feet and saw the wheel going around like a buzz saw; over it went one way then back again the other so fast it looked like a pinwheel and I could not see the spokes. Then, just as it was about to spin back again, Bill grabbed it and I scrambled around to leeward and took hold again, but my left arm was powerless. As I took inventory of my remains, I found I had been thrown over the wheel. My oilskin coat had caught on one of the spokes, which yanked me forward so my elbow struck one of the revolving spokes and threw me bodily over the wheel, ripping my brand-new oilskin from front to back around the waist where my belt held it.

The felt lining of my so'wester, together with my now-heavy head of hair, had eased my fall on deck. I gave Bill the benefit of my opinion of him in no choice language and, but for my disabled arm, might have done more.

Things were whistling when we went below that night and we had to wait for our chance to go forward, when the water was not too deep on the main deck, and then jump into it and scramble forward; though sometimes the water was waist deep. Once in the fo'c'sle, with the doors and windows tightly closed, the howl of the gale outside was hushed to a faint humming sound such as you hear among telegraph wires on a cold, windy winter night.

Everything in my bunk was wet, but I turned in anyway, just taking off my boots and oilskins. We all smoked a pipe or two to try and warm us up before going to sleep; but our matches were so damp we only got about one in every twenty to strike fire.

It was a sorry-looking sight that met our eyes the next morning. Harder than ever blew the wind, and the seas came in long high hills as high as our topsail yards. During the morning we were sent up to put extra gaskets around the main upper topsail and then we felt a sample of the wind's force. It was all I could do, as I climbed up the main rigging, to hold myself away from the shrouds so as to have room to lift my knees up. The wind, like a giant hand, seemed to press on my back, flattening me against the rigging. But that was not the worst of it, it kept getting under the back of my so'wester and lifting it off my head like a balloon, nearly strangling me with the string buttoned under my chin. One minute the shrouds were up and down and the next, as the bark rolled over, they were like a ladder laid horizontally, and the wind boosted me along faster than I cared to go.

It was a grand sight to look around from the height of the yard we were on and see the wild play of those Cape Horn seas all around us. Down to leeward we saw another bark, evidently an iron vessel with a straight stem, hove to under the same sail as ourselves.

Things got so bad about noontime, the captain ordered all hands to stay aft where the decks were higher; and when our watch was up we went down into the cabin and slept in our oilskins on the polished hardwood floor.

That morning the mate put three oil bags over the weather side, one outside the rigging of each mast, but it was hard to see what effect they had on the water. No doubt they did some good, but things were so bad it was like a drop to a bucketful.

Every watch, we had a spell at the pumps. It was so difficult to get a true sounding of the well, so the mate kept us pumping to make sure the water shouldn't gain any. This job was hard enough in the daytime when the mate kept watch on the poop and gave us warning when a sea was coming aboard so we could jump and get into the rigging around the main bitts, but at night it was very dangerous. Many a time we were heaving the heavy flywheels that worked the pumps around, with the water washing back and forth knee-deep, when, without warning, there was a flash of white and a sea broke on deck that sent every mother's son of us washing into the lee scuppers, soaked to the skin and choked with salt water. Many a narrow escape we had from going over with the sea to leeward; but none of us were lost, so it was simply an incident, just one of the everyday occurrences in a sailor's life.

About two o'clock in the afternoon, the fore staysail blew out of the bolt ropes and left nothing but a few flapping ribbons that soon followed the rest of the sail, but it made no difference to the bark, she lay hove to as before.

There was nothing we could do but wait, so when it was our watch on deck and it was not my trick at the wheel, I crouched down in the lee of the wheel box, where the deck was dry, and let my thoughts run as they chose.

I noticed as I looked astern that the gulls, the strongest birds that fly, were unable to fly to windward, but kept close down to the water in the lee of the swells In the lee of the bark's hull, floating on the water, were a number of them, glad enough no doubt for the protection it afforded them. From there my eyes gradually went forward to the bow of the bark and I watched her sluggish rise, followed by a drunken, drowning kind of lurch that made me think she must have water in her. The more I looked, the firmer I became convinced she was slowly drowning. She seemed to lack the buoyancy she formerly had, and an unconquerable dread crept over me. I tried to shake it off, but it seemed impossible to do so. I cannot remember ever feeling so blue as I did then, seated on deck with my legs stretched out and no heart to move myself.

My feelings seemed to be shared by everyone else and a haggard-looking crew we were, with dark circles under our tired-looking eyes crusted with dried white salt and sunken washed-out cheeks.

Once I asked Captain Freeman what he thought of the weather and his reply was that if the gale didn't break by morning, there would be nothing left of the *Wright* by nighttime.

And so another, a third, black night passed with the sea hissing over the bark in showers that looked like snow squalls and all hands hanging on with their teeth chattering, half frozen in the cold night wind.

The gale increased and reached its height that night and it was a wonder we ever lived through it. There was only one spot on deck where it was safe for a man to stand and that was clear aft by the wheel. All the forward part of the bark was sometimes under water and every movable object had been smashed to kindling wood and gone over the side. All the ladders, casks, etc., were gone and one sea broke over the forward house and smashed in the bow of one of the boats on top of it, smashed in the galley windows and as it came aft, broke in the cabin door and skylight. That was when the lifeline came in handy and saved us from probably going over the stern into the sea; for all that sea shot aft over the cabin top and struck us at the wheel square in the stomach, a good-size waterfall.

At daybreak things looked a little brighter overhead. The captain said the barometer was rising, and his face looked hopeful. Sure enough, by ten o'clock that morning, the fourth day since leaving Staten Land, the gale broke. For about an hour it blew with more strength apparently than any time previous. It was a wild, furious outfly that tested things aboard the bark to their utmost, but it did not last long and then there came an apparent lull.

The old man was in a hurry to get the bark headed the other way, for all this time she was going bodily to the eastward, the direction opposite to which our course lay. During those three days she had drifted one hundred miles sideways. About noontime he decided it was safe to wear the bark around and we did so, but things were interesting about the decks while doing it. Then we hoisted a reefed main upper topsail, set one jib, and the main topmast staysail.

During that afternoon we again passed the iron bark we had seen from the top-sail yard and she also wore around and came after us.

Chapter 8

The second mate's dirty trick—Cold weather—Back again to Staten Land—Company off the Horn—Another gale—The homeward bounder—A fair slant of wind—My meteorite—Cold work at the wheel—The fo'c'sle is washed out—The second mate's surprise.

Sunday, October 20th, found us worrying our way slowly back toward Cape Horn through a heavy cross sea. The bark had been put in order about the decks after her hard shaking up, and we hoped to get a hot dinner and some sleep for we were all tired out, and cross as bears. The second mate and his watch relieved us of the deck at half past twelve and our watch got the steaming pans of hot soup with "dough boys" and a pan of duff and molasses on our way to the fo'c'sle, laughing and trying to be cheerful in anticipation of the coming feast, for a Sunday dinner at sea is something to look forward to. As soon as we had closed the fo'c'sle door, after us there came a call of, "All hands reef topsails!"

"Oh! The dirty blackguard!"

"Dot ish a put op yob!" and stronger expressions were the various opinions we expressed of the second mate. That it was a "spite job" everyone knew, but what could we do? The meanest officer aboard the ship could spoil all our comfort under the mask of his authority, and this was apparently what he was trying to do. I then remembered a threat he made one night when his watch was called out to furl the foresail. Things did not go fast enough to suit him and he swore our watch was taking it easy and so trying to keep him and his watch up longer than necessary. This was to square up for that night.

So, pulling on our oilers, we carried the pans back to the galley and asked the cook to keep them hot for us. But no; he was in the job with the second mate and it made us boiling mad to look aft and see him watching us with a sneer on his face. So we put the pans in the fo'c'sle and went aloft and reefed one topsail after another and then to make sure our food should get cold he made us put the watch tackle on the braces after the yards were hoisted. This was a job one watch could easily do, and it proved he was trying to keep us up.

His revenge must have been complete as far as we were concerned for everything was not only stone cold, but the rolling of the bark had spilled all our pea soup into the bunk where we had carefully bolstered it up with a blanket. And so the only decent meal of the week, Sunday dinner, was a sorry disappointment for us; but we swore as a watch we'd get even with him, and so we did.

He tried his tricks too long. We went to pump her out one night and no matter how hard we pumped we couldn't raise any water. So the mate took out the top valve and fixed it, but still no water came. Then he took a sounding to see if there was any water and found there was. It was over an hour before we found out why the pumps would not "catch." Upon taking out the lower valve we found two handfuls of coal stuck in it. All kinds of things had been washing about the decks lately, but not any coal; there was none on deck to wash about except in the galley, and the second mate was there a great deal.

The mate was more than mad when he saw it was a trick, and a number of times afterward our watch had the satisfaction of seeing him call out the other watch and keep the second mate up an hour or so furling the mainsail and, remembering his trick we kept him up with a vengeance. So things ran on and the work that was hard enough was made harder by dissatisfaction.

Cold weather followed the gale, and chests and clothes bags were rummaged over for heavy winter clothes. I put on my heaviest winter red flannel underclothes, a thick pair of woolen socks, a blue flannel shirt, a heavy pair of breeches, rubber boots, a thick blue sweater, and then the ever-reliable oil skins strapped and tied at wrists and waist and lashed to the boots to keep the water out. I found nothing so warm on my head as my so'wester, with its flannel lining and ear flaps. While I had them I wore a pair of mittens, but they were forever getting lost so I had to pull a pair of socks on my hands instead. For use at the wheel, I made two bags out of the tail of a long overcoat I had, which we could slip our hands into. They were novel-looking things but, being of such heavy material and reaching to the elbow, were very useful; each man as it came his trick at the wheel shared in putting them on.

On the morning of October 26, I was up on the fore upper topsail yard making up gaskets; it had been snowing and hailing so hard I had to turn my back to it as I worked, and the hail rattled like pebbles against my stiff and frozen oilers. When the squall blew over I heard the mate below me on the fo'c'sle sing out, "What's that on the weather bow, Davis?"

I looked and there was the same rugged snow-topped peaks of Patagonia we had left a week ago. "Land!" I shouted back.

At noon we tacked ship and headed once more for the Horn. Toward nightfall the breeze hardened until the *Wright* was plunging against the head sea at a rate of seven knots. Several times in my lookout, from two until four A.M., she put her bow clean under and sent the water ankle deep over my feet. Every time she did so, the bell at the heel of the bowsprit gave one loud ominous clang.

The second time we sighted the Horn, we found quite a fleet of vessels cautiously poking their noses around the corner, waiting for a chance to slip around when an old Cape Horner was not blowing, and then go spinning off up the west coast.

One iron bark we passed close enough to signal and found she was the *Coromandel* of Glasgow, bound from Brazil around to the west coast. One ship followed the example of another; if one set a main to'gansel, all the rest followed suit. And more than once we wished there was not another vessel in sight, for the captain did nothing but keep his glasses fixed on the other craft and give orders to set or take in sail.

But another short-lived gale put us under reefed topsails again, and with yards fore and aft we made the best course south we could. Ships and barks were heaving in sight on all tacks; one outward-bounder came along with both his topgallant masts snapped off at the caps; and then the sight of a homeward-bounder sent a pang of regret through us to see him under a press of sail making a fair wind of a breeze that kept us practically hove to, rolling rails under and decks and scuppers running with water. How I wished then that we, like him, were homeward bound, but wishes were of no avail.

On the twenty-ninth, however, a shift of wind came and a godsend it was to us. We shook out the to'gansels that had been stowed for some time past, and drove the bark for all she was worth. Fair winds in that part of the world are not to be lost, it is so seldom ships get them.

On lookout one night I walked back and forth across the fo'c'sle head from the large black flukes of the anchor stowed there to the network of jib sheets that melted up in the shadows of the dark patches of jib. I thought of home and made up my mind to stay there if I ever got back. Suddenly something struck the deck just beside me. I couldn't imagine what it was.

It must be one of those meteoric stones I have read so often about that fall on the decks of ships. I couldn't imagine anything else that could fall from the clouds above. It wasn't as if I was in a city, where it might be anything; something off a roof, a tree, or a telegraph pole, or someone at a distance throwing a stone. But out here, hundreds of miles from land, it couldn't be any of those and surely there was no one aloft for, on looking aft, I could see two black shadows moving back and forth that I knew to be Peter and Joe, while Bill was at the wheel. So I looked all over for the stone, thinking what a relic it would be, but found nothing and finally decided to look for it at daybreak.

But when daylight broke that morning I was snoring away in my bunk, glad enough to be there and not thinking of meteoric stones. After breakfast when our watch came on deck, the second mate asked us if any of us knew where a heavy bolt he held in his hand came from. "We found it when we were washing down the deck this morning," he said.

I told him I had heard something drop when I was on lookout, and going forward we found where it had struck and made a dent an inch deep in the plank. "It's a good thing it didn't land on my head," said I, but I didn't tell him I had thought it was a meteorite.

For several days we had fine weather with little or no wind, but the cold was simply painful. Sometimes we would get a flurry of cold, dry snow or hail and we had to keep in motion every minute we were on deck to keep ourselves warm.

Standing at the wheel was the worst job of all and it became so cold we had to relieve each other every hour instead of every two hours as the custom was. It made no difference how much clothing we wore; standing still, all exposed, we soon became chilled. I would put on two pairs of woolen socks, a heavy sweater, and two coats with my oilskins strapped over all of them, which made me look like quite a portly person. Over my ears I pulled a skull cap and put my so'wester over it. About my neck I wrapped a soft undershirt for a muffler and, in lieu of mittens, wore a couple of pairs of socks.

During this fine spell we had royals and everything set, but they soon had to come in, for dirty weather again overtook us and reefing topsails was again the call. We got a half a gale from the so'east and drove along with all the sail the bark could stagger under.

One morning our watch had just gone below after furling the mainsail, for the wind was hardening every minute. Joe and I were standing in front of our bunks, trying to light our pipes with one hand while we hung on to the edge of the bunk with the other; for the bark was rolling so we couldn't keep our footing without hanging on. We had not yet taken off our oilskins and Joe, to get light enough to see to undress, had pulled the wooden slide back from the window on the outside, as our side of the fo'c'sle was to leeward and so in no danger of being broken by the sea. Just as he struck his fourth match and got it to fire, I heard a shout on deck, but didn't know what it was about. Then a shock ran through the bark as if she had struck a rock, and the next instant there was a cannon-like report and I clutched the edge of the bunk and held on. I didn't know what had happened, but thought I was overboard. I felt volumes of water washing me about, choking and blinding me. I felt the icy streams flow down my neck until I was chilled through. What had happened? I still had hold of something with one hand and hung on to it with all my strength. Finally, I felt the water leave my face and, gasping for breath, I opened my eyes. In front of me was a square of light that I recognized as the window, and the door, too, stood wide open. Then the bark rolled to leeward and again my feet were washed from under me and the water came up to my waist.

The water poured out of the open doorway and a dark object passed me, going out with the current. I grabbed it and found it was my blanket; so, wiping the brine from my eyes, I looked for more and, standing in the doorway as the water poured through it, I caught coats, hats, shoes, and all kinds of odds and ends. Inside, Joe, Bill, and Peter grabbed things as they washed back and forth around their feet and threw them into an empty upper bunk.

All the lower bunks were washed completely out and the beds and bedding ran with water. There were no scuppers to the fo'c'sle, so a couple of barrels of water were left as it was not deep enough to flow over the raised doorsill. This we baled out with our pans and a deck bucket, and were a tired and disgusted watch when once more we had collected our belongings and relit the lamp that had been washed or blown out.

The mate came to the door and looked in when we were fixing things up. "Didn't you fellows hear me shout?" he asked.

"Yes, I heard someone yell, but I didn't know what it was about," I answered.

"Why, I saw that sea a coming up to leeward," he replied. "It broke aboard as high as the sheer poles, smashed in the galley window, and washed out the carpenter shop."

We made the best shift we could; some of my clothes that were tied up in my clothes bag were dry and these I put on. But my mattress and all my blankets were soaking wet, while my small wares such as tobacco, matches, etc. were lost and it was over a week later before I found them jammed in back of an old water barrel that was stowed in the space between two bunks. The tobacco I dried in the sun and managed to smoke; it was the last package I had and, as I did not like to smoke the strong plugs of black tobacco we got from the slop chest, I was anxious to save it.

Not liking to use any of the other fellows' bedding, I turned into my own bunk, but after sleeping for an hour or so I woke up with a terrible headache and a suffocated shrunken feeling all over my body, and had to get out, my bed was so wet. Kaiser had offered me the use of his, so I climbed up into it and slept the rest of our watch there.

The sea, when it broke aboard, had smashed in the thick glass window right in front of which Joe and I were standing, but the glass never cut us, although Charlie, who had the top bunk on the opposite side of the fo'c'sle, found pieces of it there when he turned in. Such a surprise party as it gave us. It puts me in mind of what happened a few days later. Our drinking water consisted of one bucketful a day, but down in these cold latitudes no one seemed to want to drink much. We kept the bucket on one of the benches that were lashed fast in front of the forward bunks, so as not to slide. But somehow, on this particular occasion, just as the second mate stuck his head in the fo'c'sle door to call the watch, as all his men were up stowing the to'gansels, the bench carried away and shot down toward the door, striking the sill with considerable force and shooting the whole contents of the bucket square into Mr. Stevens' face. And such a swearing time he had, it tickled our watch immensely. It was one more grudge paid off against him.

Chapter 9

The grub question again—Baking our wet clothes—Boils—We break into the ship's stores—Fair winds—Overwork and no sleep—When the sea took charge of the deck—Falling asleep at the wheel—Nearing land—The mate smells the shore—My surprise at the first sight of Chile—Picking up a pilot—The pilot's fee—Valparaiso—We lose an anchor—At anchor—Letters from home—Anchor watch.

We were now in what was called bad weather and had been in it for some time, but there was no mend to the grub question. We got coffee with our dinner, to be sure, but the food was even worse than before; sometimes the cook was unable even to light a fire. Then our watch wanted the other fellows to keep their promise, made up in flying-fish weather, to kick for more food, but now that the time had come they refused to do anything and would rather suffer. More than once we went to bed hungry, and even went so far as to steal slices of the raw salt pork from the cask forward to eat between slices of bread. To make matters worse, we all broke out into saltwater boils. Our food was all salted stuff and we were wet continually with the salt water. Old Bill, in our watch, was disabled from doing any work about the ship or aloft, and could hardly hold the wheel. Charlie, in the other watch, could only use one arm and the rest of us could work, although we all suffered more or less with boils, except Fred, and he had one on his wrist so big he had to cut the sleeve off his shirt and coat to get his clothes on.

I had a small boil on each instep, just where my boots bent as I walked, and no wonder, for I hadn't had dry boots for more than a month. Our only means of drying them was to put on two pairs of socks and let them absorb the moisture from the felt lining of the boots while on watch. When we went below, we'd put the wet socks under us, roll up closely in our two blankets, and "bake them," as we called it. By repeating this operation for a couple of days, we got the boots fairly dry; but what good did it do? Next day a sea would surely soak us through and through, and then we'd have to begin all over.

To draw out my boils, I did as all hands were doing. I cut a thin slice of raw salt pork and tied it over them with a piece of linen. Mr. Stevens, our second mate, was the surgeon of the ship and he lanced the boils for the men and dressed them with strips of lint the captain gave him.

There was not much to be done in bad weather. Water was running all about the decks, so it was the custom of the mate to put the three men on watch down in the half deck to rip up the sails and pick out the stitches. One day Joe, Peter, and I sat around under the booby hatch in the half deck, picking stitches out of an old topsail, when we heard the mate come near the hatch. He stuck his head into the slide and looked down to see that we were all working. I was hard at it; but as soon as he was gone Peter dropped his canvas and disappeared in the dark alleyway that extended aft all along the sides of the cabin, in the wings as they are called, to the lazaret at the stern. Here was where all the ship's stores were kept. Barrels of hardtack; barrels of flour, beef, and pork; beans; canned stuffs; sugar; and, in fact, everything in the eating line. It looked suspicious to see him going in there and when he came out in the light again he was eating something.

"What you got?" I asked.

He looked up at the hatch to make sure the mate wasn't looking, and then pulled out a hardtack from the bosom of his coat.

"Where'd you get it?"

"In there," he answered motioning to where he had just been. "There's plenty more there."

In the meantime, Joe had slipped out of sight, and while he was gone the mate looked below.

"Where's Joe?" he asked and I thought the jig was surely up; but just then Joe came into view with a bundle of old canvas in his arms and, opening them out, he began to pick, so the mate left the hatch.

As soon as I was sure he was gone, I scurried across the deck into the darkness where the alleyway or wing commenced. It was too much of a temptation for a hungry man to see Peter and Joe eating their fill of good, clean, hardtack, so I decided to do as they had done: steal some. It was black as night in there. I could hear the wash of the water past the outside of the hull and hear the groaning and creakings of the woodwork, but my main fear was that the mate would look below and, not seeing me under the hatch, might suspect something and come down and catch me. So with feverish haste I felt about for the barrel the others had got their bread from. All I could reach were sealed up tight, probably barrels of beef or sugar. I felt all around the hoops, but they were all sound, so over the top of them I crawled on my stomach until I got so far in I felt sure the mate would look below before I could get back. I was on the point of giving it up and retreating when I ran my hands around a barrel and felt the top hoops were slightly loose. How I did work then, I had the strength of two men for inside that barrel was all the bread I could eat, and so near my grasp. Without making a sound, I worked the hoops up so the top was loose and pried out one board with my sheath knife; in went my hand and "Oh!" I thought, but didn't dare let the exclamation escape me. "Bread! A whole barrel of it."

I shoved my arm as far in as I could and felt smooth, hard crackers as far as it went. I didn't take any off the top, they were chipped and broken, but felt deep down and pulled out about six whole, smooth crackers and stuck them into my oilskin coat, which was like a bag with my strap around my waist. Replacing the cover, I hastily jammed the hoops down and scrambled back over the barrels. I felt as if I had been gone a week and was glad to see the mate was not on the half-deck waiting for me.

The rest of that watch we all three munched crackers and for once had our stomachs full. What we had left we ate with our tea at suppertime and were a jolly watch.

Nearly every day after that, until we emptied the barrel, we filled our coats with crackers, but had some narrow escapes from being caught. Once, I had just stuck five or six crackers into my coat when the mate called us on deck and had us put new lashings on the booby hatch. This required a good deal of leaning over and, in spite of my careful movements, one cracker worked its way out and fell on deck. But the mate had his head turned and by the time he looked around there was no telltale left.

These crackers were probably intended for cabin use, for they were sweet and fresh. We had the same kind the first two weeks we were out, only they were stale and full of maggots and weevils. But what could we do? We were hungry enough at that time to eat gum boots and little things like maggots didn't spoil our appetites. We found a way of getting rid of some of them by soaking them in our tea. First we'd stick the point of our knives into the seam and split the crackers apart. There on the inside were the inhabitants, white mealy looking worms laying in smooth grooves they had bored out, and they were so near the color of the cracker they were hard to see; while sprinkled about like pepper were twenty or thirty little black bugs. I examined one of them closely and noticed it had a long tapered bill like an anteater with a hard kind of black shell. By hitting the two sides of the cracker together, most of these would fall out. Those that did not would float to the top of our pot of tea and then we'd skim them off with our spoons.

One morning, when we were off the Horn, the cook reported to the captain that someone had unscrewed the gratings in the galley window and stole his pan of ginger cake during the night. Who it was they never found out, but we knew well enough it was Peter. The cook then, as I afterward found out, put a pie with a dose of jalap in it to try and catch the thief; but since no one made the second attempt, no one got caught.

Now that we were around the Horn, we had fair winds. Gale after gale sent the bark booming up north with a flood of water pouring off her decks and a crew tired and dragged out from being constantly called out in their watch below to reef or furl sail. When it blew down in that part of the world, it did blow and no mistake. It needed the entire crew to handle anything below the gansels.

Watch after watch we were called out until all were ready to drop with fatigue. It was no sleep and man-killing work. We got in such a state that, when relieved of the deck by the other watch, we'd stagger forward like a crowd of Eskimos in our oilers, slam the fo'c'sle door after us, and roll into our boxes with our boots, hats, and everything on.

I was so sleepy many and many a time that all I remember was sitting on the edge of my bunk, where I fell asleep and rolled over into it, snoring for all I was worth and accompanied by like music from three other bunks.

And then while in that helpless, exhausted condition, we would be aroused by "All hands reef topsails!" More than once I awoke to find myself crawling up the jumping ratlines with a crowd of dark figures all about me. Up to that moment I had been unconscious. My sleepy, tired faculties refused to awaken, and the wonder of it was I didn't go overboard.

On such nights it was so black I couldn't see my hand before my face. Feeling my way, I'd climb aloft knowing where I was going only by the touch of things. What a grand sight it was, when I was wide awake enough to appreciate it, to look down from the fore yard and see the white phosphorescence in the water as the bow plunged clear out of sight into a sea whose presence could only be determined by its impact with the bow. Shocks, as if the bark had plumped down on a rock, ran through the craft from stem to stern with each sea; and a cloud of spray, white as milk, came up and wet us on the yard, so high did it spout into the air. As it struck the sail or ropes, it turned to ice and to stow the sails we had to pound and kick the canvas.

On deck the sea would be running waist deep; then, as the stern settled and the water drained aft, things again assumed their black shapes. First the fo'c'sle appeared out of the suds. Then the fo'c'sle head, off which ran a waterfall. When the capstan and anchors appeared, the water filled the decks to the rail aft, dashing back and forth and making one end of the ship inaccessible to the other.

It was a pleasure to be ordered aloft in comparison to a job on deck. Up there we were out of the water that made it really dangerous below.

Imagine a man so bundled up in oilskins, gum boots, and a hat like blinders on a horse, with everything strapped and tied on, so he can't move half as quickly as he should, trying to keep out of the water. Imagine such a man trying to keep his footing on the deck when the seas are breaking aboard with force enough to stave in the side of a house and the bark rolling so her decks are at an angle of forty-five degrees each way. The water washes back and forth across the deck as the bark rolls with such force that every obstruction in its path sends it up in spouts three and four feet into the air. Every eyebolt makes a fountain.

More than once I was carried clean off my feet, as if I had stepped on ice, and went across the deck on my back with my legs in the air and my arms helplessly grasping for something to stop myself, plump into the water in the scuppers, out of sight and half drowned. Then back I shot, carried by the water, with no more control over my movements than a chunk of wood; and when I did catch something and held on until the water drained away from me, I sometimes got so mad to think how helpless I was amid the wild rush of water that I shook my fist at the scuppers and cursed the old bark for using me so badly.

But every day found us farther north and the cold hail and snow squalls gradually grew less and less, until the day came when we could leave off our boots and once more wear shoes. Flying-fish weather again, and we got flying-fish jobs with it, such as slushing down the mizzen and topmasts. But before we leave the cold weather I must tell you about standing at the wheel.

It was when we were so tired and dragged out from being on deck so much; I was at the wheel one trick, but had not been there an hour before I became so sleepy I positively could not keep the lids of my eyes up. I did all sorts of things to keep awake, such as moving one step back and then forward again, or sideways. I couldn't go far as I couldn't let go of the wheel. Or I'd stand on one foot and then on the other, but it was no use. My muscles would move quickly enough but I could not keep my eyes open. I tried slapping myself on the cheek, but every little while my eyes dropped and I came pretty near sleeping. The light in the binnacle box made my eyes heavy to look at it.

This lasted for about half an hour more when, completely overcome by sleep, my knees thumped down on deck and the shock awoke me. Jumping up, I grasped the wheel again but again my muscles gradually relaxed until I again sank, exhausted. Every time I struck the deck, it woke me and I determined I'd keep awake from then on, but all the rest of that trick I kept falling asleep.

Day after day the bark tore along, heading northward until it became apparent that we were getting near land. The mate put us at such jobs as scraping down the royals and topmasts, scrubbing all the paintwork with canvas and ashes, and tidying up the bark generally to give her a good appearance upon entering port.

Then came the job of heaving up the cable out of the chain locker and shackling it onto the anchors and getting the latter over into the shoe on the rail. They had been lashed together across the fo'c'sle head all the passage out and the hawse pipes had been plugged.

Just how near land we were none of the crew knew, and none of the officers would tell. Why they kept us in ignorance on such subjects I did not know, but imagined it was done so no schemes would be hatched up about what we would do when we came to anchor. Some of the crew might try to run away.

On the morning of Saturday, November twenty-sixth, our watch had the deck from breakfast time, eight o'clock, until twelve-thirty, dinner time. I had the first wheel eight to ten and never for a moment thought we were near land; in a week or so I expected we would see it, but as the mate kept looking off over the starboard bow I did the same. There was a thin mist or fog on the water and our horizon was limited, but the sun was breaking it away and I watched to see if some other vessel was not in sight.

The mate came aft and, going to the rail, he sniffed at the air like a dog. Then, turning to me, he asked, "Don't you smell land, Davis?"

I twisted my nose in vain to catch an odor that might suggest the shore, but smelled none.

"No! I can't smell it," I answered.

"Well I do," he said. "It's right off there." And he pointed over the starboard bow, but all I could see was fog.

At four bells Joe relieved me at the wheel and the mate had me throw all the rigging off the pins along the rail on the poop and coil them back again clear. I was busy at this job when the captain came on deck; the sun had come out good and hot and the breeze also freshened, so the *Wright* was walking through it in fine style, a broad band of suds floating past on each side.

"Yes! That's it! Right ahead there! See it Mr. Hill?" I heard the captain say.

"Yes sir, I see her, it's a whaleboat. I'll get a line clear to heave 'em."

The mate sang out to Peter to get a line clear to heave to the pilot and I stopped coiling down to see what the pilot looked like. Only a small speck was in sight dead ahead of us, but I knew it was a boat and let my gaze sweep along the horizon to starboard to see if any land was in sight, but the horizon ran clear in a line of mist. I was about to resume my job of coiling down, wondering why the pilot should venture so far out in a small boat, for we could see a distance of some fifteen miles from the deck. Then I noticed a dark line, up, pretty nearly over the main yardarm, that I at first thought was a bank of clouds. But as I paused and looked steadily at it, I could make out the gullies and promontories that seemed the edge of a nearly perpendicular cliff, thousands of feet high.

I was not prepared to see such a coast. I was looking for rolling mountains and plains with forests and bays, but here was a towering cliff, vertical on its face, that made me think of the Palisades along the Hudson River in my native state. It was certainly a grand sight, and in open-mouthed astonishment I drank in the view.

The base of the cliffs was still hidden in the mist, but the height to which they towered above us convinced me that we were close in under the land.

My attention was then called to the pilot boat that came sweeping down to our bow as the bark rushed along. Peter hove them a line from the fore rigging and such a chattering as they set up, it sounded like a boatload of monkeys. There were six dark-skinned men in the boat, all dressed with oilskin jackets and wide-brimmed hats. The swell thrown off to leeward by our bow nearly swamped them, but they caught our line and took a turn with it around a thwart. Their boat was a long double-ended whaleboat, which I afterward learned was the only kind used on the coast. One man, the ugliest of the lot, seemed to be the boss; he had an oar over the stern and kept the boat away from the bark, which was sailing along so fast as to nearly tow the boat under. It was dangerous work hooking onto a sailing ship, but they knew their business and gradually hauled up on the line and then sheered in under our main chain.

Two of them, the pilot and another, jumped into our rigging and came over the rail while the boat sheered off as far as the line would reach; her sharp stem shearing through the seas and sending a shower over the men who, as soon as they were clear of us, rolled themselves brown-paper cigarettes and did nothing but smoke one after another.

I was amused watching the pilot and the old man arguing about the pilotage. For a long time they could not come to terms, but finally it was agreed that the pilot was to get so much money and a big piece of salt beef—a big piece was especially stipulated.

The captain sang out to set the gansels, but the pilot stopped him with a wave of the hand. We were just sounding a low rocky front that forked out some distance into the sea, when all hands were called to stand by.

Then, as the view of the bay opened up, we saw a large fleet of steamers and sailing vessels at anchor. Built up on the side of a mountain that ran up from the shores of the bay, lay the city of Valparaiso, basking in the sun.

As we sailed in, a ridge of land, which came out from the mountain to the point we had rounded, shut off the view to the south'ard. To the north'ard the mountains gradually sloped down to a level plain backed in the distance by mountain ranges.

Two "coffee mills," as they call their side-wheel tugboats out there, came splashing and rattling toward us, hoping to get a job. But our pilot held on without them and we gradually clewed up sail. When we were near the berth he proposed to bring up in, he ordered everything clewed up and the bark forged ahead under what headway she had.

The mate had already cleared away the starboard anchor and when the pilot sang out he hit the trigger on the cathead with a top maul. For the first time since leaving New York, one hundred and fifteen days ago, our anchor splashed overboard and the heavy iron cable sent thundering echoes through the bark as it rattled out through the hawse pipe.

I was aft on the poop with two or three others and we hurriedly threw over the side ladder and man ropes for the port captain, who came out to us in a puffing little white, canvas-topped launch.

He came over the rail dressed in gold lace and was joined by sailors dressed in typical man-o-war costume, white duck suits and blue collars, accompanying him.

Then came a hail from the mate on the fo'c'sle head. "Anchor's gone, Sir!" and I noticed the bark was still forging ahead.

All the officers ran forward and looked over the bow and the mate let go the port anchor. The starboard one and forty-five fathoms of chain were lost and the hawse pipe had broken off with it.

The captain went ashore with the port captain in his launch while we went up and furled all the sails and stripped off some of the chafing gear. Then we sent down the fore and main course, unbent the spanker, and stowed them all away in the sail locker.

I was sweeping off the poop when the captain returned from shore that evening and was more than surprised when he handed me a bundle of letters. I stuck them in my shirt and went on sweeping and read them that night after we had knocked off work and had our supper. All hands ate together that meal and we had fresh beef procured from shore. We thought we were going to have all night in until the mate came to the fo'c'sle door and told us we'd have to stand an anchor watch. Of course we kicked, we wouldn't have been sailors if we hadn't, but we chose watches just the same.

To pick watches, Kaiser took a piece of chalk, which he used to keep tally of the days, and marked a circle on the top of his sea chest. He divided this into eight equal parts and each man made a mark or sign in one of the divisions while Jim waited outside of the fo'c'sle. Then Jim was called in and he numbered each one of the divisions. He unknowingly left my mark until last. I had made a circle and as he numbered it eight, he said "This one is round like the sun and that's what the last man on watch will see, so I'll just number it eight." So I would have the last watch, from four to five the next morning, which was Sunday. Then all hands turned in early to make up for the sleep we had lost during the day.

C.C.DAVIS

Chapter 10

Home news—Sunday at anchor—The shipping—Working cargo—
Daily routine of work—Making a landing at the mole—"Gringos"—Our
tallyman—In the hold—Sugar to burn—Ferryboat work at night—The
ship Thomas R. Dana—Peter and Kaiser are paid off—Our plaza men—
Beach combers—Making an arrest—Fred is put in irons—I get a fall—
Cargo fever—The lighters and launcheros.

Kaiser woke me at four o'clock next morning and I dressed and went on
deck while he turned in. It seemed queer to feel the bark lying still. The
anchor light, swinging on the forestay, was still burning and it was quite
dark, although dawn was not far away. Everything was still as death and a light mist
made all the shipping in the bay look hazy and indistinct.

I took my letters with me, some of which I had not yet opened. As soon as the
sun gave light enough to see by, I read them all through, one after another. Those
from home I read twice. I was still reading and walking back and forth when the
cook came forward to light his galley fire and first thing he asked me for the news
from the "States."

One large envelope from my chum Bob contained a lot of newspaper clippings and these gave us an inkling about what had happened during our absence. They showed there had been a heavy gale on the coast, told about the cholera scare and how the ships were quarantined at Sandy Hook and their passengers landed on Fire Island, told about politics, fires, etc., but the news that was most appreciated of all was the clipping that told how James Corbett had defeated the champion boxer John L. Sullivan in New Orleans.

There were pictures of the two men and the whole crew eagerly passed them around when we gathered at breakfast time Sunday morning.

This was our first Sunday at anchor and we had the day to ourselves. Land was such a welcome sight that I hung a long time over the rail, just gazing at the city and the other ships. The city seemed stuck up on the side of the mountain's base and was composed almost entirely of square, flat-topped houses either a gray or brownish color. Down in the heart of the city, though, there were many white marble buildings; grand old affairs with all the finery of Spanish carving under the eaves and on the columns. What few trees there were looked dried up and stunted on the bare, brown hills.

A large square building on the point to the south'ard looked like a convent, but we were told it was a government building. Along the eastern shore, just inshore of where we were anchored, were two or three mud batteries and a railroad that disappeared on the flat valley to the north of the city.

The harbor was full of vessels of all nationalities; from a little full-rigged Chilean bark of about one hundred tons, whose fore yard could be reached from the top of her forward house, to a monster of a four-masted German ship with double gansels and more apprentices than there were men in our whole crew, and whose tonnage was close on to two thousand.

All the ships lay anchored stern and stern in rows across the harbor. From the mud batteries there was a stone seawall built around the shore of the bay, with a mole or landing stage projecting out from the main street, where all the rowboats landed. Along the wall at intervals were placed iron cranes to hoist the cargoes out of the lighters that ferried the cargoes to and from the anchored ships.

The lighters were large, clumsy open boats built from lumber hewn out of native wood and with the adz marks visible on every part. Extending across from side to side near each end of the boats were two heavy beams a foot square to strengthen them. They carried from eight to ten tons each and were rowed by two "launcheros" using immense oars fully twenty feet long.

These lighters were anchored just off the seawall. Seaward of them, the first row of vessels consisted of old hulks—old iron hulls that have been condemned for further use at sea, stripped of all their machinery and spars, with roofs built over their decks. Some of these were used as storehouses, some as machine shops, boiler shops, etc., while opposite the mole a short distance out was moored a large floating dry dock painted white. The next row were coasting steamers and outside of them the sailing vessels.

There was only one dock in the harbor and that was an iron pier built by a German company for the use of their own vessels. Off under the point of land we rounded as we came in, lay the men-of-war at anchor. The *Esmeralda,* a low, black, modern iron-clad with a wicked look; the *General O'Higgins,* a fine-looking square-rigger of the old school; the *Wasca;* and a few small craft and torpedo boats.

We lay at anchor about a mile from the fleet, but next day we moved to the outer row alongside of the French bark *Carolina* of Bordeaux. Astern of us was a small coaster, then the wreck of the Yankee ship *Benj. Sewall.* She had only two short stumps of masts, the rest having been torn away off the Horn. Astern her, moored alongside an old hulk, was the Yankee ship *Thomas Dana* unloading the Sewall's cargo.

In near the mud batteries were two little clippers; two Puget Sound four-masted schooners that had come down with sixteen thousand feet of lumber as a deck load. The Chilean papers called them the two American rafts when they came into port.

One of the schooners, *The Golden Shore,* was the finest looking craft I had ever seen and later, up the coast, I got a chance to see more of her.

We had a feast for our dinner on that, our first day in port: a whole roast of beef and fresh vegetables, a whole boatload of which had come out to us during the morning. I spent the rest of that day writing letters to send home.

Monday morning we turned out at four-thirty A.M., had our coffee, and then hove up short on our cable and waited for our pilot, or rather the port captain. A little fat German dressed all in blue came off in a whaleboat rowed by four Chileans. Then we hove up our "hook" and were towed in by a small propeller to within about a mile of the mole and then dropped anchor. A "coffee mill" came out, dropped an anchor astern of us and brought the cable up to our stern. We hove taut fore and aft and were all moored before ten o'clock.

We cleared all the barrel staves out of the half deck in the afternoon and piled them on deck, ready for the first lighter the next morning. Peter and Kaiser both refused to work and the next day they were taken before the American consul and paid off.

Our work was the same each day, so if I tell you what we did one day you will know just what was kept up day after day with very little variation until all the cargo for Valparaiso had been discharged. At five-thirty A.M. I was awakened from my peaceful slumbers by "Come now lads and get your coffee!" from the second mate. All hands dropped out of the boxes that formed our bunks, some all dressed, some half-dressed, but all sleepy. Joe or I, the youngest, then went around to the galley and got the coffee pot and a pan with just eight slices of bread in it for the crew. This is what is called "coffee," and is kept up the whole voyage, in port and at sea. After a few minutes, just time enough to let our coffee settle, the second mate called Joe and me aft; we lowered away the small boat that was now slung on davits from the poop, and rowed him ashore to get the tallyman.

It was a pull of a mile or more into the mole and there was such a crowd of native whaleboats when we got there that it seemed impossible to reach the iron steps. Mr. Stevens, however, was equal to the emergency. Our boat was much heavier than the light Chileans' craft so we would get her going as hard as we could lay it on, and they did some lively scattering to make way for us. If they didn't, they went away with the print of our stem on their boat, cursing the "gringos" at a great rate. It didn't worry us any, we couldn't understand the swearing, but they soon learned to make way for the "Gringo Americano" as they called us, when they saw us coming. Gringo meaning a foreigner in Spanish.

Our tallyman was a dandy young Spaniard, very proud of Chile and his countrymen. Many a time we met another tallyman going out to some ship in a native boat and the result was a race, and our tallyman urged the rowers in the other boat to beat us. They rowed their boat by standing aft of the oar and shoving it, as if they were rowing a gondola. They made their light, double-enders fairly fly, but heavy as our boat was, she was easily rowed and by bending our backs with a will, we held them every time and beat them out in the end. They had not the endurance we had and always gave up, defeated.

When we got back aboard, the rest of the crew had the hatches off and a platform made with them from the hatch to the rail for the man who tended gangway. Joe, the second mate, and I then went down in the hold and broke out cargo, Charlie was on the gangway hooking and unhooking the falls, Jim was at the lowering fall, and the rest on the winch heaving the stuff out. Joe and the second mate "broke out" the stuff and rolled it to me under the hatchway. I then rolled it onto the slings, which I had to adjust each time, hook on the fall, and sing out to those on deck to "Haul away!" And I could sing out as loud as the next by that time. When I shipped I was a boy, but living with men, doing men's work, and being thrown upon my own resources developed me into a man.

By breakfast time, eight A.M., one lighter was loaded and another one partly so.

We had forty-five minutes to eat and rest, and then all the long morning it was "Haul away!" "Haul away!" working as I had never worked before and thinking all the time of home scenes and planning what I should do when I got back.

Then came an hour for dinner and back to work again we went. The bark had a general cargo: first came oak staves, then barrels of oil, then cases, and one thing and another until finally we struck some barrels of cube sugar. When we saw these, stowed up as high as our heads, we started a barrel, then let it drop and smash on deck. Of course the head flew out and cube sugar spilled all over the place. Mr. Stevens helped himself to some and said, "Fill your pockets boys." Then he headed up the barrel and I sent it up through the hatchway.

Our fourth and last lighter was loaded about two or three o'clock, then we rowed the tallyman ashore and all hands went below and "broke out" cargo, rolling it under the hatch to be ready for the lighters in the morning.

At six o'clock we stopped work, put the hatches on, swept down the decks and loafed about until suppertime. After that important event was over and the inner man had been made comfortable, we smoked our pipes, spun yarns, and turned in.

The first few nights we were left to ourselves, but one night I had just taken off my clothes and lay in my bunk, smoking and listening to the yarns being spun, when the second mate opened the fo'c'sle door and told me to come aft. I didn't know what was up, but dressed and went aft. When he said, "Get your coat and come in the boat," I knew I had to help him row the old man over to the *Thomas R. Dana* to make a call. Once there, the captain went down in the cabin, our second mate hunted up the second mate of the *Dana*, and I went forward to talk with the "boys."

They were nearly all "Cockneys," as Englishmen are called, and according to their story they did pretty nearly as they pleased. I found one man by the name of Yates who hailed from Harlem and had been nicknamed "Yorkie" by the others because he came from New York. He and I walked back and forth across the fo'c'sle head until the captain was ready to return and the second mate called me aft to the boat.

The *Dana,* according to Yorkie's tale, had been on the coast for several months and during that time she had had three different mates and two second mates. The crew, being all of one nationality, stuck together and did as they pleased; one mate had struck a man and in return he had been kicked down the hatchway by others in the crew, so he left the ship for the hospital. The second one, after being hove overboard, decided she was no ship for him to stay aboard of. And the second mates had been treated the same way. One Sunday when I was aboard, I had an example of their independence. They went aft and asked leave to go ashore, but were refused. So, dressing up in their good clothes, eight of them went aft, lowered away a boat and went ashore anyway.

Some nights when we went visiting, the captain stayed until midnight and I had to go in the *Dana*'s fo'c'sle and sleep on the benches until called by the second mate or else I went down into our boat and slept in the bottom of her.

There was one thing about this night visiting I never tired of admiring, and that was the zigzag flashes of phosphorescence as the fish darted away from the bow of our boat. Every oar dip left a whirlpool of fire and the bow wave trailed off in thin yellow threads of gold on either side. We had to hoist the boat up out of the water each night. If we didn't get back until midnight, the four of us on watch had a heavy pull; but when all hands got hold it was a race to see which end of the boat came "two blocks" first.

Peter and Kaiser, having been paid off, were replaced by two hands from shore, "plaza men" as they are called. One of them was a short fat Scotchman who went by the nickname of "Scottie," and he was as comical, both in the cut and make of his dress and his actions, as a circus clown. He regaled us night after night with yarns of when he was in the "sarvice" and told us all the old man-of-war jokes to laugh over. He was a typical old salt and a thorough seaman. In the course of his conversation, he told us there were between two and three hundred "beachcombers" ashore in Valparaiso. Sailors who had run away from ships and were now begging a miserable living around the streets and docks rather than undergoing the hardships of rounding the "Corner" as they called the "Horn." He also said that all these beachcombers had been gathered by the police and locked up. Several American men-of-war were expected any day and the authorities feared another outbreak such as had occurred a few months ago and resulted in the death of a sailor named Riggan from one of the American war vessels.

The beachcombers, he said, slept in caves in the mountains or about the streets, and early in the morning they went about from house to house offering to empty the slops for the price of a drink. There were no sewers and everyone had to dump their slops off the seawall. As soon as a beachcomber had earned a few centavos he went and got drunk and so lived from day to day.

But there was one thing the beachcombers feared, and that was the mounted police. Nor do I blame them, for I saw one man arrested and it was a wonder he ever lived to reach the station house. I was ashore on leave and wandering up and down, noticing the peculiarities of the place, when I heard the clatter of hooves coming along the stone pavement. It was a policeman or "gendarme" as they are called, in hot pursuit of a ragged, tattered tramp whose bare feet went pat, pat, pat as fast as he could go, the very picture of desperation. As quick as a flash he dove around the corner, thinking to gain on the horse. But with a reckless bound, the horse cleared the pavement at the corner. Just as I got there, I saw the gendarme swing a lasso around his head and then let it fly, catching the tramp just below the shoulders, pinning his arms fast to his side. I expected then to see the officer dismount and arrest his man, but no, on went the horse with the poor tramp, already exhausted from his flight, endeavoring to keep pace with it. Just before they reached the corner, the tramp fell, but without a halt the gendarme galloped on dragging his victim along the stones.

Scottie and his mate, Baker, worked "plaza," which is by the day, for eighteen American dollars a month; in Chilean money this represented forty-five dollars.

I had Captain Freeman change the five-dollar bill Johnnie Walker had given me and I received twelve dollars in native money, which I gave to the steward to buy me sugar, condensed milk, and chocolate, and so made my living a mite more comfortable.

Fred still had two painful boils on his wrists and wanted to leave the ship, as Peter and Kaiser had done, but the captain would not pay him off and finally he refused to work.

One morning we were eating our breakfast when Fred was called aft. He did not come forward again by the time we turned to hoisting out cargo. That night, at the captain's orders, I took Fred's bed and blanket aft to him. I found him handcuffed and tied to a stanchion down in the lazaret and felt sorry for the poor fellow. He wasn't quite right in his head and before the voyage was over we learned he had come out of an insane asylum, having previously been aboard the U.S.S. *Monocacy* in the China Seas. His parents were well-to-do people in Switzerland. Once or twice he took me into his confidence and told me bits of his home life, which showed he was no common loafer. I smuggled two cakes of chocolate aft with his bedding, and his looks of gratitude repaid me for the sacrifice, for all he was given to eat was bread and water.

Outside of the dark, gloomy hole in which he was confined, quite a gay scene was being enacted that night. An English mail steamer was just leaving port for England with two-hundred-and-forty Chilean man-of-war men aboard, going out to bring back a new war ship for Chile.

The sea and sky were mellow and soft in the tender light of the setting sun, a fitting background for the departing steamer. As she passed the Chilean man-of-war anchored inside the point, the two-hundred-and-forty sailors ran up the rigging and gave three cheers of "Viva! Chile!" that echoed and re-echoed across the still water and was returned by the crews of the *Esmeralda, O'Higgins, Wasca*, etc.

And then came the notes of the *Esmeralda*'s full band playing the national air of Chile, which runs very similar to our "Hail Columbia," and made me think for a moment of home and the Brooklyn Navy Yard.

Then followed a dipping of colors and a salute of guns, while the steamer rounded the point of land and disappeared from view.

The next day was Sunday, and a day of rest. Poor Fred missed his whack of duff, molasses, and soup with doughboys that always made a Sunday dinner a thing to be looked forward to.

On Monday, Fred went ashore with the captain to the American consuls, and when he returned he had to turn to and work. I was alone in the fo'c'sle, having hurt my back, when he came back aboard and he gave me a banana he had bought ashore in return for the favor I had done him.

That morning I had taken my pot of coffee up on the fo'c'sle head to drink and when I tried to come down my shoe slipped on the wet copper and I fell a distance of about five feet, landing flat on my back on the main deck. It was some minutes before I could rise. Old Jim sat on the fore hatch drinking his coffee, but never spoke or helped me. I gave my spine such a twist it hurt me terribly, so I lay down in my bunk and rested all I could. I worked cargo until noontime, but when I stopped for an hour or so to eat dinner, my back stiffened up and hurt so, I did not return to work in the afternoon.

Once the captain called me aft and asked, "Well! What's the matter? You got the cargo fever?"

I told him about my back and he gave me some liniment, which Scotty kindly rubbed into my back that night. He was a kind-hearted old chap and as a token of my gratitude I gave him one of my blue knitted watch caps, the kind that is used in the navy. In return, he made me a present of a pair of rawhide moccasins that I had admired very much.

Our lighters came out just at sunrise before the trade winds, which blew hard between sunrise and sunset, began to blow, for it was no easy job rowing those heavy lighters. Up in the bow, forward of the first heavy crossbeam, were two or three boards laid across, forming thwarts for the launcheros to stand on. The boats were very bluff forward, giving a good spread for the men, who stood on the opposite side to which they were rowing, to handle their long sweeps.

All the lighters were painted black outside, with a round white circle on each bow, in which was painted in red a distinguishing letter. All the lighters of one firm had the letter N, another V, and so on. Inside, the boats were devoid of paint and were open from the beam forward to within three or four feet of the stern. They were wide, square-sterned boats just like a big rowboat about fifty feet in length.

When we turned out there were usually two of them alongside and I was much amused by the way the launcheros cooked and ate their meals. Each boat carried a crew of two or three men; dark, powerfully built fellows, quick as cats, with straight, oily, black hair, who looked like a cross between an Indian and a Spaniard, which they no doubt were.

Each man carried his cigarettes rolled up in his sash and continually smoked them. Their dress consisted of a cotton shirt, straw hat, and cotton breeches; while about their waist was wrapped, as tightly as they could bind it, a red or yellow sash some ten or fifteen feet in length when stretched out straight and which, I was told, strengthened them by its tension about their middle. Mr. Stevens used to say if you took the sash off of them, they couldn't lift a pound.

They cooked their meals in the bottom of the lighters, over a coal fire built in a tin can filled with sand. One of the principal exports to the West Coast is case oil; we had something like eight-hundred cases for Valparaiso alone. Each case contained two tin cans of oil and it was one of these cans, about a foot square and sixteen inches high, that they used as a stove.

The man who did the cooking first cut up some bread into square chunks, then fried either some cheese or some sliced onions in a pan with sweet oil. A piece of meat he cooked by holding it over the coals on the end of a stick. When all was done, he cut the meat into portions and put pieces of it on small bits of clean paper on a beam.

Each man helped himself from the pan of onions and filled his cup, made from the horn of a bullock with the end cut off and plugged, with some kind of liquor they heated in a can over the fire. They drink various kinds of liquor out here: malorica, anisour, frisco, and something that sounded like watch-a-ki. When a man gets drunk on these liquors they say he's nearly crazy for a week afterward.

While we worked cargo down in the hold, several ship carpenters from shore were putting in a new hawse pipe and patching up the trail boards, part of which had carried away when the anchor chain parted. They also mended the boat on top of the fo'c'sle that had had its bow smashed in by a sea off the Horn; and made a new door for the coach house that led into the cabin.

Chapter 11

The Tobey arrives in port—American men-of-war—Lawrence and I have a Sunday ashore—Can't buy ice cream—Conductresses on train cars—We visit the men-of-war—I get hit with a cargo block—The cargo protest—A floating church and a Christmas Eve entertainment—A hot Christmas—Working overtime—The "Coffee Mill"—We leave Valparaiso bound north—The geese—New Years afloat—Autofagasta—Mooring ship—Heavy cargo—The seals and mackerel—Stubborn launcheros—I buy bread—The market steamers—Apprentice boys.

On December 9, several new vessels arrived in port. Among them was an American whaler with single topsails and rows of boats swung on heavy, clumsy davits along her side. Another was a clipper-looking bark with a main skysail and a hurricane deck. Our old man knew the captain of the latter vessel, so early the next morning Lawrence, the darky cabin boy, and I rowed him out to her. We lay a long time under her stern, on which was painted her name in large white letters: *Gerard C. Tobey*. But I didn't mind waiting. It was far better out in the breeze and sunlight, where I could look out to sea and watch the ships coming and going and the hundred and one interesting things going on in the busy harbor, than to be down in the hold of the *Wright,* handling boxes, kegs of nails, barrels of oil, and cases.

When the two captains did come down the gangway, our old man had a little white puppy in one hand. It was so small it couldn't climb over the handle of an oar that lay in the bottom of the boat. We rowed in to the mole and as the captain landed he said, "Go back aboard and get your dinners, then come in and wait for me here." We did as we were told and lay all afternoon with our boat moored to a large iron can buoy just off the mole, waiting for him. There were about a dozen other boats around us, most of them clinker-built English boats with two or three apprentices in each. These boys did nothing but swagger about and boast among themselves, trying to assume a sailor's recklessness. Most of them were young boys between fourteen and twenty years of age, but they were passing a whisky flask around and some were already half drunk.

One of the men on the *Tobey* had given me a package of old novels and I had a fine time, lying along a thwart of the boat, reading *Snarle Yowl the Dog Fiend*.

The next day a man came aboard to take Peter's place. He was a Swede named Albert, a tall lanky fellow whose face and hair were the color of a boiled lobster. Another man, a little short German just the other extreme from Albert, came aboard during the afternoon to replace Kaiser.

On Friday, December 16, the long-awaited American men-of-war came in and dropped anchor all in a line. A beautiful yet powerful-looking fleet they were, painted a pure white with the Stars and Stripes at the stern of each. Each ship fired a salute as it anchored. There were four of them on their way back from New York, having taken part in the "Columbus Celebration" held there in 1892.

The following Sunday I went aft and asked the captain to let me go ashore. Charlie had gone the night before. He consented, but said to take Lawrence with me; so dressed in our best we were landed at the mole about half past nine that morning. We didn't know where to go or what to do; so we tramped up one street and down the next, taking in all the novel sights and seeing so much we couldn't remember half of it.

I had gotten some money from the captain, so when I saw a candy store I went in to invest in some of it. The place was kept by two French ladies and I could hardly make my wants known. I had to point to things.

"Have some ice cream, Lawrence?" I asked, seeing a sign I recognized as ice cream.

"Yaas!" he answered.

So I asked for a quart, but they refused to sell it to me. "Oh! No! We only sell to accommodate de ladies," was the answer.

"What's the difference who you sell to as long as I pay for it?" I asked. But it was no use, so when a tramcar came along we jumped aboard. It was the queerest contrivance I had ever ridden on. It had two decks with a winding pair of iron steps connecting them.

We went up on the top where the passengers sat back to back with an iron guardrail in front so they couldn't fall off, and here we watched the ever-changing scene along the streets the car ran on. The driver sat up top where we were and was so wrapped up in blankets and capes I thought he would have roasted. His breeches were slit up the sides from the bottom nearly to the knees and were wide and highly ornamented with braids and buttons. He wore a broad, round sombrero with buttons all around the rim. Instead of a conductor, each car carried a conductress. I couldn't believe my eyes at first, but sure enough every car that came along had a girl conductress dressed in black with a white apron and a straw hat set jauntily on one side.

Our fare was two cents up on top, while inside the fare was five cents. I was surprised to see the number of fine stone buildings, stores, etc. At the mole a couple of streets back from the water, we saw the depot and a train of cars that were just going out; where, we couldn't tell as all the signs were in Spanish. One thing I noticed, instead of saying Brown and Co., the signs all read Brown y Ca.

Once we passed a church and I saw all the people reverently lift their hats to the priest as they passed by. All the women looked alike to me, fat-faced things with clear white skin and rosy cheeks that gave them a babyish look. They all dressed alike in black gowns that made them look like nuns.

Lawrence and I sat eating candy and cakes when a fat Spaniard sitting next to me turned around and in a most polite voice said something that I took for "Excuse me," and helped himself to just one candy from my box. I offered him more, but he wouldn't take any.

We rode to the end of the line and I could see from the position of the ships in the bay that we were in the northern part of the town. There were lots of drivers, conductresses, and carmen here; changing horses and turning the cars around. We got in the same car and came back, only riding "in the 'tween deck," as Lawrence called it.

There was one beautiful little park we had passed and when we came to it we got out and sat on one of the benches. I feasted my eyes on the fountains and different varieties of flowers and palms that filled the park. We didn't know what to do or where to go when we got back to the mole, so we sat down on the seawall and looked off over the bay at the ships at anchor.

All the grog shops were called storehouses and I saw such names as "Cape Horn Storehouse," "Liverpool Storehouse," "San Francisco Storehouse," and "New York Storehouse." Lawrence wanted to buy a pair of slippers, so we tramped about the lower part of the town until he got them and I had invested my remaining cash in towels and chocolate. About five o'clock we went back aboard, but the mate sent us back again for the old man. While we waited for him, we saw Admiral Gebhard land at the mole from one of the men-of-war boats.

The next day was Monday. We had discharged most of our cargo for this place and all hands were kept scrubbing and painting the bark. The captain took Joe and me in the boat and went around to all the American vessels and got their skippers to go make a visit to the men-of-war. There were the captains of the bark _Gerard C. Tobey, Seminole,_ and _Lottie Moore._ Two other sailors from the other vessels were taken along to help row and we pulled out to the man-of-war _San Francisco_ and landed all the captains at her gangway, then we pulled up forward and hung onto a rope from her boatboom. The blue jackets asked us aboard, but no one else would go, so up I went alone and the crowd of men I saw as I looked along the berth deck was enough to make my eyes swim. It was like a hornet's nest; I felt as if I had suddenly dropped into Broadway, with its busy hum and hurrying crowds, and I was glad to get out in fresh air and back to our tidy, roomy bark.

As it was getting on toward Christmas time, our captain purchased two geese and several chickens and the forward part of the bark was transformed into a barn-yard.

One afternoon I was working down in the lower hold with the mate and a couple of others, cleaning up the dunnage, while the rest of the crew were shifting the cargo tackles forward to the fore hatch. I was standing under the hatch when suddenly something struck me on the head and sent my teeth together with a snap, and for a few seconds I knew nothing. When I came to, the mate was standing alongside of me asking, "Where'd it hit you? On the head?"

"What was it?" I asked.

"That's what it was," said he, kicking a large twelve-inch cargo block that lay near me. It was so heavy it was all one man wanted to carry.

"Good Lord!" I exclaimed. "It's a wonder it didn't kill me."

"It would have if it had hit you square; it must have hit you slanting."

The others all looked on and, when he saw I was all right, the mate went on deck and gave Fred, as he was the one who had dropped it, an awful laying out.

The next break in the monotonous job of loading lighters and working cargo was when Joe, I, the two mates, and Lawrence rowed ashore one morning and all but Lawrence, who was left in charge of the boat, went ashore to the American consul's office. We were joined by the old man, while the consul read a cargo protest to us, which stated that everything possible had been done by the officers and crew to save the cargo from damage during the gale off the Horn; this we all had to sign.

It seems some of the bales of goods were damaged by salt water that had leaked below around the pumps and this protest, as it was called, protected the captain and ship from any loss therefrom.

That same evening, washed and dressed in our best, Joe, Bill, and I, with the cook, cabin boy, and second mate, rowed in to a Christmas Eve entertainment given aboard the "church ship" *Bethel* or "Battle Ship," as it was called. What induced us to go more than anything was the promise that we would be given tea and biscuits. The *Bethel* was made from the hull of a small English iron bark that had been dismasted off the Horn and brought back to Valparaiso and made into a floating church for seamen. A long, narrow hatchway had been cut in the upper deck, over which a roof was built with the sides left open and protected by awnings. This hatchway enabled those on deck to look below and hear the preaching as if from a balcony. When we rowed up to the gangway, we found the decks underneath the awnings lit up with Japanese lanterns and a good-size crowd already assembled. There were sailors of all nationalities, with mates, bos'ns, a-b's, ordinary seamen, and a large percentage of apprentice boys, togged out in their blue dress suits.

There was a stairway leading down to the lower hold and, after tying our boat at the boat boom, along with some twenty-odd others, we went below and took seats on the benches, which were arranged like the pews in a church.

At the forward end was a raised platform draped with a flag and lit with lanterns. I was quite surprised at the number of English and American ladies who seemed to be managing the affair and were dressed up in great style. They sang and gave recitations when the performance began and I sat lost in meditation. I was back in Brooklyn then. Some of the songs were joined in by all hands and many were songs I knew well. But there was one song, sung by an old bewhiskered salt, as near like Dick Deadeye as a man could be, that brought down the house. It was called "Billie, the Longshoreman" and seemed to be a favorite ballad with the English sailors.

There was an intermission in the middle of the performance and tea and cake were passed around by the ladies. I could have drank a dozen cups such as they gave us, as it was sweetened with fresh milk and sugar, something I had not tasted for four months; but I was ashamed to drink more than two cupfuls, although the ladies pressed us to take more and were, to us, such bewitching-looking creatures that we didn't like to refuse them. Joe looked at me after he had drained his cup at one swallow, and I knew by his looks what he meant: the cups didn't hold but a taste compared to his appetite.

We spent a very happy Christmas Eve and it was well on toward Christmas morning before we came away.

I hardly realized the next day that it was Christmas. There was no snow or ice, no snowballing, or going skating for me that winter. The sun burned down on our decks so that by nine o'clock we perspired even in our undershirts and breeches. All morning long I was kept in the boat, "ferryboating" as we called it. Charlie and I took the captain around to all the other American ships, collecting stuff that we then took to the *Benj. Sewall*, aboard of which a grand supper would be given for all the American captains. Each ship contributed something, and we rowed about getting it. One gave crackers, another a turkey, another chickens, another celery, etc. Then we went in to the mole and brought off a boatload of ice and champagne; the ice I learned was manufactured ice.

Then we went aboard the *Wright* and had our dinner, and a good one it was, too. I turned in and slept for about an hour in the afternoon and then Bill and I rowed the captain ashore and lay at the buoy off the mole all afternoon in the boiling-hot sun, waiting for him to come back. We had nothing in the boat to shade us and the white paint was so hot you couldn't lay your hand to it. I was much amused by watching a little steam tender from the British man-of-war *Pheasant* come in loaded deep with blue jackets going ashore for a frolic. It was quite comical to note the difference in their appearance and actions when they returned. One belated old sea dog came down long after the launch had steamed off to the ship. The boatmen all made fun of him, but he was too drunk to resent it. They kept their boats off just far enough so he could not get in and I expected to see him stumble and splash in at any moment. Finally, one Chilean in an old punt backed in and took him aboard. He tried to sit up, but it was too much for him and he slid down into a helpless heap in the stern, with his feet on one rail and one arm trailing over the other side. He had had his Christmas celebration.

We loaded our last lighter the next morning, but were short two cases of Luberline, a kind of oil. There were two-hundred-and-fifty cases of oil stowed aft in the lower hold and we had to carry them about twenty feet and re-stow them, looking for the two missing ones. Finally we found them; they were the same size and weight as all the rest, only the marking on the case was a little different.

That afternoon we hove some castings, weighing more than a ton each, aft near the main hatch so as to trim the bark. Before supper, a steamer came alongside with a new anchor and forty-five fathoms of chain to replace what we had lost when we came to anchor. It was ten minutes to seven, when the mate asked in a sarcastic tone, "Is it six o'clock yet, Steward?" He might have known it was by the muttered curses and scowls among us, for we knew very well it was long past "knocking off" time.

The following morning we took in all our fenders, hoisted in the gangway, and then a "coffee mill" came alongside, hoisted our anchor for us with her powerful winch, and towed us out between the barks *Seminole* and *Gerard C. Tobey,* which were waiting to sail. Here we moored to one of the can buoys to wait for our papers before sailing up the coast to Autofagasta, our next port.

The *Tobey* slipped her moorings when the offshore trades began to blow, and was followed the next day by the *Seminole,* leaving us alone in the outer row. We bent on our fore and main courses and the spanker that had been unbent, but could not sail, as our "lay days" were not up yet.

On December 29, about two o'clock in the afternoon, our captain came aboard and said we would get under way. We signaled a tug to tow us out, as there was practically no wind in under the land. Without the least regret, I watched the high, brown mountains, the shipping, and the city fade from view. I was all eagerness to see what our next port would be like. Offshore we got a good quartering breeze and piled on the canvas until the old *Wright* was smoking through it once more and all hands felt happy to be at sea again, having watch every four hours.

One of the geese the captain had brought aboard for a New Year's dinner had died of some disease and we hove it overboard. The other one had also disappeared and had not been seen since the day we unmoored in Valparaiso. We found it one day; the mate and two men went down in the chain locker to stow the cable and there was the missing goose, dead, its neck broken by a heavy chain.

We saw the Old Year out and the New Year in, in a way I had never seen it before. From eight until ten that night, I was on lookout and when relieved by Joe at ten, I rolled up in my blanket and went to sleep by the pumps, with the coil of the buntline for a pillow. At eight bells, midnight, we called the other watch, wished each other a Happy New Year, shook hands all around, and then our watch went below to have our first sleep in the year eighteen hundred and ninety-three.

The mate was in an ugly mood the next morning, probably last New Year he'd promised himself he'd be a captain by this time and was mad to think he had not yet got a ship. But we got the benefit of his humor; he kept us washing down the decks from half past five until eight o'clock and even then we were not through. I had never carried so much water since we'd left New York. When the morning mists rolled away under the hot sun, the coast was in sight all along inshore of us. High mountain peaks with rolling undulating plains between that were as barren as a desert, with not even a tree or a blade of grass as far as the eye could reach. It seemed queer to be coasting along shore and not see any schooners or coasting vessels as we would in America. The only sail we saw was sighted early one morning, dead ahead. As we overtook and passed it, we saw it was an open lighter rigged with two square sails and loaded with bags of stuff that looked like saltpeter. Her crew of two men and a boy crawled out from under the tent stretched over the after part of the boat and watched us pass. I was going up with the union jack to lash it on the tie of the fore royal yard at the time, and in the distance ahead I noticed the spars of several vessels. It was toward this place that we steered and soon came into plain view of the port.

We counted thirteen craft at anchor and in the background, built on a level grade of ground that sloped down from the mountains to the shore, lay the city of Autofagasta. To the north, the coast circled around and ended in a low point of land that jutted out into the sea and formed a bay open to the south'ard. All the ships lay at anchor in a row off the city. There was a cut or pass in the mountains just back of the town, through which we saw a winding road leading down. Way up on the mountainside was an immense anchor standing out as white as chalk against the brown hills, perfect in its outline.

We hove to three or four miles out and got our breakfast while we waited for the pilot to come out to us. His boat was visible as it rose on the top of a sea, coming out with a large flag in the stern. He was less gaudily dressed than the port captain at Valparaiso, but knew his business. We filled away and ran down to the anchorage, clewing up sail as we ran in and rounded up smartly between the English bark *Berwickshire* and a Yankee ship called the *George Skofield*. I thought we were going to cut the latter in two, we forged ahead at such a rate, but we just fetched into a berth alongside and let go our anchor.

Then we took a small anchor out astern in a lighter rigged with a winch. Before we knocked off for supper, we had the bark moored stem and stern and the courses unbent and stowed away.

We hardly expected to get a lighter the next day, so the mate mixed up a barrel of paint and was just sending us off to paint the outside of the bark from stages made of a plank slung over on ropes, when we saw a lighter heading our way. Paint pots and brushes were hurriedly stowed under the fo'c'sle head and we went aft to the hatch and got ready to load the lighter.

Most of the cargo for this port was heavy stuff; there were three locomotives in sections, the boilers alone weighing six tons. There were several hundred long iron pipes, car wheels, and several hundred cases of oil, oysters, etc. I was down in the hold again with Joe and the second mate, so I didn't see much of what was going on in the harbor until all the light stuff was unloaded and we began to hoist out the boilers and heavy locomotive frames.

Then all hands were needed on deck. We put preventer backstays to the topmasts and then hoisted the spare main yard, which lay along the main deck in the scuppers, up on end as a derrick. Turn upon turn of heavy hawsers were passed from the masthead to the yard to bear the strain of the heavy boilers, and the heel of the spar was cut round and stepped into a heavy oak block with a hollow in it for the spar to set in. Below decks we shored up from beam to beam down to the keel and then we hoisted the boilers out. It took all hands and the launcheros all morning to heave out one, using the capstan on the half deck for the job.

On deck we were able to look around as we worked, and saw the lighters going back and forth in tow of small, open launches. Next to us, the crew of the *Skofield* was discharging timber out of her bow port, and the *Berwickshire,* lying on the other side of us, was all discharged and rode like an empty cask on the water. Behind the *Skofield,* anchored in a row one alongside the other, stretched a line of barks and ships to within a mile or so of the city.

My chief amusement came from watching the seals and sea lions eating fish. The waters swarmed with fine plump mackerel, swimming in schools so thick that as you looked down and over the water you saw nothing but a mass of moving fish. Deep down, as far as could be seen, they moved in countless thousands, now all swimming one way, then suddenly turning, thousands of them in the twinkling of an eye. Some leaping out of the water as those below crowded them up, in haste to escape the hungry maw of the seals that were eating them.

It was a comical sight to see the shining bald pate of an old sea lion rise slowly up out of the water, his big round eyes fixed on the ship, his tusks and beard hanging down for all the world, as the mate said, like Old Bill when he's eating pea soup.

It was astonishing to see the speed those fat, oily creatures could go in pursuit of the fish. On the surface of the water they did not go very fast, but deep down we saw the flash of their whitish bellies as they sped along belly up, going like a shark with a peculiar sculling motion of their tail. After they had eaten their fill of fish, they showed the same trait as a cat; they would catch a fish and let it go, slightly crippled, then catch it again. Rising to the surface, as a man would come, head up, with the fish in its mouth, the seal gave its head a jerk and tossed the fish up in the air. Then, when it sank so far it seemed the fish must have escaped, the seal turnèd over and dove, reappearing maybe on the other side of the bark to go through the same antics.

One morning about a week later, we saw two native fishermen in a rowboat catching fish; they did it in a novel way, too. One man was at the oars, while the other, standing in the stern, threw over a lit dynamite cartridge, which sank some distance before exploding. The second it went off, in a radius of about fifty feet all about the rowboat, hundreds of mackerel jumped out of the water like a fountain and floated about, stunned. Then the men rowed around and scooped them up in a net. Two explosions filled their boat with fish, so thickly did they swim in these waters.

The lightermen, or "launcheros," in this port were independent fellows and took no bullying from the mate. Once he tried to make them haul their lighter a little further aft and threatened to throw a piece of coal at one of them. He came near getting his head smashed in when one of them rushed at him with an iron bar. But he scrambled up on the bark and never ventured onto another lighter.

He did not give them any water to drink either, and the heat from the sun was something cruel, but they got revenge. The bark was floating very light, with her copper well out of water. The launcheros came head on into us and the sharp stem head of the lighter as it rose on a sea skinned the copper off like an apple peeling. In vain, the mate swore at them and tried to get a fender over, but they sheered the lighter so her stem came against the *Wright*'s coppered bottom.

In a little over two weeks we had the bark unloaded and painted outside so that her sides shone as black and glossy as the day she was launched. We painted inside after that, and also varnished the 'tweendecks. Some days it blew so hard no lighters could come out to us. The anchorage was simply an open roadstead, exposed to all southerly winds, and for a couple of days we caught it; the seas broke clear over the reefs that lined the shore and made the one little inlet through them impassable. Those days we hung over the side, painting, two men on each stage.

In hoisting out one of the boilers we had smashed a piece out of the rail. On one of those windy days Joe and I rowed the captain to the bark *Janet McNeil*, lying astern of us, and brought her carpenter aboard to repair it.

Then we saw the size of the seas that were running. It was like coasting down a hill into a hollow, and the ships and land all sank from view and we seemed to be down in a deep hole with towering walls of water meeting the sky all around us. Then up we rose like a bird to the crest and found it a difficult thing to catch the gangway as the bark rolled.

Besides Tobey, the little white puppy we got in Valparaiso, we now had another, a black dog. Tobey was a comical little puppy and was growing nicely. The black dog was an older one and as sly as a wolf.

We caught him stealing food out of the fo'c'sle several times and were obliged to watch him continually. He would run away with coats and shoes and made lots of trouble.

He never came around when we were eating our meals or in the fo'c'sle, but as soon as the order was given to "turn to" and we all marched aft, he snuck forward around the other side of the house and got into the fo'c'sle. Several times when I got a chance, I ran forward and caught him drinking up our fresh water or eating in some man's bunk. And how he bolted aft when he saw me. Once I caught him just as he came out of the door. He knew he was caught and let out a howl that made the fellows aft at the winch double up with laughter, for I caught him square with my toe and sent him aft faster than he expected to go. He finally got to be such a nuisance that we gave him to our tallyman, a fat little man from Bolivia, who took him ashore.

When we took the tallyman ashore at night, the mate never came with us, as at Valparaiso, but let Joe and me go alone. The landing place was a small iron pier built out into the water for a couple of hundred feet. One morning we were sent ashore for the tallyman and took with us all our remaining money, which did not amount to much. He was not on the pier when we arrived, so I jumped ashore and went up to town to try and buy some bread. I asked in a couple of restaurants for "pan," but they had none to sell. I went all around the square and came out by a large store kept by James Imbrea, one of the parties to whom part of our cargo was consigned. He was a little, short, sandy-haired Scotchman. When I told him what I wanted, he showed me a man going down the street leading a donkey with two large covered baskets slung one on each side; he was a baker. So I ran after him and invested all my money in small round loaves of bread. When I regained the boat, I found Joe and the tallyman waiting for me. We stowed the bread in our coats and smuggled it forward, unseen, into the fo'c'sle.

There was a line of English steamers that ran up and down the coast, stopping at all the ports. Called market boats, twice a week, regularly, they came in and anchored at this port. The country being a desert, the people depended upon these steamers for their produce. When the day came that the steamer was due in port, the population flocked down to the waterfront with bags and market baskets, eagerly awaiting its arrival.

The minute she was sighted as a smudge of black to the south'ard, there was a wild scramble into the boats, and such a shouting, go-as-you-please race as they indulged in made me think of a crowd going to a circus; young and old alike eager to buy. Some looking for food for their families, some to buy trinkets and luxuries, for the steamers carried everything. The lower deck was filled with cattle; the next, like a market, had bins of corn, onions, potatoes, beans, etc., ranged around the entire ship; and inside the cabins were fancy things, dry goods, etc.

Some of the rowboats from shore were loaded down with a crowd of men and women, with maybe a barelegged urchin sitting astride the bow or on a little short deck that was at each end of these whaleboats. Dogs barked and the people shouted across to one another in a tongue that was foreign to me, but sounded musical, with its long drawn-out o, o's and a, a's at the end of each call.

The steamer soon loomed up, a large iron craft with two schooner-rigged masts and a black funnel. She gradually slowed down until the hoarse grinding of her cable announced that she had anchored. The flotilla of boats hung back while a government barge containing the port captain and doctor, swept up to her gang-way, with the ensign of Chile flying from the staff in the stern. The officers mounted the gangway and not a boat moved until they came down again into the barge. But then, such a commotion; the townspeople's race out was nothing com-pared to the wild scramble for the gangway they had, all trying to be the first aboard and get the pick of the market.

It was a wonder to me some of the boats were not sunk; six or seven, going at full speed, met at the gangway, all coming from different directions. Sometimes the steamer stayed in port until the next day, but sometimes she proceeded north or south, whichever way she was going, that same night.

One Sunday when one of these steamers was in port, Joe and I took our cap-tain and the *McNeil*'s skipper aboard her and then lay alongside, nearly suffocating with the stench coming off the lower decks, where the cattle were stowed in bins.

From there we took them ashore and lay all afternoon at the little pier, talking with some English apprentice boys. One young fellow, fifteen years old, to whom I was talking, said he had been four years on the ship he was now on and would have to serve a year more before he could ship as an ordinary seaman. He was amazed when I told him I had shipped as an AB, although it was my first voyage. Another apprentice, a young Scotch boy not as old as the one I was talking to, was staggering about the pier, drunk as a lord and evidently thought that made him ap-pear like a sailor. During the afternoon, the boat from a large iron Liverpool ship called the *Wray Castle* came ashore. It was a beautiful boat, clinker built with brass oarlocks, varnished wash strake and gratings, and bright oars, rowed in man-of-war style by four apprentices dressed in white duck suits with the ship's name worked across the breasts. Their captain was a regular "lime-juicer" and sat in the stern on an English flag thrown over the seat. This boat also lay at the pier and we "spun coppers" with the apprentices about our ships and officers. When the English cap-tain went ashore, he gave his apprentices some money. As soon as he was out of sight, two of them went up the street and returned with a couple of bottles of wine or some kind of liquor and passed them around until they were empty and our young Scotch friend was so full he fell asleep in the bottom of his boat.

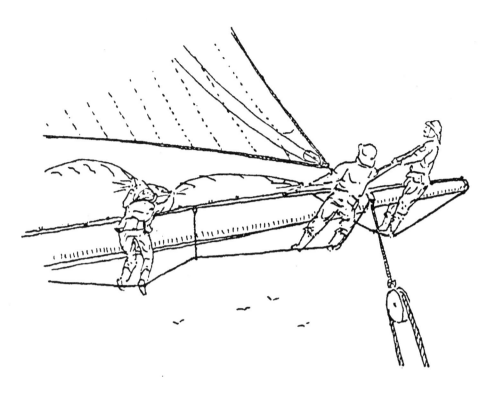

Chapter 12

Take in ballast—Unmooring—We sail but have to anchor again—Off at last—The officers quarrel—Putting up the platform—Jellyfish—Anchor off Caleta Buena—Discharge ballast—The town—Saltpeter and the ceremony of heaving in the last bag—Dynamite fishing—A sailor's gratitude—Moored waiting for saltpeter—Hot work and hard heaving—The Golden Shore goes out.

On Monday, January 16, we began to heave in our ballast as all our cargo had been discharged. The bark was so light with nothing in her that the captain was afraid to sail without some weight in her bottom. We hove in about three lighter loads a day, each lighter carrying about fifteen tons of coarse brown sand. This was shoveled into baskets in the lighter by the launcheros and hove in with the winch by four of us, with two men standing by to spell us; Charlie tended gangway and Old Jim was at the lowering fall. In all we took in about two hundred tons.

It was an odd sight to see them loading the sand into the lighters from the beach. Two men shoveled and filled the sacks, which were made from the hide of some animal, while others, naked except for a cloth about their loins, carried these skins full of sand out into the water and up a sloping plank to the lighter, where they dumped it. It took two men to lift the sacks onto the shoulders of the carriers.

Saturday, January 21, we had been just eight weeks on the coast and that noon the pilot came out and we began to unmoor, preparatory to going to sea again. But such a time we had getting our anchor up. We started to heave short just before dinnertime; our port anchor came up all right, but every time the starboard one came "up and down" the cable slipped back over the wildcat of the windlass. We hove and hove, and the mates monkeyed about until we discovered that the chain, which was the new one we took aboard at Valparaiso, was too small for the wild-cat. There was some swearing then. We had thirty fathoms of chain out and the only way we finally got it aboard was by heaving on the windlass and also on the fish tackle made fast to the chain and stretched along the deck, and then we had to use a luff tackle. The pilot got mad and threatened to go ashore and his men stopped work at six o'clock, although it took us until half past eight to cat the darned anchor.

Then we warped ahead about half a mile and moored to the can buoy, ready to slip out to sea when the wind served us.

We didn't get a fair slant until Monday morning, just as we were washing down. All day Sunday we had waited in readiness to get underway, but no wind came. This morning, however, it came out good and strong. We let go our lines, sheeted home our topsails, and crowded on sail as fast as we could set it. The wind, however, which had struck in so suddenly, died out altogether in a short time. We then braced the yards back and forth, trying to use the cat's-paws until about three in the afternoon, when we had to anchor as the current was setting us on shore.

We furled everything, coiled down the gear, and spent the remainder of the day heaving all the starboard chain up out of the locker and shifting it end for end so the small chain would stay in the locker when coming to anchor.

After supper that night, the mate, Joe, and I sailed back in the boat to the harbor and got some "holystones" from the *McNeil*. We went in under our spritsail, before the trade wind, and at a rattling pace, but coming back it fell a flat calm and Joe and I had to row back four or five miles against the sea. Everybody was snoring in their bunks when we regained the bark, except Old Jim, who was standing anchor watch.

At half past ten we were roused out again to get the bark under way as the land breeze had begun to blow. It was dark as a pocket on deck and everybody was as cross as two sticks. We hove short and waited for orders, but the mate and captain got into an argument over whether the anchor was up and down. The captain would not take Mr. Hill's word for it, but sent the second mate forward to check. The mate threatened to quit work and go to his room, so, while they argued, we rested and waited.

Finally we broke out the anchor, set all sail, and at two o'clock, everything being coiled down, our watch went below until four A.M., when we were called out to take the deck. We had an easy time of it then, the mate let us do as we pleased and never gave an order; but from the way he walked back and forth and kept muttering to himself, I knew he was mad clear through at the captain and second mate.

We had very light winds most of the time running north from Autofagasta, but once in a while we caught a fresh puff. On the third day, about five o'clock in the afternoon, we passed a city called Iquique and hove to that night with the bark heading offshore, although this was not necessary as it was dead calm all night.

Both watches ate breakfast together and then stood by, ready to come to anchor in Caleta Buena, the port where we were to load for home. I was astonished, as I hung over the rail with the rest of the crew, to see the beautiful, large, various-colored jellyfish through which the bark was passing. In shape they resembled an immense mushroom with a long trailing mass of roots or feelers. They were beautifully marked with alternate pink and white stripes that radiated from the center like an umbrella, and were covered with pink dots in the white stripes and white spots in the pink stripes. Some of them were as large around as a dinner plate, and the mate told me a yarn about a sailor who had struck one of them while swimming. The mate said it was like an electric shock that nearly stunned the man, causing his flesh to break out in red blotches like prickly heat.

My study of jellyfish and the other marine matter floating past was interrupted by the mates ordering us to get the port anchor cleared away. The masts of the shipping in the bay ahead were visible when we took our pilot aboard, and about ten o'clock that morning we clewed up everything and let go our port anchor about a mile to the north of the town. Here we would discharge our sand ballast overboard.

We were used to furling sail by this time and had everything stowed aloft, cargo tackles up, and awning spread by dinnertime. All that afternoon we hove out baskets of sand and dumped them over the rail. I was on the winch with four others and the sun was enough to boil one's brains, and caused the perspiration to run in drops off our chins and noses. We were on deck and could look about and see what kind of a port we were anchored in. It was simply an open coastline with a slight dent not more than half a mile in depth and a sheer wall of loose dirt, sand, and pebbles shutting out the world to the eastward and sea and sky meeting in the haze to the westward. At the base of the cliff, nestled on the narrow, sandy strip of beach were two rows of dirty little hovels, built of all kinds of cast-off boards and patched up with pieces of sheet iron and matting. At the northern end of the town was the evaporating works, with its high chimney; all the water they had to drink here was salt water, which was boiled and the steam condensed. One street ran between the rows of huts and ended in about the middle of the bay, at a small iron pier built out something like the one at Autofagasta.

From this pier, straight up the mountainside, ran what is called the saltpeter slides. Two tracks with a car on each connected one to another by a cable, reaching in three lifts, or sections, to the mountaintop, where the houses appeared not more than an eighth of an inch square. During the day we saw the cars going up and down; the one going down was filled with the heavy saltpeter, and hauled the other up, which was full of coal; a sort of gravity railway.

Saltpeter is about the heaviest kind of a cargo carried in ships, and the process of loading a vessel with it is the hardest work required of a sailor. In any other part of the world the ship would have been loaded by stevedores or coolies, but here we had to load our own ship. Each bag of saltpeter weighed about three hundred pounds and was hove in, one at a time, by five men on a single barrel winch. Some days we unloaded four lighters and some only three.

That night, our first in port, we saw an English bark finish loading. It was quite late and we had all had our suppers when cheer after cheer came over the still water. I got to the rail just in time to see the last bag being hoisted in. On the bag, as it swung in midair, sat a little darky, the cabin boy, waving an English flag in one hand and the Chilean flag in the other, while the crew sang some appropriate chantey. When the bag, darky and all, reached the yardarm, they made it fast and all the crew lined up on the rail and gave three cheers, first to one ship then another, until we heard them cheer the *Wright*. Then all our crew lined up along our rail and gave them three rousing Yankee cheers in return. When the last ship had been cheered, we saw her colors go floating aloft to her mastheads, a happy sign for her crew, but it made our fellows feel blue to think we had yet to load our bark. Then, keeping time to a sort of chant, they lowered the bag and darky to the deck and the tableaux was over.

All the next day, Saturday, we hove out ballast. I discovered our old friend the four-masted schooner *The Golden Shore* anchored way in under the land, deep in the water. One of her men came in our fo'c'sle that night, having brought her captain over, and told us she had nearly completed loading; she had been seven days at it so far and three more would fill her up. She had a donkey engine for hoisting sails and anchor, and with this she could heave in two bags at a time.

Sunday morning, after our breakfast, Joe and I were called aft to lower the boat down and go dynamite fishing with the old man and the mate. We rowed a couple of miles to the north'ard, up where the long Pacific swells came thundering in among the boulders and rocks that lined the shore. It was rather dangerous work so close inshore, but the captain fixed his charges and started in to work. The dynamite came in round packages about four inches long and a half inch in diameter, carefully wrapped in oiled paper. He untied one end of this package and made a hole in the brown powder with an ivory knitting needle; in this he inserted a brass cap about an inch long, with one end opened to receive the fuse. Then he bound the oiled paper tightly about the fuse with twine and the charge was ready for its deadly work. The fuse he cut off about nine inches in length and when Joe and I had backed the boat in far enough, he lit it from his cigar and threw it astern.

We pulled off a couple of strokes and watched the yellowish brown smoke curling up from the water, until we heard a sharp clicking sound, as if a handful of tacks had been dropped onto a sheet of tin, and a shock ran through the boat, telling us the charge had exploded.

Then we backed in over the spot and watched the white bellies of the stunned fish as they floated to the surface. With each charge we got about three fish. Once we ventured way in between two rocks and fired a bomb, and were rewarded by getting an immense rockfish, fully eight pounds in weight, but came near wrecking the boat in doing so. Just as we backed in so the mate could scoop him up with the net, an immense white comber came rolling inshore on us. We were caught where the water poured like a sluiceway between two rocks and the captain, when he saw it coming, shouted, "Pull! Pull like hell!"

We bent our backs at the oars, but could not stem the upslope of the oncoming sea. It broke before it reached us and nearly swamped the boat. We were carried stern first inshore among the rocks and could not get out until the backwash helped us.

We kept at it until we had a mess of fish, then started back for the bark. On the way, we passed through several schools of small herring. The mate threw a cartridge into one school and the stunned fish actually covered the water all about us. He took a basket that was in the boat and scooped up fully four hundred of them and Joe and I leaned over the side and scooped them up in handfuls.

All hands were called to the scuppers to clean fish when we regained the bark, and the cook gave us a royal fish dinner; he made the herring into fritters with about ten fish in each.

We hadn't washed down this Sunday morning and the fellows couldn't imagine what all this leniency on the part of the mates could mean. When they gave us an old sail to rig up as an awning over the fo'c'sle head, the older ones in the crew shook their heads in apprehension. Old Jim remarked, "Never knew it yet when they did a good turn but what there was some work-up job a-coming."

"Dot's right," chimed in Joe. "Ve'll get vork now sure, fer dey gets so kind."

Such is a sailor's way of appreciating a kindness. We were so used to abuse that we regarded the least sign of a favor with suspicion. You have seen a dog that has been kicked. He crouches and looks with suspicion at the man who tries to pat him. That's the way sailors are. A good illustration of this was given one day at break-fast. The cook had killed and cooked two chickens and they were more than enough for aft, so he sent some into the fo'c'sle with our mess. And what did the men do? Were they grateful for it? No indeed! Albert jabbed his fork into a wing and held it up. "What's this?" he asked looking around at the rest of the crew. "Chicken?" and he threw it back in the pan and helped himself to some tough salt horse. "Do you think I'd eat that? Not much."

"If it was fit to eat it would never be sent in here."

"It's rotten or it would 'ave been sent aft," said Jim.

And so on . . . The men turned up their noses at what the officers were, at that moment, eating and glad to get for a change.

The following day, Monday, we continued heaving out ballast while a gang of six or seven Chileans was hoisting in a couple of lighter loads of saltpeter so the bark would not capsize. We also stripped the bark of her sails and prepared to paint the masts and yards. By Wednesday, February 1, we had discharged our ballast, warped into the harbor, and moored stem and stern, as was the custom on this coast, with our stern toward the shore.

For several days we could get no saltpeter, and this gave the mate a chance to get his painting well along. All day long we swung up aloft with a paint pot or else worked on stages over the side. The job of painting the name and scrollwork at the bow and stern was given to me, and I made it last. The mate couldn't see me from the deck and I lay on my back and took it easy while I had the chance. Our captain had stayed ashore for a couple of days to see about getting a cargo, and on February 4 we got our first lighter.

A peculiar thing about loading saltpeter is the way it is stowed; one man stows the entire cargo of the ship. Our stevedore, as this man is called, was a short, fat little fellow. He took a bag on his shoulders and trotted along until he came to where the bag was to be stowed, then, with a quick toss, he sent the bag off his back and came back for another. He never touched a bag with his hands to stow it, except, of course, the last top tier, which had to be shoved in between the deck beams. When a bag left his back, that settled it, and he stowed them as fast as we heaved them in.

Charlie was in the hold on the platform, as it is called, which is simply bags of saltpeter stowed in a square pile under the hatch to the height of a man's shoulders. The bags were landed on this and Charlie rolled them onto the stevedore's shoulders. Old Jim was on deck at the lowering fall and the mate or second mate tended gangway, hooking on the falls, etc., for we had to heave it in on one tackle and then Jim lowered it into the hold on another, with several turns around a short spar he had lashed to the rail and a pair of leather palms to keep the rope from burning his hands.

But the hardest part of all was on the winch. It was a single wooden barrel mounted on an iron frame with no gearing whatsoever, and the bags were hoisted out with a single whip rove through a block on the main yard, or fore yard, as the case may be, according to which hatch we were loading, direct to the winch. It took four of us heaving with all our strength to bring the bags up out of the lighter. Sometimes there were five of us heaving, with another man standing by to relieve us one at a time after a certain number of bags were hove in. In this way we all had our turn at a rest and gave our overheated blood a chance to cool down.

For several days the mates would not give us an awning at the winch to protect us from the sun, although every other ship in port protected their men in this way, and all during the morning it was killing work. We dressed as lightly as possible, but even then the perspiration ran off us in streams. Joe, whose feet perspired badly, left two wet prints on deck where ever he had been standing. Up to noontime there was not a breath of air stirring, but just at dinnertime a good, stiff trade wind came offshore and made the work a little cooler.

Oh, how I wished then that I was back in the States. I was just about ready to desert such a hard-working packet as the *Wright* proved to be; and yet our stevedore told us one dinnertime she was a "home" the voyage previous. She was no home, as sailors term a good living ship, to us and a madder crowd of men were not in port. And it was all because we were a mixed crowd and could not trust one another. If we had all stuck together at the start, it would have been all right, but we let the mates tyrannize over us at first so now there was no letup. Many a day we hove in three lighters while other ships had only hove in two; as a reward, another lighter came off when the other ships were washing down, preparatory to knocking off work, and we would not stop work until after six o'clock, while all the other crews had had their supper by that time.

On the day the schooner *The Golden Shore* got under way, how I envied her crew, for she was bound up the West Coast to California, a fair-weather voyage all the way, with no Cape Horns to round. She hoisted her anchors and sails at the same time with steam, and inside half an hour she was standing out of the bay with every stitch set and I cannot remember ever seeing a finer-looking sight than she presented with her well-set, snow-white cotton sails, red Oregon-pine spars, and well-blacked rigging and hull; the latter setting low in the water and relieved by a narrow yellow band along the plank sheer. And, best of all, the American flag, old gridiron as we called it, was floating at her peak. She had our boat in tow as our captain was aboard her. As the schooner disappeared over the western horizon, we saw a little speck returning, which soon grew into the proportions of our boat with a sail set.

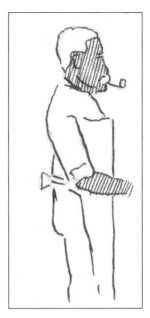

Chapter 13

*Fast heaving—I fall sick—The cook's pity—We get shore leave—
The saltpeter slide—All hands drunk—Back aboard.*

O ne day the stevedores, for there were two of them for a day or two, were bantering us about heaving in the bags, and said they could stow faster than any crew in port. So when we went to work, all hands agreed to make them hustle. Lord! how the bags came in that day. Round and round flew the winch handles like a steam engine, and the stevedores cried out at last to hold up a bit. They could not carry them away from the hatch fast enough. By half past six we had unloaded four lighters; the first contained two-hundred-and-forty-five bags of saltpeter, the second two-hundred-and-eighty, the third two-hundred-and-eighty-five, and the last two-hundred-and-forty, making a total of one-thousand-and-fifty bags, which, at three hundred pounds each, was one-hundred-and-fifty-seven tons hove in that day.

But we could not keep this pace up long for two reasons; first because we could only get so many lighter loads each day and, secondly, because the work was too hard and would make us all sick. All the next day I was sick at my stomach and felt quite miserable; whether it was heaving so hard on the winch or the change in drinking water, I didn't know. Jim and Charlie had both been laid up with the same complaint. As a soother, the Chilean informed me that nearly all the deaths on the coast were caused by stomach derangements.

That night I grew worse; I couldn't sleep a wink and had such cramps in my stomach they doubled me up in a heap. I tossed and turned and spent a most miserable night; then I thought of home and friends and wished I was among them to receive proper nursing. I didn't turn out next morning, nor could I eat anything, but lay in my bunk in agony. The mate came to the fo'c'sle door and asked me what was the matter. Soon after he left, I felt stifled in the close fo'c'sle and went up on the fo'c'sle head to lie under the awning, where I could get a breath of fresh air. Just as I got there, I was seized with a violent vomiting spell that left me as weak as a mouse. I couldn't stand up and lay for a spell near the rail before I ventured back to my bunk, for now that I was out in the air I was so chilled that my teeth chattered. I sat down and shuffled along, afraid I would fall if I tried to stand. I reached the fo'c'sle and fell exhausted into my bunk, and lay for an hour or so panting like a dog. I was so distressed in my mind for fear I had the coast fever and I completely broke down and fell asleep sobbing.

I was awakened by the crew coming in the fo'c'sle with their pots and pans to eat dinner and the smell of the food almost sickened me. Our stevedore was the most kind-hearted of the lot, and when Old Jim and Bill began to smoke he made them go out on deck and not stink the fo'c'sle with tobacco fumes.

"He's bad enough as he is without that," said he and asked me what my symptoms were. He patted me affectionately on the cheek when they turned to again, and told me to keep up heart.

He must have said something to the captain about me, for I was soon called aft to see him. He looked at me for a minute and then asked, "Well! What's the matter with you anyhow, you got the nitrate fever?" I told him I was sick at my stomach and was weak, so he took me below and gave me a dose of medicine. Then, after a few remarks in which he implied I was shamming sick to escape the work of heaving cargo, he ended by saying, "Well! You get the hell out of here now!" And I went back to my bunk. I was given two or three more doses of the medicine during the afternoon and after a good night's sleep was able to turn to next morning, although rather shaky on my legs.

I couldn't help laughing at our steward, or cook, a couple of days later. All through the week he sang ballads and comic songs, or swore as hard as any, but Sunday morning always found him with a clean white shirt on and all day he did nothing but whistle or sing hymns and religious tunes as he worked away in the galley or sat in his doorway, peeling potatoes.

In the afternoon, the second mate got permission to go sailing in the boat and he took me along with him. We set the spritsail the boat carried and ran ashore to the pier to get some stones for ballast.

That was the first chance I had to step ashore at this port, and while the second mate stayed with the boat, I walked up the pier and went down on the beach to get some rocks. I was surprised to see how smooth and round the stones had been worn from constantly rolling up and down the beach in the surf. I picked out one that was about as heavy as I could carry. Just as I lifted it up, something shot out from under it so quickly I didn't see where it went. I looked all about and finally detected a little brown lizard, about eighteen inches long, mounted on a rock whose color exactly matched his and accounted for my not seeing him before. His forelegs were bowed apart with its toes spread out like a chicken's foot, and his head was stretched out to the full length of his neck, with two little bead-like eyes fixed full upon me. I was as surprised as he, but the minute I moved he was off in a series of bounding leaps from rock to rock in a zigzag direction, landing upon the rocks with beautiful precision when you considered the rapidity of his flight. Then he stopped and again stretched his little turtle-like head to see if I was after him. I was glad enough to be rid of him and carried three rocks out the pier to the boat. Then we sailed about for a couple of hours and had quite a good time, Mr. Steven's being an old hand at dory fishing and used to small-boat sailing.

The only trouble with him was his love for cursing. He cursed at the men in the lighter and the stevedore in the hold, and he looked at us every time he swore to see that we appreciated his accomplishment in that line.

Saturday, February 11, we had the bark nearly loaded and the boys wanted to go ashore the next day. After breakfast the next morning they coaxed me to go aft and ask for a liberty day.

When the old man appeared on deck I went aft and "braced him" for permission to go ashore.

"How many of you want to go?" he asked, and I told him. "Well, you can go," he added in a rather hesitating tone. "But mind you all come back. The last voyage I let the crew go ashore, and they never came back. I had to ship a crew of Japs in their place,"

"Oh we'll come back," I assured him. "We only want a chance to stretch our legs on dry land."

"I suppose you'll want some money too, won't you?" he queried.

"Why, yes," I said, and nearly laughed in his face, for in back of him, around each side of the fo'c'sle, I saw anxious faces wondering what we were arguing so long about and anxiously hoping my request would be granted.

I repeated the whole conversation in the fo'c'sle, and when they heard we could go, out came the long-hidden shore clothes and the bottom of clothes bags were explored for a clean shirt or the shore-going shoes that had been carefully stowed away.

It was comical to see the care the boys bestowed upon their toilet and dress. Joe's hair fairly shone with the polishing of soap he had given it to make it lie smooth. Bill screwed his face about before a fragment of looking glass he had in endeavors to comb his beard into something like decent shape. Joe donned a loud checked shirt that made him look like the thoroughbred Dutchman he was. Old Bill togged out in a badly creased dress suit and rubbed up his derby, or "hard hat" as he called it. Joe capped his blond face with an immense soft felt sombrero, while Hansen—a little German we had shipped in Valparaiso to take Kaiser's place— squeezed his little feet into a small pair of dancing pumps with real shoelaces in them. All my shoelaces had gone long ago, but to dress up I rove marlin laces in place of the rope yarns used every day. My shoes were the ordinary convict-made dollar ones, but I cut them down so they made pumps or low shoes with only a short lacing in front. A brand new cotton shirt from the slop chest and the blue serge suit I had shipped in at New York completed my dress. I beat Hansen in the way of head gear, as I had a regular felt hat, while his best shift was a peaked uni- form cap that contrasted strangely with the rest of his getup. Old Jim and Fred rowed us ashore, as they were going to stay aboard, and landed us at the pier. A motley-looking crew we were when the surroundings of shipboard were replaced by those of shore.

We each had five dollars in Chilean money, equal to two and a quarter in Amer- ican coin. Our idea was to get into a saltpeter car and ride up to the top of the mountain, where we were told there was quite a city. But when we inquired, we found there was no car going up until five o'clock that evening, so we turned to- ward the village to see what amusement we could find there. At the entrance was a high picket fence with a soldier standing guard at the gate. We passed through without being challenged and walked the whole length of the one dirty lane. On each side were built one or two decent frame houses, and the rest were small hov- els filled with dirty children and their parents. In several, a pig lay sleeping on the floor, as much at home as any of the family. Everybody came to their doors as we passed and stared at us, but that didn't bother us any. We walked to the end of the street and found further progress impossible, as the shore came up from the sea so steep it was dangerous, and in most places impossible, to walk. So we started back and stopped at every gin mill we saw. Out of about thirty huts, there were six that sold liquor. But the last place we came to, near the gate, was the largest and best store in the place. They had everything for sale, and the proprietor could speak

English. Here I invested all my money in brown sugar, condensed milk, cocoa, crackers, and some maple sugar that came wrapped in reed.

It was too early to return to the bark, so Joe and I proposed a climb up the mountain. I didn't drink and I knew if we stayed there long, everyone would be blind drunk. Charlie had run across one of our launcheros, who sported a spotless white starched shirt without a coat, vest, or collar; but he did have on a pair of cuffs. Where he got hold of such things I couldn't imagine.

We left them in conversation and started to climb the mountain. We intended to go to the top, but after an hour of hot climbing under a tropical sun, we were glad enough to stop at the first saltpeter lift, which was only about a third the distance up the mountain. We had to zigzag our way as it was too steep to climb straight up. At the first station, or "lift" as it is called, we found a narrow ledge of level ground with a shed alongside the slide and the keeper's house in back of it. A car on the slide or track held a large iron tank full of water, for the people on top of the mountain depended on the condensing works at the beach for fresh water. We dropped down on a bench in one corner of the shed, glad to get under some shade. The glare of the sun on the light brown sand was most trying to the eyes.

Here we sat and looked over the queer contrivance of wheels and brakes that controlled the speed of the cars going up and down the slide by a couple of turns of the cable around a drum. Below us lay the town on the narrow crescent-shaped beach and, with the ships anchored in the bay, it looked as small as a child's toy. We were already many times higher than the masthead of the tallest ship and looked down on their decks and saw little black dots that indicated men moving about on them.

Right at our feet, at the bottom of the slide, the little pier ran out into the water with tracks for the cars to run on. Small iron cranes were used to hoist cargo out of the lighters and the saltpeter slid from the cars down chutes into the lighters. Off the end of the pier to the left lay the fleet of thirty or forty lighters at anchor, idle for the day. As far as the eye could reach to the westward, the calm blue waters of the Pacific lay sparkling under a cloudless sky, but not a sail was visible. After studying the toy houses and ships below us, we decided to descend. Before we went, I tried the faucet of the tank car and succeeded in getting a drink. Then Joe and Hansen each had a drink, for the climb had parched our throats. But we could not stop the water, and with dismay I saw the valuable fluid running to waste. There was a large wrench hanging in the shed, much too large for the faucet, but by putting a little stone in the jaws of it I succeeded in shutting off the water. Then we began the decent, and by running and jumping reached the bottom in under fifteen minutes.

The rest of the afternoon, until about four o'clock, we spent in the store, talking with several men among whom was a Spaniard or a Frenchman, it was hard to tell just which, by the name of Charlie, and he got into earnest conversation with Bill and Joe. It seems he wanted those two to run away from the *Wright* and ship on a Chilean bark in Pisagua that was going to San Francisco. Joe asked me to go and I told him I would think it over. So they carefully made all arrangements to desert the bark. I was amused by a procession of natives that was going by the door. They were having a carnival we were told, a kind of a masquerading time. There was one character, the center of attraction for all the young urchins of the place, called the "Mexican Barber." He was so smeared with chalk, bluing, and some kind of bright red and yellow powders that his naturally hideous face was a fright to look at. Up and down the street he staggered, getting a drink wherever he stopped, until he finally ended up in the store where we were and was fell to sleep in a chair. The proprietor told me he came from Mexico and that was why they called him the Mexican Barber. No one thought of such a thing as harming him, although he was the butt of the town.

Charlie had gone off somewhere, so Bill, Joe, and I shouldered our heavy bundles of supplies and started for the bark. At the gate, the soldier stopped us and felt of our bags to see if we had any liquor; finding none he let us proceed, but I noticed he followed at a distance. We set our bundles down alongside the house at the end of the pier and Joe and Bill got into a conversation with him. The result was that all hands had to go back and get a drink. I tried to persuade them not to go, but finally agreed to guard their bundles until they returned.

While they were away, several young Chileans came and hung around in a suspicious manner. When my mates next hove in sight, Bill was trying to walk the figure of eight and Joe was luffing him through the squalls. They were a very affectionate couple and were vowing eternal friendship in grand style. Then they gave three miserable drunken cheers for Frisco. "Hurray for Pisagua!"

"Full moon (hic) it never grows whiskers!"

"To hell with Captain Freeman and the bloody old *Wright*."

"She's nothing but a work house! Hurray for Frisco!"

They were leaning up against the side of the house, hugging each other and both trying to talk at once. The guard was near them and the other Chileans were laughing at them. I went around the house and hailed the bark as loud as I could, for she was about a mile out. When I came back to my mates, I saw them in a fight with the young Chileans. I jumped for two of them who were trying to steal some of our supplies, but they took to their heels and fled, all but one. The guard caught him and gave him a severe punching, knocking his hat overboard and making his nose bleed, and finally marched him off to jail. This was more justice than I expected from the guard. I thought he would side with his countrymen, but I guess the liquor made him loyal to us. I was glad to be rid of them. I had enough to do to keep my two drunken mates from going overboard without having to watch the supplies.

I hailed and hailed, but no boat came, and Bill insisted on coming near the iron steps that led down to the water. Finally, his derby blew overboard. He threw off his coat and pants, in spite of my efforts to stop him, and fell, rather than walked, down the steps and overboard, shouting as he went, "I want my hat! I want my hat!"

I started down the steps after him when Joe, who was nearly as drunk as Bill, came after me. "Go on back you!" I shouted. But he was determined to save his mate. I forced him back up the steps and hung onto him until Bill, who had now reached his hat, swam back to the pier. Then I had to let go of Joe and help Bill, who nearly drowned himself every time he raised his arms to catch the steps. Every time he went under, his hat floated up and when he grabbed it and stopped to put it on his head, down he would go again and come up for all the world like an old sea lion, hundreds of which were swimming all about him.

I was afraid he would drown before I could get him out, yet I didn't dare jump in after him for Joe had followed me down and was trying to do that very thing. "Hold on, Bill! Hold on!" he shouted. "If you drown, I go get a bloody big stone and we'll both drown together." But Bill finally caught the steps and Joe and I hauled him out. And such a sight he was. He was not by any means stout and his wet underclothes clung to him like glue.

In his drunken good humor, Joe immediately began to undress him. His shoelaces were swollen so he could not untie them, and he ripped Bill's underdrawers off in strips and flung the pieces overboard. When Bill saw this, he wanted to swim after the rags, but we held him back. Joe took his own dry shirt off and made Bill put it on, while he wore Bill's wet one. We couldn't make him put on his breeches, so he walked around the dock with the rags of his underdrawers trailing after him, his long shanks bare and the tails of Joe's shirt fluttering in the breeze. But he had his hat, it was jammed clean down to his eyes, and his long beard hung down dripping wet. This was the way we bundled him into the boat, still singing, "Full moon it never grows whiskers," and as Charlie had arrived by that time, the whole party returned to the bark. I thought the mates would die laughing at old Bill as he came barelegged up the gangway, carrying his breeches under his arm.

Chapter 14

*Joe's scheme—We desert the bark—Go ashore in a boat—Bill's chest—
Hard climbing—We hide under a house—Our scare—Hot quarters.*

The following week we couldn't get much saltpeter, so spent the time painting the ship and such like jobs. We were nearly loaded and one day went in the boat with the mate, towed out the freshwater lighter, and pumped all our casks and beakers full.

The hot weather had bred bed bugs so thick in the fo'c'sle that we were compelled to take our mattresses and blankets up on the fo'c'sle head to sleep. Here, as Joe and I lay side by side on our mattresses one night, he told me the stevedore was going to bring him a note from Charlie, the runner ashore, next day and give the final arrangements for deserting the bark. Would I go, too, was what Joe wanted to know. Bill, Albert, Hansen, and he had already decided to go. After arguing the question in all its lights, I finally said, "Yes, you can count me in."

I reasoned it this way. We were nearly starved coming out and no provisions had been laid in to ensure better food going home. The bark was deeply laden and none of us cared to face the days and nights of hardships off the Horn. The runner promised us a berth on a vessel bound for Frisco, which, if we got, would land me in my native land and my folks would send me money to go overland home. I would be willing to forfeit my pay and even my clothes to get clear of the vessel. Here was a chance, I thought, to get clear of the *Wright* and yet save my clothes, for it was arranged that each man would take his clothes bag with him. Even if we failed to get the desired chance, I would at least have a little liberty ashore and be able to see the country, for I might never again come out to this God-forsaken land. Now I was here, so I might as well see all I could. Certainly I could not get on a harder-working craft than our bark. And so we decided we should run away from the *Wright*.

The stevedore brought the note the next day. When the eventful night came around, it was a guilty crowd that rolled up in their blankets and lay down on the fo'c'sle head to sleep. The bright anchor light burning overhead on the forestay left the fo'c'sle head under its awning in total darkness, which favored our scheme. Strangely, it was only those intending to desert who found the fo'c'sle too hot to sleep in. To all appearances, all hands were soon sound asleep, in fact Bill was, and his snoring could be distinctly heard. The night was pitch black, without a star in the sky, and the calm water rose and fell in long smooth swells and a mist hung over all, making the neighboring ship look faint and ghostly. It was impossible to tell whether the officers at the other end of the ship were asleep or not, but that was a risk we had to run. More than one pair of eyes kept a bright lookout to give a warning should any moving form be seen aft. Joe rolled over until close to me and, in muffled whispers, told me the plan of escape laid out by Charlie, the runner. He would come out in a shore boat between eleven and twelve o'clock to take us up the coast to Pisagua. How he was going to do this I could not see, for there was a guard ashore who allowed no boat to leave or land at the pier or on the beach after sunset, and there was no other place where it was possible for a boat to land except on this strip of beach.

The signal would be three matches struck in succession, the last dropped, burning, into the water. So about ten o'clock we stole one by one into the fo'c'sle, packed our clothes bags, and put on our best clothes to run away in. Quickly but noiselessly we worked in our stocking feet, leaving our shoes until the last. The lantern burned low in the fo'c'sle, and the three sleeping forms in the bunks snored peacefully on—sometimes giving a restless grunt that sent my heart into my throat for fear it was the mate looking in the door at me. One look would have been enough, for I had on my best clothes and the ready packed bags told their own tale. But all went well. Each man packed his clothes and lay down again to wait for the boat. Slowly the time dragged on, according to the small watch I carried, until eleven o'clock.

Then I climbed over the bow to watch for the boat and be ready to strike the matches where the bow would screen me so no one aft could see the glare from them. Joe stuck his head over the rail every once in a while to see if I had seen anything yet, but nothing happened until just about half past eleven. When Joe and I began to think we would be disappointed and were discussing the advisability of going back to our bunks, I saw a faint object moving across the bow and we grabbed each other in breathless excitement. It was the boat, sure enough, and as soon as we were sure of it, Joe scurried back to rouse the others, for every one but us had fallen sound asleep. The boat crept slowly across our bow until just ahead, and then it stopped and a faint spark appeared for a moment, followed by a second and a third that dropped, burning, into the water.

I could almost hear my heart beating as I struck the matches in answer to this signal, for on came the boat straight for us. I was down on the head rigging when the boat came under the bow and I made out four men in her, two rowing and two in the stern. One of the two in the stern whispered up, "Is all right?"

"Yes," I answered. "Stand by for our bags." Just then a large swell ran under the bark, and the boat, settling down as it rolled, came across the ship's hawser and was nearly capsized. The grating of the cable and rattling of oars gave me another fright, for the night was still as death itself. The two men in the stern of the boat muttered some curses in Spanish at the boatmen for having allowed the boat to get across the cable. But everything remained quiet aft and one after another we lowered the bags to the men in the boat on the end of a jib down haul. Joe and I were doing this part of the job while Hansen and Albert brought the bags from the fo'c'sle until only Bill's fine camphor-wood chest remained, and that he had not even tied up. He acted as if he didn't want to go now that the time had come. Joe nearly lost his patience with him, for the men in the boat were getting restless. But Bill finally went to tie it up with several fathoms of a new down haul he cut off.

"Be sure and wrap your blanket around it so it won't make a noise, Bill," I said.

After a delay, they passed the box along, but instead of wrapping the blanket around the chest, he had folded it to protect only the cover, so it made a great clatter that brought out another volley of oaths from the Spaniards. Then one by one we dropped into the boat from the martingales and I found myself in the bow of a long, narrow clinker-built boat loaded down with bags and five extra men.

High above us loomed the bluff bow of the bark, and, keeping her end on, the rowers pulled softly out to sea until the gloom almost hid her from view. Then they bent their backs with a will and sent the phosphorescence buzzing past in eddies of fire. I thought we were bound up the coast at first, but noticed after a while the boat was making a gradual curve so as to bring her toward the shore.

Once in under its shadows we were safe, the gloom there being as black as ink. It was so black the rowers had to stop every little while and listen for the wash of the sea on the rocks. I was way up in the bow so I could not ask what they meant by rowing for the shore, but I was anxious to know why they had changed their plans and did not row on to Pisagua. Joe and the rest of the crowd were aft and probably knew what they were up to.

The next thing I knew, the rowers stopped and backed the boat around in toward the rocks. I didn't think it was possible to land, the seas were breaking so and swirling about in dangerous whirlpools and eddies, but it seemed we were in back of a large rock that broke the force of the sea. Here, as the stern of the boat rose, the men jumped ashore one after another. Old Bill, of course, slipped and went in up to his waist; when a Spaniard grabbed him and hauled him up on the steep slope of the rock.

Then I climbed over the thwarts to the stern of the boat and tossed the bags ashore to be caught by those on the rocks. It was all I could do to heave them clear of the short space of water between the rock and the stern of the boat. I got them all over safely and then laid hold of Bill's chest. Of course it was upside down, and when I picked it up the cover opened and out poured a multitude of trinkets. Then it was my turn to swear, and I did. As I hurriedly stuffed the things back in the chest, I thought nothing would give me more satisfaction than to punch Old Bill's stupid head.

But we got it ashore and, watching my chance when the stern of the boat rose, I gave a leap and landed on the rock, into the arms of Joe and the runner, Charlie.

What became of the boat we never found out, for there was no time to be lost and the Spaniards showed us a crevice where there was a level strip of sandy beach about a hundred yards from where we landed. Then they left us, with instructions to bring all our bags to this place while they went ahead to see if the coast was clear.

The rocks were sharp and ragged, and in the darkness we could not see where we were stepping. Shouldering our bags, we set out for the crevice. Joe and I were in the lead and thought we were traveling the same road as before. The rocks seemed steeper, however, but I supposed it was partly my imagination due to the heavy load I had on my shoulder. Joe stumbled and swore as we climbed along, sometimes on hands and knees, for the rocks sloped down to the sea so that none but a goat could walk them with ease. I was picking my way along carefully when suddenly I heard what sounded like a landslide coming down the rocks at me. Joe, who had taken a higher route than I, landed bag and baggage at my feet. He was so mad he was swearing in Dutch, the meaning of which, of course, I did not understand.

We didn't know how the others made out. We were all lost in the darkness. After a hard stumbling climb, we found the crevice and were glad to sit and rest. Then Hansen came shuffling along and we heard Albert calling to know where we were. We kept shouting to him and, guided by our voices, he also found us. By the light of a match, with which Joe was lighting his pipe, I noticed both knees of his breeches were cut from falls on the rocks. Bill did not show up at all. We waited, to give him time to reach us if he was still on the way, but he didn't come. We shouted and shouted and then all scattered to look for him. When I got back after a fruitless search up the rocks, I found him sitting down, smoking, with Joe giving him a lecture.

"Where'd you find him, Joe?" I asked

"Setten' down smokin', right alongside here."

"Didn't you hear us shout, Bill?" I asked, but he sat smoking in moody silence, not even raising his head.

"I guess he's sorry dot he come," said Joe. "I vish he'd never come, he's a bloody nuisance," he added. And when Hansen and Albert came in, Bill wouldn't answer their questions either.

"Ye'd better go back aboard, we don't want no such mops as ye a draggin' on us!" was Hansen's remark to him, and then we all sat in silence on our bags, with only the glow of the two pipes visible as the smokers puffed on them.

I began to think the undertaking would prove a failure. In the first place, Charlie did not take us up the coast as he had agreed. Then again he and the other man had gone off and left us, and there was no telling what treachery they might be up to; they were not breaking the rules of the port for the fun of it, but for some gain. Who would furnish this gain I could not imagine, unless it was ourselves. I was almost tempted to shoulder my bag and clear out by myself, and probably would have had it been possible to get away with my deeds. But the steep mountains on all sides showed me how foolish such an attempt would be, so I decided to stay with the crowd.

Joe looked over the pile of bags for his own and then noticed there was no chest there.

"Where's your chest, Bill?" he asked. And then we found out what Bill was mad at. He was mad because none of us would leave our bags to help him carry his chest. We thought he could carry it himself, but as soon as we found it was back where we landed, Hansen and Albert went after it.

They had just returned when Charlie came back, accompanied by the three men who were in the boat with him. They gave us a lift with the chest and bags and, in single file, we climbed about a hundred yards farther over the rocks and came to the end of the beach on which the town was built. We walked quietly toward the village until near the condensing works, whose high chimney towered above us, a black shaft against the starless sky. One electric lamp that lighted the works threw a circle of light on our path and we halted again. Then at a signal from Charlie, we stole one by one across the lighted space and handed our bags in through a window of a small hovel, to a pair of arms that were thrust out to receive them.

Then Charlie turned us over to another man and told us to follow him. We demanded an explanation of his plans in regard to us. The man told us we could not get up to the top of the mountain before sunrise and by that time mounted police would be riding the plains in search of us. He said he would hide us until it was safe for us to come out and proceed.

So we followed our guide down along the beach to about the middle of the town. All the way we stumbled over refuse thrown to rot on the beach, for there was no such thing as sewerage here. Tin cans, straw bottle covers, and old brooms kicked about our feet while once I nearly took a fall by getting tangled in the remains of an old hoop skirt. All the while there was the most infernal racket made by the dogs; there seemed to be one in every house and every one was doing his best to betray our presence by his infernal barking. I was surprised that the guard did not investigate and catch us, but I found out later on that all that had been provided for. In fact, the very man whose job it was to watch and arrest any man found landing was one of those who had come out and helped us ashore.

We filed up an alleyway and halted in front of a high wooden door until the men on the inside rolled a large pipe back so the door could be opened. The passageway was so narrow the pipe completely blockaded it and we had to climb over it and crawl on our hands and knees through a small hole into total blackness.

Where we were we didn't know, except that we were under some building in the middle of the village. I was the first one in, and so I crawled in as far as I could go. When I had gone about thirty feet over pieces of sheet tin, straw bottle covers, etc., I came to a partition and, in feeling about, found a large basket filled with straw in the corner. There was only about three feet from the ground to the floor above us, but I sat in the basket and leaned up in the corner to sleep. We were all tired and curled up and slept soundly until morning.

I felt rather cramped when I awoke and saw my four shipmates stretched out, still sound asleep. Hansen lay full length on a piece of old sheet iron and Joe on a wooden door. Bill and Albert had collected straw and made a shift for a bed. Right in front of me were three hens, their heads tucked under their wings, sound asleep on a crosspiece that served for a roost. At my left I heard talking and, looking through a crack in the boards, I saw a whole Chilean family in the hut adjoining and watched, unseen by them, their mode of living and eating.

The hens in front of me annoyed me. It was bad enough to have to hide, without the humiliation of sleeping with chickens. Lifting one foot, I caught an old brown hen in her afterquarters and sent her sailing across the place, cackling and clicking in righteous fright, and with her went the other two, scurrying over the sleeping men in mad haste. The one I kicked landed square in little Hansen's face and I guess he thought the "Old Scratch" had him by the way he awoke. The noise awoke all hands and we were afraid the chickens would betray our presence to the police, who we knew would soon be looking for us.

The captain would certainly come ashore to try and find us, and it gave us no end of amusement throughout the day to picture the looks of astonishment that would appear on the captain's and mates' faces when they looked in and found the fo'c'sle nearly empty. The old man would be obliged to hunt for us, for every man he brought from New York would have to be accounted for when the bark again reached the States. Not only that, but men were hard to get out here and he would have to give a new crew more money to get them to ship. But then, we had each left some forty or fifty dollars behind that was due us, so the ship would not really be the loser. Having been out now seven months, it might seem that there would be more money coming to us, but when you deduct the thirty-five that was advanced in New York, five that we'd had on the coast, and more than a month's pay that had been drawn out of the slop chest, it is easy to see where the money went.

About breakfast time, a man brought us something to eat. After handing the food in, he rolled the barrel back against the opening. There was tea, a luxury to us, bread, and some fish. When he came back in an hour or so for the dishes, we asked him for a pack of cards and some "agua" as they called water. When we started to play, we found the cards were Spanish and entirely different from any we were used to, so we had to give that up. The water he brought was in a red clay bottle with a long slender neck. He also brought us a bottle of red wine. He told us, before he closed the opening, that the captain and two policemen were searching every building along the street. "I'll let you know if they come in here, and if you hear me say, 'Fly!' you get out of sight quick, you can go through there." And he pointed to a small opening that led in under the floor of the front part of the building. All the houses were built on spikes two or three feet off the ground, and it was under the back part of one of these buildings, a restaurant as we afterward found out, that we were hiding.

Just before dinnertime we heard a scuffling of feet on the floor above us and recognized our captain's voice. When our friend appeared at the hole and shouted "Fly! Fly!" we needed no second bidding. All hands dove for the hole at the same time, but it was only large enough to admit one. When I squeezed through, right on Joe's heels, I found the ground more hilly than in the other place; shells and pieces of bottles were scattered about, but the queerest part was the density of the cobwebs that hung in festoons and sheets from every beam and post. It was simply a network of them all covered with an accumulation of dust. How many years those cobwebs had been forming I did not dare guess. I didn't care, either, but lowering my head I butted a passage through them headfirst as I scrambled along on my hands and knees as fast as I could go toward a projecting corner of the building. The others went in every direction, like so many rabbits, and then we all lay flat on our stomachs behind the little bumps and ridges in the ground, hardly daring to breathe.

After a while I began to think we were safe, so I raised my head for a look around. While I was peering through the network of cobwebs, Hansen stuck his head up from behind a hump of earth and I nearly laughed outright at the comical sight he presented. He had festoons of cobwebs hanging from the peak of his cap, his nose, chin, the buttons on his coat—in fact all over him. We were all just as bad and it took us quite a while to clean our clothes after the scare was over and our friend called us out.

We had a good dinner of soup, fish, beans, and bread, and spent the afternoon trying to keep cool. It was stifling hot where we were and, even with our coats off and shirts loosened, we could not stand the heat. So we crawled out into the yard and sat on the steps of the back porch, where we could get more air. Even here it was fearfully hot; the high fence kept the air from circulating and the tropical sun scorched down unmercifully. We felt the heat more because we were so used to the open water, where there was always plenty of air moving.

By going up to the top steps of the porch we were able to look over the fence and see the *Wright* at anchor across the bay, loaded deep and nearly ready to sail. I could see that they were sending up and bending on the sails and almost wished I had stayed aboard; for there I knew inside of a few days we would be homeward bound, whereas now everything ahead of us was an uncertainty.

I thought the long afternoon would never pass and was glad enough to go to sleep at sunset, although we were given a short candle to use if we wanted to.

I found the basket I had slept in the night before contained a lot of chinaware beneath the straw, so I made up a bunk on the floor and fell asleep with the others. Hansen found a grating in the floor above and lay down under it to get more air, but shortly after suppertime someone poured the dishwater through the grating and Hansen came near getting baptized with it.

C·C·DAVIS.

Chapter 15

We start to walk to Pisagua—Joe gets lost—I take the lead—A steep climb—We leave Bill cursing at us—Played out—The silver mine—Waiting for daylight—We start to walk over the desert—Our fresh water gives out— Joe gets drunk—Albert drops behind—A mirage on the desert.

I had fallen into a sound sleep, when someone woke me and I heard Joe's voice saying "Come along, Davis," and had my senses about me in a second. I knew something was about to happen, and as I crawled out after the other fellows I put my hand to my sheath knife to see if it was still there and ready for use. I never felt so dependent on anything before in my life as I did on that knife. It was the only weapon of defense I had and I guarded it with care, keeping it strapped to me night and day.

When I joined the crowd in the room above where we had been hiding, Charlie, the runner, was telling the others that we would have to walk to Pisagua. All the windows had been carefully closed and the conversation was carried on in whispers for fear of detection, although at this hour, midnight, not a soul was stirring. He said it would be impossible to launch a boat to take us up the coast as an extra guard was now watching the beach. So he told us to take what we needed from our clothes bags, which we found stowed along the wall of the front room that served as a bar room in the daytime. He gave us each a quart wine bottle full of water and one bottle of red wine extra for the crowd, some crackers, and some dried-up German sausage.

I took from my clothes bag my small blanket, a brand new suit of dungarees I had drawn out of the slop chest before I ran away, and three cans from my stock of condensed milk. We didn't have much time, or I would have gone deeper into my clothes bag and taken a small diamond scarf pin and seven other small valuables that I should have known better than to have brought to sea with me; but Charlie kept urging upon us the necessity of starting early so as to get to the plains above before sunrise.

He gave us minute directions as to how to get to Pisagua, but Joe insisted that he knew the way well enough, he'd walked the same distance before. I listened attentively, however, to what Charlie said.

"Go straight up the mountain from here and at the top you will see three paths; follow the middle one and you will come out all right."

When we were all ready, Charlie looked out to see if all was clear and as we stepped out into the street he gave Joe a letter to a man by the name of Antone, in Pisagua, and said that Antone would hide us until our ship sailed. Then, bidding us goodbye, he closed the door and left us in the dim starlight.

Some of the fellows began to murmur about having to walk, but it was no time to stand and argue. The dogs had scented us and one after another joined in a chorus of unearthly howls that momentarily increased until I expected to see the armed guards come down the street in pursuit of us.

Joe started off as guide to lead and the procession followed. We passed the condensing works and left the town behind. But Joe, instead of going up the mountain, kept close along the beach and before we had gone a mile the shore became so steep that it was impossible to proceed farther. Any step might send us down the rocks to be tossed and crushed in the surf at the shore. Here we came to a halt and, on hands and knees, retraced our steps until standing was safe and held a council of war. What were we to do? Joe certainly did not know the way, in spite of his assertions that he did. He had not followed Charlie's instructions from the start, for he told us to go straight up the mountain until we reached the plain above, and then to follow the sea.

"Come on, fellows!" I said. "Follow me. I know the way better than this." I realized something had to be done and done quickly. As long as Joe was leader, I was content to follow, but when he failed I used my own judgment. I had studied the face of the cliff from the ship many a time and had made up my mind how to get to the top. So, with Joe at my elbow and the rest following in line, I led them back to the condensing works and started straight up the cliff, following the zigzag course of a crevice that looked as if it had once been the bed of a stream.

It was hard climbing. Our feet slid back with every step; the loose sand and gravel rolling under our shoes. The dim, uncertain starlight was deceptive, for in some places the ground was light and in others dark. One looked like a ridge and another a gully, yet when we got there it would be all level ground, and other places where it looked smooth we stumbled into small, unseen gullies and over unseen ridges. It tried the endurance of all, and we had not gone a mile before we had to stop and let Bill and Albert rest. When the fellows looked back and saw the village laying a dark mass at their feet and the anchor lights of the ships seemingly not a stone's throw away, they began to get uneasy.

"Vich von is the *Wright*'s light?" asked Joe.

"Dere it is, next to de last out dere. See it next to dat bright light?" said Hansen.

"Yes! The bloomin' craft is too mean to burn much oil," chipped in Albert, and the rest of us gave her like compliments. We were glad we were clear of her and every little while one or two of the men would look back and burst out into a torrent of profanity accompanied by a shaking of the fist at the innocent light on the bark's forestay, which looked like a star far below us.

After another climb straight up, the top of the mountain seemed farther off than ever and the lights in the bay were still directly under us.

When they saw this, the fellows began to get uneasy and suggested that we go north up the coast so as to get out of sight of the ship. I argued and argued in vain with them. They had no more sense than a lot of sheep and I either had to go along the coast with them or continue to climb straight up by myself.

Remembering the old saying that in unity there is strength, I went with the crowd, but kept telling them my arguments in favor of going straight up.

True, it was easier to walk along the face of the cliff than to climb up it; but in the gully we were making pretty good headway and I wanted to continue there. Going north we gradually left the lights in the bay behind us, but the top of the mountain still towered a long way above our heads.

About four miles north of Caleta Buena, the mountainside ran out in a steep promontory into the sea and its sides stood almost vertical. As we neared this point, climbing became more difficult with every step until, exhausted with our efforts, all hands sat down to rest again.

"If we don't get to the top pretty soon," said I, "it will be daylight and then they will be able to see us from the ship; there's no place to hide here and we'll be like flies on a wall, and you bet the old man will have his glasses on the mountain as soon as it is daylight."

"Why, what's the matter with the way we are going?" asked Albert. "We have made more headway since we started along the coast than we did before."

"Yes," I answered, "it seems so, but you'll find you've got to get to the top before you get to that point, or walking will be impossible. It is getting steeper and steeper all the time and when you come to climb up now you will find it much harder than if you had gone straight up in the gully, as I wanted to."

But they wouldn't be convinced until, as we progressed, we found it got so steep it was dangerous to proceed. The mountain went down in a regular landslide from where we were to the sea. Then it was go up or nothing and, after a short spell of climbing almost on our hands and knees, the others soon admitted their mistake. However, there was no time to go back to the gully now, we had to get to the top from where we were. Joe was leading, I was next, followed by Hansen, Albert, and Bill in the order named. Not only did the darkness make climbing difficult, but the ground was loose and stony, making it necessary to use our hands as well as feet in climbing. This work soon tolled on Old Bill and we were continually stopping to let him rest, until he got so he would only walk about five minutes and then want to sit down for ten. Joe told him we could not keep up that kind of pace or daylight, which was fast approaching, would find us not yet over the mountain. We had all agreed to keep together, but when Bill sat down and refused to go any farther, we threatened to go on without him, and for a reply he began to curse us.

"Go on! Go to hell!" said he and followed it up with some vile language directed at us. So we went back to him and divided our crackers and sausage, and Joe gave him a dollar in native money from the five dollars Charlie had furnished us when we started. We tried to reason with him, but it was no use, he was tired and ugly. So leaving him, we hurried on as fast as we could, slipping and sliding back with every step. Once or twice we stopped and shouted down, asking Bill if he wouldn't come on that we would wait for him; but he refused to reply except once when we heard him cursing.

I was getting very tired in the knees myself now, but Joe seemed as fresh as ever. I stuck to his heels with determination and for a couple of hours we had the hardest climbing I had ever had in my life. Albert was the next to flag, and finally poor little Hansen began to pant and fall behind. But he was still game, so Joe and I waited for him to catch up. Finally Joe himself showed signs of distress and while he and Hansen sat down for a rest I pushed on, for I felt it was not very far to the top of the mountain, yet to look at it, a black ridge across the sky above, it seemed miles away. When I had gone half a mile or so I suddenly came to level ground and saw the land rising in a gentle slope a short distance ahead to the very top of the mountain. So I shouted down, "Hey! Joe! Come on up, here's the top right here. I'm on it!" And I could hear stones rolling down as they scrambled up, followed by Albert, who had also heard me say the top was not far away.

None of us were tired then. The walking on level ground was easy after the climb we'd had. We took a pull from the water bottles that we carried in our hands, and started up the slope for the top. As we crossed the level ground, we passed close to the black yawning mouth of a cave with a derrick at its mouth and knew then where we were. We had often looked up from the bark's deck, when heaving in cargo, at this cave, which we were told was a silver mine and wondered what kind of an affair it was. If it had been daytime and I had been doing anything except running away, I should have liked nothing better than to have gone into the mine and seen how they worked it. But as it was, we hurried on up the slope of ground. We passed a number of the miners' huts and were nearly scared to death when five or six heads rose up out of the ground and jabbered something in Spanish at us. "Pisagua! Pisagua!" said I, and one of them pointed north. They were sleeping in holes for all the world like graves, with their blankets laid over the top; and we had to walk carefully among them so as not to step into one.

Upon gaining the summit of the hill, we saw a broad tableland stretching as far as we could see in the uncertain light preceding dawn. There was, as Charlie had said, three distinct trails leading north. Crossing the first, we ran across the sand to the second, but to my astonishment we found it was no path at all, but a strata of light-colored earth with not a footprint visible.

We followed it for about a mile and then lost all traces of it. We had no idea which way to go, so decided to stay where we were until daylight, when we could see where we were going.

I unstrapped my blanket from my back, lay down, and wrapped up in it to rest. The earth was like flour for about six inches in depth and was coated with a crust of hard earth formed by the heavy dews at night and the hot sun during the day. It was a poor country to run away in, being a total desert without tree, shrub, or blade of grass for hundreds of miles around; not a drop of water or anything to afford one shelter from the noonday sun. Many a sad story is told by the natives of sailors who had run away. Ignorant of what kind of a country it was, they had perished in the hot sand hills. During our walk that day we came across the whitened bones of mules that lay scattered over the plains. Occasionally a mound of earth showed where someone had perished of thirst and been buried. The natives traveled on mules and, as we were doing, carried water in bottles to drink.

When I awoke after a short nap, I found it was light enough to see and Joe was off to the eastward, walking in a wide circle, his eyes fastened on the ground about him, looking for tracks. When he got around to the north of where we were encamped in a slight hollow, he shouted to us and beckoned us to come on. Strapping up my blanket, I ran with the rest of the crew up the hill and saw in the sand the tracks of a herd of mules that gradually formed into a defined trail as we followed it. It led up to a low range of hills and, anxious to know what might be in sight on the other side, we pushed on, not stopping to eat our scanty breakfast until we reached the other side. There we saw the land stretching north as a sea of sand flooded with the glare of the rising sun.

Crackers, sausages, and water constituted our meal, topped off with a can of condensed milk; and all but myself took a pull at the wine bottle.

It had been very pleasant walking so far, but when we started on again we found the sun was uncomfortably hot. All hands took off their coats and vests and strung out in Indian file, following the narrow footpath across the sand. My shoes were heavy awkward things, the kind that are made by convicts and sold to sailors and laboring men for a dollar a pair. I took them off, tied the laces together, and slung them over my shoulder along with my blanket, which was rolled up and strapped to my back, while my coat hung on in front. Walking was much easier barefooted and with my bottle of water in one hand and my trousers rolled up to save them from the dust, I followed Joe, who led the procession.

We were happy as schoolboys to think we were, for the time at least, our own masters. We sang, whistled, and cut up capers in our joy; sometimes turning back and waving farewell as if the ship was in sight, saying, "Goodbye *James A. Wright*, you old workhorse," comparing her, as sailors do a hard ship, to the penitentiary. "Ta! Ta! Captain Freeman, sorry to leave you, but we're bound for Frisco, thank you, not for Cape Horn."

"Bye! Bye! Mr. Hill, you can swear all you want and find another crew." Such like sarcasms were hurled at the bark all morning and served to arouse and cheer us, but along about noontime, after we had covered some fifteen miles, jokes were given up and the more serious side of the situation contemplated.

It was no small undertaking without a guide, to attempt to walk thirty miles over a desert where it was the easiest thing imaginable to lose your way. Empty and broken bottles took the place of milestones, only there were close to a hundred of them in a mile; and every little while we passed a small mound of earth at the side of the path with a collection of stones piled upon it to mark the resting place of some unfortunate who had perished on the plain. Occasionally we came across what at a distance looked like a broken barrel with only its hoops sticking up, but which, on closer inspection, turned out to be the skeleton of a mule with its large skull and rows of grinning white teeth.

About noon we saw another ridge of hills ahead and, as before, the road led up through a shallow valley. There was just one spot where the banks were steep enough to throw a shadow, and here we sat and enjoyed the coolness the shade afforded, but even that spot was soon claimed by the sun, so on we went.

All that dizzy afternoon we tramped over another sea of sand and, about three o'clock lost the trail completely. Our water by this time was reduced to one swallow and I refrained from drinking mine as long as I could. My throat became dry and choked with dust and my tongue was parched, yet I would not drink my last drop for it was a source of great comfort to think I had at least one swallow left. But finally the time came when I could stand it no longer and greedily swallowed in one gulp what remained. It seemed but a drop and before I could roll my tongue in it, it was gone.

Joe, who was carrying the wine bottle, finally suggested that we drink what wine remained. He had been walking in the rear for some time and I did not notice until we gathered in a group that his condition was anything but a sober one. When he held out the bottle, I saw he was drunk and, sure enough, the wine bottle was nearly empty, save for a swallow or two.

We each moistened our lips from it, but it had a vile taste and burned my mouth, so I quickly spat it out.

Then we pushed on again, a rather dubious-looking lot by this time, covered from head to foot with a layer of the fine, white dust. Joe, to make matters worse, commenced to pick a quarrel with Albert as the liquor mounted to his head. Poor Albert was nearly fagged out as it was and could hardly swing his long gaunt form along fast enough to keep up with us. Joe wanted to go faster and flourished his sheath knife, threatening to fight Albert. I was afraid to let Joe rest, so I hurried him along to try and walk off the effects of the liquor while Albert, to avoid trouble, dropped about half a mile behind. I looked aft from time to time and his red flannel undershirt would appear astern as he came to the top of a hill, then disappear in the hollows as we pushed our way over the rolling hills of sand.

I felt sorry for Albert, poor fellow, it was bad enough to be nearly dead with thirst without having to be deprived of the comfort of companionship. Still it was better as it was, for if he came near Joe, there was sure to be a fight and one or the other would be done up. We had no means then of helping a wounded man, in fact we were sadly in need of help ourselves and I dreaded to think of leaving one of our number to whiten his bones on the sand. Bill was already gone, but that was no fault of ours, only his own mulishness.

On and on we walked with a mechanical stride, hoping against hope that we would come across some water. As far as we could see in all directions it was nothing but burning-hot sand and we could see the heat throbbing in the air over the surface of the plain.

Once Joe thought he saw green trees and a lake.

"Look! Look! Vot is dot?" he exclaimed and pointed to the eastward, where not a moment before there was nothing but a clear horizon of sand. Now as I looked, I saw a large patch of green trees whose tops waved to and fro as if a strong breeze was blowing over them; but what interested me more than the trees, and the grateful shade they seemed to offer us, was a sheet of beautiful white water that lay between us and the forest, to all appearances a large lake. Oh, how tantalizing it looked to us so parched for thirst. How I should have liked to throw myself into that lake and drink my fill. But I knew there was no lake there and tried to keep down my disappointment. I couldn't trust myself to look that way until I heard Joe shout.

"Look! Look! Ye dom it, de whole bloomin trees is goin' hup in de hair!"

And sure enough, I looked just in time to see the bottom of the trees snap up in the air and disappear, leaving a clear horizon again. Every little while after that some one of us would cast a longing look to the eastward.

Chapter 16

Nearly played out—Water at last—The sea in sight again—Junin and the store—Albert joins us again—On the edge of the mountain—The point below Pisagua—Down a narrow footpath to the city—A spy— We find Antone's saloon—A Chilean pepper—The little fat gentleman in black—Captured by the police—Locked up.

Bout four o'clock we saw a line of telegraph poles ahead of us and, picking up heart at the sight, we pushed along faster. "Surely we are near civilization now," I thought. But after traveling several miles from pole to pole and then seeing nothing but the same line of poles as far as we could see, our spirits suffered a decline.

"If we could only get up on that cussed wire and ride on it," said Hansen, "we might get somewhere."

"I vonder if ve can hear vot dem is saying?" said Joe, and he laid his ear to a post and listened.

"I only wish they would telegraph us some water," said I. "But I dare say they are telegraphing the police to look out for us, if anything."

This set the others in a stew for fear such might be the case. And Joe suggested, "Let's climb hup and cut de dom vire."

"Yes," I said, "then you'll have someone come and help us in a hurry."

There was a wagon trail following along the line of poles that looked as if it might have been made by the wagon and men who first erected these poles.

At last we came to a more hilly district and followed the poles toward a line of hills ahead. Here, as we mounted a hummock of earth, we saw a road running from inland out toward the sea and saw a wagon train going west, just disappearing in a cut in the hills.

My head was burning up with feverish heat and my whole system seemed on fire, but at the sight of moving horses and men ahead, we three broke into a run. We soon gave that up, however, and when we finally struck the road, the caravan was nowhere in sight.

The road sloped steeply to the west and disappeared in a deep gully between the mountains. We followed it down, down until I thought every moment we would emerge into sight of the sea. We supposed we were within a mile of the coast, while in fact we were away inland behind a mountain range.

The road was deeply worn by the wheels of heavy wagons, and dust lay nearly a foot deep on the road. Every step took us down, down into the gorge between the mountains, until I began to think we must be going down into some mine. The steep, vertical sides of the mountain rose on either side, so abrupt it was impossible to see the tops of them.

We were beginning to despair of ever finding water and were well nigh played out, so when we came to a slight widening in the gorge and saw a low hill to our right, we painfully climbed it in hopes of seeing some aid.

Right at our feet was a small hut nestled against the side of the hill, and a branch road running past it joined the one we had been following a little farther on. We ran down the hill but came to a halt as a large bloodhound made a jump at us. His barking brought two Spaniards out of the hut, who stared at us in surprise. We held up our empty bottles and asked for "agua," but they knew well enough what we wanted. While one of them held the dog so he wouldn't break his chain, the other pulled aside some pieces of sheet tin, exposing a large, round iron casting, like a basin, full of water. We dropped on our knees around the edge and plunged our faces, nose and all, under the water and drank our fill.

"Muchee agua, no bueno!" said one of them, noticing how much we drank; but we didn't care whether much water was good for us or not, we drank all we could hold. Then with the Chilean's consent, we filled our water bottles and proceeded along the road we had been traveling, as the Chilean told us it led to the sea and a place called Junin.

The road continued to twist and wind downhill all the time and at one place it was just wide enough for a wagon to squeeze through. Shoved up the steep side so as not to blockade the pass, lay the grinning skeleton of a mule with its shriveled-up hide hanging over the white ribs like remnants of old gunny cloth.

The water put new life into us and made us hungry, so we ate and sipped water as we walked. Finally we turned a corner in the road and emerged from the mountains onto a broad, level plain some three or four miles across, with the blue waters of the Pacific just visible beyond. On the edge of the plain, just above the sea, was the town of Junin.

Although the plain was a tableland, as flat as a board, it was very hard walking as we sank in at every step over our shoe tops. It wasn't sand, it was a fine dust like flour that rose in a cloud behind us as we walked.

Halfway across this plain we met a caravan coming inland from the coast. It consisted of about twenty mules hitched in pairs, one ahead of the other, drawing a great lumbering truck with broad, tired wheels that sank nearly to the hubs in the fine dust under the load of bags and boxes. Behind this one came another with an immense iron tank on the wheels, drawn by mules like the first one.

We met a Spaniard mounted on a spirited little white pony and wearing a broad sombrero, the rim of which was decorated with a great many little round buttons. He wore a smart little coat highly ornamented with braids, and breeches that opened up the sides to the knees, the flaps of which nearly hid his small feet, but left wicked-looking spurs sticking out behind.

As we drew near to the town on the coast, we saw them blasting out saltpeter in a mine to our right. Behind us, like a huge wall, the mountains extended north and south to the horizon, while ahead it seemed as if we could run and jump off the edge of the plain into the sea below. As we neared the town, we noticed what at a distance looked like quite a city, resolved itself into a few rows of miserable little huts. The first thing we came to was a lot of horses and mules grazing in a large fenced enclosure, while farther on were others under a rude shed, harnessed and ready for work. The shanties were laid out so as to form a street running seaward to the edge of the coast.

A group of ironworkers in a shed, forging iron at their anvils, stopped their hammering to gaze at us as we passed. Halfway down the row of huts, a sign displayed "Store" and into this we stepped.

It was a dark little box of a place with only one small window to light it, and was piled so full of barrels and cases there was hardly room for all of us to crowd in. A typical-looking frontiersman stood behind a counter at our left as we came in, just such a looking man as you would expect to see in Texas: a big sombrero on one side of his head and hide boots up to his knees. There was everything imaginable packed into this little shanty, but the most noticeable thing of all was the number of flies. I have never before or since seen the equal of that room. The flies actually covered everything and when the proprietor moved anything they rose in a swarm and made such a buzzing it sounded like a beehive instead of a store. We purchased some eatables and asked the man what the name of the town was.

"Junin," he answered.

"How far is it to Pisagua?" we queried.

"Between three and four miles," said he. "You can make it before dark."

"How is the road?"

"Follow along the edge of the cliff, it runs out on the backbone of the point above here and just the other side of that is Pisagua."

As we left the store, we told the man to tell Albert we had just left and to come on, that we would wait for him. "He's a fellow with a wide-brimmed brown-felt hat and a red flannel shirt on, you'll know him when you see him, tall and thin he is, with red freckles all over his face."

Continuing our way down the street, we came to the edge of the mountain. Looking over at the surf rolling in among the rocks on the shore miles below, I couldn't help thinking what would be the fate of a man if he fell over; he would not stop until he went splash into the sea, and long before he reached the bottom he would be a corpse. Here was where Joe said the railroad had given away and hurled a number of people down the incline to death. He pointed out to us a narrow ledge cut in the face of the cliff that zigzagged its way to the beach below. That, he said, was where the cars had run, but it was now used only as a footpath.

There was a slide here, as at Caleta Buena, only this one had but one track and we saw the clumsy windlass at the top by which the cars were worked. Far below us, so small she looked like some toy at anchor, lay a ship; we could see her decks as if drawn on a piece of paper and looked down upon the tops of her masts. The little black dots moving about her decks were men hard at work loading her with saltpeter from a lighter that lay alongside. We walked along the very edge of this sandy cliff until Junin lay a mile or so behind us, and then we sat down to rest and eat a bite or two.

There was a peculiar growth of snake-like vine covering the ground in places, that had small sharp thorns upon it and looked as if it had grown up during the night and then been scorched into a dried-up stem during the day by the sun. Sitting in a spot that was free from the vine, we were eating some bread and sipping water when who should come over a hill not a hundred yards away but the familiar figure of Albert, with his flaming red shirt and wide hat.

He was glad to see us again, as we were to see him. Joe, now that he was sober, insisted on supplying Albert with whatever he had.

"How did you come to find us?" was the question we all asked him at once.

"Why, I filled my bottle at the same place you did, the old fellow there said you fellows had just left when I came along. He took me into his hut and gave me a plate of soup," he said.

We were a much happier crowd when we resumed our walking; we were no longer tortured in mind with fears for the man we had left behind. All were united again and a feeling of good fellowship seemed to have sprung up among us.

Ahead of us, a point of land running far out into the sea shut off the view to the north, but looking back we could see the shoreline for miles and miles to the south'ard. As we neared the point, the path became a mere ledge cut into the face of a perpendicular wall of earth, and in some places we had to leap over breaks where the path had been wiped out by small landslides.

Stopping again to rest, I threw an empty condensed-milk can down the cliff and as long as I could see it, it went rolling on and on down toward the sea. But it was too small an object and I lost sight of it long before it reached the bottom.

It took all the nerve I possessed to make some of the jumps across places where the path had been wiped out. On level ground it would have been only a short jump, but it took the courage out of me to look across and see a narrow ledge only about eighteen inches wide for me to land on, and the cliff going almost straight up and down from it. Then, as we followed the path out onto the point of land, we found in some places it was a steep ridge or backbone of earth about two feet wide and so steep on either side it meant death to fall. It was like walking on top of a fence, as I had done many a time at home in my younger days.

About half an hour before sunset, we came to the edge of the point of land and cautiously looking over beheld Pisagua, a good-size city at our feet, with about a dozen ships anchored in the bay. The city itself was well laid out; the houses were neatly painted and all bore the appearance of prosperity. There was a moor, or landing stage, at the center of the town; the streets were all paved and had sidewalks of flagstones or brick. I also noticed a railroad track and could trace its course far to the north, across a plain and up a mountainside that was not as high as the one on which we stood.

A line of telegraph poles also cut crosslots from the city over the mountains and was probably the same line we had been following back in the country.

Farther out on the point we were on, where the rocks were steep and jagged, was a sort of signal tower erected and I could just imagine the wild and lonely view that must be presented from its windows.

We were afraid to show ourselves over the cliff for fear the police might be looking for us. Charlie had told us the night we left that Captain Freeman had telegraphed to Iquique, a city south of Caleta Buena, for a new crew and said that by the time we reached Pisagua the *Wright* would have sailed.

Nevertheless, we laid low until the sun had set behind the western sea line and things began to get dusky in the fading daylight. Then, in single file, we started down the narrow shelf-like ledge that formed the path; so narrow and steep was it in places that I dreaded to pass one foot around the other in stepping, for fear the movement would over-balance my body and send me crashing through the roof of one of the huts below. We had to lean in against the cliff and keep our weight in away from the edge, sometimes feeling along the wall with our hands.

But we reached the bottom safely and, running down the incline at the base, found ourselves walking into the city. As we came into the populated part, we noticed a Chilean across the street who appeared to be following us. When we stopped on a corner while Joe rubbed up his memory as to the location of the saloon kept by Antone, the Chilean crossed over and asked us where we wanted to go.

"None of your business," we replied. "We know where we're going."

He followed us, however, until we found Antone's saloon and stepped inside. What became of him then I did not know. I lost track of him in the crowd, for there were several people sitting around in the saloon at tables and a continual string of people kept passing the door.

His dogging our footsteps made me uneasy, however, and I was glad enough when Antone, a heavy, dark-whiskered man, made his appearance and read the note Joe handed him.

"I suppose you fellows are hungry," he said. "Sit down and I'll get you a bite to eat."

So we sat down at a table where there were four chairs and waited. All hands were glad our hot tramp was over and looked forward to a good bunk for the night, at least a couple of days ashore, and ultimately shipping on some coaster bound for California.

In a few minutes a waiter brought in a platter with the remains of a good-size boiled fish on it and gave us plates and things to eat with. As I didn't care particularly for fish, I devoted my time to filling up on bread and butter.

On a butter plate in the center of the table, I noticed something I finally concluded were the kernels of some kind of nut unknown to me. I had a particular fondness for all kinds of nuts and those four round things about the size of a hazelnut shell looked a good tempting mouthful. So I shoved one into my mouth and bit bravely into it.

"Holy Mackerel!" I cried. My mouth seemed on fire, my tongue puckered up, and tears ran in streams out of my eyes. I thought I should never get the sting out of my mouth and swallowed several glasses of water, endeavoring to quench the fire that seemed to be scalding inside. It was not a nut I had bitten into but a Chilean pepper, the hottest thing that grows.

When we had finished eating, Antone said to follow him and he would show us to a place where we could sleep. "I suppose you are pretty tired after your walk," he said.

We certainly were tired and sleepy, having been awake most of the last two nights, and looked eagerly forward to a good night's rest.

He led us across the street and up a side street to a small cigar store, which he also owned, and here we sat on benches in the front while he, we supposed, went to prepare a place for us to sleep. In fact, he went around the corner and notified the captain of police, for as we sat waiting, a fat little man, dressed in black, stepped into the store and sized us up. Then he jabbered some Spanish and I noticed through the open doorway that a crowd was beginning to gather outside.

"What in thunder is worrying him?" I asked, turning to Joe, sitting next to me on the bench. "What does he want, a crew?" I thought he was the captain of some ship in the bay, and was just thinking well of Antone for getting us a ship so quickly, when in marched a file of soldiers with muskets and fixed bayonets. They blockaded the door, then came in and lined up two alongside each one of us.

Oh! Wasn't I mad! I could have stuck my knife into Antone at the sight of him. But he never showed up. The pot-bellied little fellow in black referred to a paper he held in his hand and said, "Cinco marinero! Bark Americano! Caleta Buena! Vamoose!" Accompanying his last word was a wave of his hand, signaling for us to get out.

The soldiers made us rise and march around the block to the police barracks. We made quite a procession. With our guards and a large crowd of natives who had been attracted by the sight of the "Gringos," we tramped down the street, our footsteps echoing on the hard stones in the still night air.

In through an archway to an open courtyard we went. We were put into a room across the way from the little gentleman in black and several uniformed officers sitting at their desks. Then, one at a time, we were taken before these officials and our knives were taken from us. Albert had a fine tortoise-shell matchbox which they tried to take from him, but after nearly coming to blows over it, they decided to let him keep it.

One thing I noticed in Chile was the terror the word "Americano" seemed to create in the natives. At the mole in Valparaiso, the cry "Americano" raised by one of the natives caused the rest to scatter like sheep and make way for the dreaded Gringos.

Outside the city it was different; to say you were an American there was to ensure a knife in your back, so I, during our walk, passed off as an Englishman. Here, the rabble was trying to get a look at us through the windows and barricaded doors. We heard all kinds of expressions that, by the tones and the gestures of the speakers, showed in what dread Americans were held. You'd think we were a lot of gorillas and even the guards, armed to the teeth as they were, kept clear of us. As a fact I was the only American in the crowd, but any man that comes from an American ship, be he the greenest Hollander afloat, is, in their eyes, a dreaded Americano.

After going through our pockets, they marched us across the courtyard and locked us in a small boxlike room, and for the first time in my life I was in prison. But I was the only one to whom this was a new sensation. Hansen, in fact, had served a term in Sing Sing (for sleeping on a gentleman's doorstep, as he told us), and learned the trade of shoemaking there.

As it was evident we would spend the night in this "lockup," I felt my way to a corner in the extreme end and, rolling up my coat for a pillow, took off my shoes, and lay down and slept in my blanket, which they had not taken from me.

Joe and the rest lay on the floor near the door and during the night several drunken Chileans were thrust in with us. Falling over, they raised a great rumpus among my crew. I slept undisturbed until morning and felt fresh as a daisy, but when I stood up to put my coat on, I found the air was foul with the fumes of tobacco and stale liquor for there was no ventilation whatsoever, no windows or anything to let in air.

Chapter 17

A Sunday in prison—Saluting the flag of Chile—A bucket of beans—Our
mate arrives—We are taken under guard to the mole—The whaleboat—
A long row—We give the launcheros a lift—Back aboard the bark.

When the guard opened the door about six o'clock the next morning,
Sunday, February 19, the sweet air and sunlight streaming in was a
blessing. The building, I noticed, was a light, frame affair enclosed in
corrugated sheet iron. "How long would such a prison hold a gang of New York
toughs?" I wondered as I looked at it. And yet what good would it do them to get
out? The perpendicular wall of mountains at the back of the city was a prison in itself and defied all escape in that direction.

The natives who had been arrested during the night were given brooms and
made to go out and sweep the streets. We were not disturbed until about an hour
later, when we were also given brooms and told to sweep out the place we had been
sleeping in. Joe was put to work sweeping off the sidewalk around the inside of the
courtyard and I swept off the floor of a small, round building in the center of the
enclosure, that looked like a summer house and had a table full of all sorts of chem-
ical apparatus that reminded me of tales I had heard about the Spanish inquisition.

To the right of the archway that led to the street were a number of small rooms where the officers lived. Across the enclosure from these was a large building where all the guards slept and ate their meals.

When we had given the boards a "lick and a promise" with the brooms, we threw them down and watched the garrison getting ready to go through the ceremony of hoisting the colors at the gateway. An attendant brought out the commander's horse all saddled and groomed; the soldiers lined up, dressed in their best uniforms, and to the strains of music from the band, playing a national air, they marched out and formed a long line in the gutter across the street from the barracks.

Here they came to a "present arms" and the band struck up a livelier air that sent the commander's horse prancing about the street, and the flag of Chile was hoisted on the flagstaff over the archway.

Then they came in again and broke ranks, and I was amused to see how quickly the musicians pulled off the military coat they had thrown over their starched shirts and collars and hastened away, probably to church.

Time dragged along wearily after that; no one spoke to us and we were allowed to walk about at will. The sun, as it drew on toward midday, streamed down into the courtyard, with its whitewashed walls. The glare, combined with the heat, drove us into a sort of storeroom on one side of the archway for shelter from its burning rays.

My appetite had been gnawing at my innards for some time, when one of the native prisoners came in from the street with a bucket of what I at first took to be slops. This he set down in the shade near us and motioned us to take it while he drew away and watched us.

"What is it, Joe?" I asked as Joe stirred the stuff about with a ladle.

"Something goot," he answered.

"By golly it may be!" said I. "But it's too rich for my blood."

"Vait 'till I stir it," he replied and sure enough the oils and grease on the surface gave way to a rich dark red fluid and out from the bottom of the bucket he fished a ladle full of big, red beans.

"Try dem," he said. I did so and never tasted a spicier dish in my life than those beans. I feasted on them and all the time we were eating, the Chileans refused to come near, but took what we left and ate it among themselves.

Soon after dinner we were surprised to see Mr. Hill, the mate of the bark, and an interpreter go into the office and have a confab with our little man in black. Afterward we were marched under guard down to the mole and made to get into a large white whaleboat that was waiting for us. Sitting at the long sweeps were four

Chileans who we recognized as men belonging to Caleta Buena, the same as had come off in the lighters that brought us our cargo.

They had left Caleta Buena at four o'clock that morning and pulled the thirty-odd miles to this place in seven hours. As we went out of the harbor and left the city of Pisagua and the fleet of ships at anchor behind us, I didn't know whether to be sorry or glad. As it was, we would soon be home on the *Wright* for the mate told us she was all loaded now. Stevedores from shore had come off and finished the job, for it had only taken two lighter loads to complete the cargo. But then, all our clothes were gone, we had nothing to wear going home, and it would be a cold job off the Horn with but one shift of clothes and no blankets. Yet, after our disappointment in not getting a ship for Frisco, I think we were all quite willing to return to the bark.

Rounding the point of land, we shut Pisagua from view and stretched out on the seats by the mate in the stern. He asked us all about our trip ashore and tried to get us to say who it was took us out of the bark, but none of us would tell him.

The four Chileans were sweating away at the long sweeps sending the cleanly modeled boat hissing and seething against a long ground swell that came dead against us from the south'ard. The mate dozed off after an hour or so of monotonous rowing and I, to stretch my legs and rest; moved way aft on the little deck at the stern, and from here I could see how easily and buoyantly the light boat took the seas. She was a typical west-coast boat, sharp at both ends, some thirty feet in length. At each end was a deck for about six feet, with a towing post at the end. The rest of the boat was crossed by five or six seats, on the forward four of which sat the rowers on the side opposite their oars, to get a purchase on the long ash. Instead of oarlocks they used one thole pin and held the oar to it by a grommet of rope.

As we passed along the shore, the mountains presented a most grand and fascinating sight; some places towering straight up from the sea a sheer wall thousands of feet in height. In others, the cliff was seared and split into deep ravines, as if some volcanic action had rent the earth at some distant period. When we were on the plains we noticed this same peculiarity; every mile or two there would be a crack or crevice running across the plain, some barely six feet in depth, others perhaps thirty.

Not a house, boat, or sign of life did we see along the shore save the hundreds of seals that lay basking in the sun on the rocks or dove about in the surf.

When the mate was sleeping, I made a motion to the rowers as if I would drop overboard and swim ashore, just to see how much we could count on their friendship, for I knew they didn't like the mate any too well, and they grinned and nodded for me to do so. They gradually pulled inshore until instead of being two miles out we were within half a mile of the rocks and could distinctly hear the boom of the surf against the shore. But I'd had enough of those bleak, barren hills and stayed where I was, and the mate slept peacefully on, ignorant of the move.

About four o'clock the rowers began to show the effects of their long pull, for they had rowed some forty or fifty miles since daylight. At Joe's suggestion, we relieved them and bent our backs until the sweat ran off us in streams.

Hansen had to quit, he was too short and small to swing the heavy oar and Albert soon tired, so Joe and I each kept an oar and the Chileans relieved each other at the remaining two, smoking cigarettes when not rowing.

They were very grateful for the rest and insisted on giving us each a handful of their brown-paper cigarettes in token of it.

We could see the masts of the ships in Caleta Buena on the southern horizon when the sun set in a flood of red light behind the sea line, but by the time we reached the bark it was pitch dark. Not a word was said to us as we came up the gangway, although the captain, second mate, and cook leaned over the rail watching us. Going forward, we turned into our now blanketless bunks and soon fell asleep.

Chapter 18

*I go ashore with the old man—In jug for safekeeping—Bending sail—
The second mate mounts guard—Lawson arrives from Iquique with a
bottle—I get a letter and money from home—Supplies—The custom of
the port—Homeward bound—Painting—I drop a brush overboard—
The captain has fun at my expense.*

W e were aroused at four o'clock next morning by the old familiar cry of
"Now then, you sleepers turn out and get your coffee!" It took some
lively scouting around to get pots enough for all hands, for five of us
had lost all our tins. After coffee, we started sending up and bending on the sails.
We had just turned to after breakfast and I was about to go up the main rigging
with the tail-block and gauntline, when the mate called me down and said, "Go aft,
the old man wants to see you."

"Gosh! Now I'm in for a lecture," I thought as I saw Captain Freeman watching me from the coach-house door.

But he only surveyed me with a queer look on his features and then said, "Do you suppose I can trust you to go ashore with me?"

"Yes, Sir! I guess you can," I answered.

"You won't try to run away again, then?"

"No, I got enough of that game," I said.

"Oh! You did, hey? Well I hope you enjoyed yourself, for it will all come out of your pay at the end of the voyage."

Then he told me to get the boat alongside and take Lawrence, the cabin boy, to help row him ashore. All that morning the captain hunted up and down the village with a couple of the guards, trying to find our clothes; but they had vanished. I showed him where we hid, where we saw our clothes bags last, and even went in a rowboat around the harbor looking for the boat that took us ashore, but not a sign of clothes or boat could we find. When dinnertime came around, I was put in the guardhouse for safe keeping, while the captain and American consul went to get something to eat.

I was given a low stool and sat up against one of the mud walls of the single room that was both prison and barracks in one. The guards were all young fellows, dressed more like hall boys than soldiers. All they did the couple of hours I was there was play cards and make remarks about me in Spanish. Sometimes a young boy or a girl hung in the doorway to gaze at me and joke. How my fists itched to get a good swing at one of their heads. But I had nothing whatsoever to defend myself with, while the four guards had swords, guns, and bayonets, so all I could do was to grin and bear it.

When the old man came for me again, he took me to the consul's office, where a sort of one-sided trial was carried on that resulted in nothing as far as getting back our clothes was concerned. About three o'clock we went back aboard and I turned to with the rest at bending sail.

At supper that night we drank our tea out of empty condensed milk cans and I had to borrow a tin pie plate from the cook to eat the hash from. I had my blanket yet, but the others who had run away had to hunt up some empty gunny bags to sleep in. The mate had saved our mattresses, so we still had them, and there was a suit of old ragged oilskins that I had cast off that I was now glad enough to get and patch up. The slop chest was nearly exhausted, so we had to make the homeward passage in the clothes we stood in.

That night the second mate marched back and forth across the fo'c'sle head, armed to the teeth with two large revolvers stuck into his belt.

We enjoyed the sight of him immensely, it was a good joke for us and he noticed we were smiling at him.

"Oh! It wouldn't be so damn funny if you tried your game again," said he. "Any boat that comes alongside will get pumped full of lead."

We were aroused about midnight by hearing Mr. Stevens loudly hailing a boat and we turned out to see what the fuss was about. It was the boat that had come up from Iquique with a man by the name of Samson to take Old Bill's place in our watch. We never did find out what became of Old Bill, who we had left on the mountainside behind Caleta Buena.

We finished bending sail the next morning, and then set up the rigging and did the finishing touches to make the *Wright* ready for sea. I was quite surprised when the cabin boy handed me a letter, and more so when I opened it and found it contained a crisp American ten-dollar bill and a letter from my brother. I was so happy I could have cried for joy. Just on the eve of sailing, when everything looked the blackest, and all the supplies I had laid in to make the voyage home a little comfortable had been lost, and with them every stitch of clothing I owned except the suit I stood in, to have received that money at that moment was a God-send to me.

I hurried aft to the captain and asked to be allowed to buy some clothes and food with the money before we sailed. The cook was going ashore for the last time at noon, to buy his fresh meat, and I begged the captain to let him get me some things, too. At first he was firm in his refusal and I felt mad enough to tear the bill into bits. Of what use was that greenback to me except to tantalize me with the thoughts of the comforts it might afford me? As it was, it was worse than useless; ashore it was equal to twenty-five native dollars, quite a sum to receive on the day of departure.

Finally the captain said, "Well, make out a list of what you want and give it to the steward. Hurry up! For as soon as he comes back we sail."

The steward said he could not buy me any clothes, but would get me all the food I wanted. So I made out a list as follows: twenty pounds of brown sugar, twelve cans of condensed milk, six cans of cocoa, two baskets of taffy (as the maple sugar was called), and five sausages.

There was another ship, an Englishman, getting underway that morning and the songs of the crew as they hove up anchor came over the water to us in hurricane notes, for she was a homeward-bounder and it was considered an honor to yell oneself hoarse on such an occasion. I could not catch all of the song; the notes rose from the low faint growl of the deep throats to the hurricane chorus of "Hurray! My boys, we're home-wa-ard bound!"

It was the custom of the port here, for one ship to aid another in getting underway. It was such a big job for one crew to unmoor and hoist all the sail that each ship usually sent a couple of men to help the one going out.

So that afternoon, as soon as we commenced to take in our stern mooring, a boat with six or eight men came alongside to help us. After several visiting captains came aboard about two o'clock in the afternoon, we hoisted in our small boat and began to heave up the anchor. When it was up and down, we went aloft and loosened everything, ready to sheet home when the anchor came up.

With a couple of mates and three extra seamen to help us, the work was quite light and the anchor came up and all sail was set in no time.

The wind was very light offshore, and the *Wright*, heavily loaded, gathered headway slowly. We hoisted in the anchor, unbent the cable, and plugged the hawse pipes before the captains called their mates and men aft to leave us. After the hard work we had gone through, we found the work aboard ship comparatively light, and had the decks well cleared up before dark.

When the boat left us and headed back toward Caleta Buena, by now far astern, those aboard gave us three cheers. Lining up on our rail, we returned it with three hearty ones and a tiger, for now that we were homeward bound everyone was in the best of spirits. The officers encouraged us when they gave an order and we were only too eager to obey, for every foot the bark sailed now was so much nearer home. Why it was I cannot tell, but the simple knowledge that we were homeward bound raised my spirits wonderfully. I suppose it was the excitement we were worked up to. We had everything to encourage us now, the four dreary months of work on the coast were over and we would be home with our friends again as soon as a hard-driven ship could take us. We knew the old man would drive her, and expected to be called out many a watch below to "crack on sail," but we were willing to do it now and each of us pulled with the strength and will of two men. Songs and chanteys were indulged in freely and all sorts of witticisms exchanged while hauling ropes.

But when I went to the wheel that night, from eight o'clock until ten, and the excitement of the day began to wane, I felt quite blue; after all it was not a matter of a few days or even weeks but all of a three-month trip that lay before us. And a great deal could happen in three months on the sea. Cape Horn had to be doubled in what was the fall of the year down there, and we were now poorly supplied with clothes for those frozen latitudes.

We had light headwinds for a week or so after leaving the coast and "Full and By" was the course the helmsman was given. Braced up sharp on the wind, with everything set, the bark crept slowly to the south'ard and eastward. This fine weather was taken advantage of by our mates to set up the rigging that had all come slack since the heavy saltpeter had been loaded into the bark. The boat was lashed on deck again and the cable hauled up on deck and blackened and then stowed away again down in the dark and cavelike box built for it under the windlass, up in the very eyes of the bow. It was like going down into a mine to climb down with a lantern into this place and haul the chain about with the chain hooks. All this had to be done soon, while the decks were dry, for we had to go down the fore hatch to get into the chain locker and this hatch would have to be battened down in bad weather.

I was kept at work painting the name boards and scrollwork on the figurehead. One day, on a board slung over the bow, with a pot of yellow paint and some brushes, I sat tracing over the vinelike ornament that adorned the *Wright*'s bow. The mate was leaning over the rail on the fo'c'sle, watching me, when I happened to knock one of the brushes overboard.

"Jump over after it," he shouted. "Jump! Jump!" He was quite excited. "That's a brand new brush. I just bought it myself with my own money, and now look! Jump! I'll throw you a line aft." At first I was going to jump. The bark was hardly moving through the water and the brush floated aft, slowly rubbing along the side. I could easily have swam and caught it. But I stopped to think a moment and the shadowy forms of four or five sharks I had seen from aloft deep down under the bark's hull came into my mind.

"Oh! no," I answered. "I guess not."

But aft we ran and, getting into a bowline the mate had made in the end of a brace, he lowered me down to the water and as the brush came along I caught it.

When we were not painting, we were messing about the rigging, setting up the shrouds or reeving new lanyards, repairing ratlines. When the captain was in a sour humor, as he sometimes got, he would give me all kinds of jobs to do, from putting a long splice in the main buntline to reeving royal clewlines. He was mad that we had run away, and as I was the one who had coaxed him to let us go ashore, he seemed to consider me the one responsible for the trouble he had been put to. He'd tell the mate to give me a certain job and then when I started in to do it he'd come and stand over me, making all manner of fun of me.

"You're a healthy kind of a sailor," he'd say. And as I'd tuck a strand in a splice he'd say, "Is that the way you learned to splice when you were a-yachting?" or "What kind of a splice do you call that?" But when he found he couldn't get the best of me that way he'd say, "I guess I'll have to dis-rate you, Davis, you had a nerve you did, to ship as able seaman."

This used to make me mad and I'd say, "Well go ahead then; I don't care a hang." But he never did, he simply talked like that to bulldoze me and pass what to him was a monotonous time. At other times he was the very opposite, coming into the fo'c'sle when our watch was below and I was lying full length in my coffin-like bunk looking over sketches or writing in my log book, and wanting to see what I had sketched lately. One morning he came in and gave me three or four small pieces of onyx, pure stone that he had picked up on the ground in Chile. He said I might have them made into cuff buttons when I got home.

Another time I was stripped to the waist trying to wash in a bucket of water one Sunday morning. The captain came forward and watched us, for the rest of our watch were doing the same. It was a warm day and we had everything on deck to air. To dry myself, I took a clean pair of woolen socks and mopped away, ignorant of the fact that my face was getting covered with lint from them. He laughed outright and said, "That's what you get for running away. Ain't you glad you went so you can sleep in gunny bags and wipe your face with socks?"

"Oh! I like it; it's out of sight," I replied. "And if I had the chance I'd run again."

When I said this he made a jump for me, but I lit out around the galley and just escaped one of my rubber boots, which he hove at me. He chased me around the house and then suddenly put on his dignity and walked aft, monarch of all he surveyed.

So things went on; sometimes he'd be ready for a joke and sometimes cross as a bear and ready to let fly fist or foot at us.

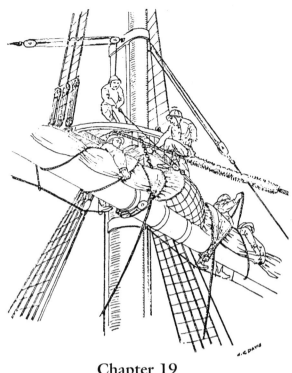

Chapter 19

*Patching clothes—Charlie's coat—Makeshifts—Tacking ship—The second
mate uses strong language—Sleeping on deck—Walking the poop to keep
awake—A meteor bursts—A flash of lightning—How I washed clothes—
The Captain says I'm a Jonah and makes me "smell the wind"—Ten knots—
Cold weather again—A fo'c'sle argument about whales.*

Every spare moment our watch had was spent patching up old clothes to keep out the cold weather we were approaching. There was nothing left in the slop chest but a few socks and one or two suits of underclothes, and these were drawn out by the most needy in our watch. Any man who says sailors are a bad lot should be thrown among them at such a time as this and they would soon pronounce such a statement a falsehood. If one man had a couple of pairs of socks while another had none, it was, "Here, you take these, I've got enough." And over went a pair to the other man. Underclothes, and in fact everything that was needed to keep out the cutting wind, were cheerfully divided among the watch.

And not only among our watch; the other fellows also helped us out. Charlie had a coat that was used continually in cold weather. He took it off when our watch came on deck and gave it to Joe to wear. It was the most remarkable coat I ever saw. Charlie called it "Old Cape Horner" and said this was the third voyage around the Horn he had used it. It certainly looked it, the patches were so thick you could not tell what the original color had been. Patches of all colors and shapes, some round, some square, some heart shaped, in fact all kinds of figures were made, and each patch had its own tale. One little black patch like a round button showed where it had caught in a block and had a piece pinched out, same as a brace sometimes catches the finger of the man belaying it when the watch lets go of it before he has a turn, and it nips a piece out of his finger.

Another long narrow strip showed where a watch mate had ripped open the coat with a sheath knife in a fo'c'sle row and Charlie had laid him up for a week afterward for doing it. And so it ran on, each patch recalling some scene of sea life. You could tell the ones that were put on on the outward passage from those that were sewn on on the homeward voyage by the stitching. The former having short, neat stitches close together, the latter genuine homeward-bounders an inch or so long.

The big mittens, or bags they really were, that I had made from the tails of my overcoat passed from one to the other of us as we took our tricks at the wheel. Hats, boots, in fact everything, were thus loaned about or used in common and no one thought of such a thing as complaining if the coat or boots were soaking wet when we got them back. That was the proof of good fellowship: When one man lent his dry clothes to another and then had to wear them himself soaking wet. Hardships are plentiful at sea, but sailors, as a class, are the most generous of men.

Sundays found me hard at work ripping the pockets off my oilskin coat to get stuff enough to patch the elbows. When the pockets were used up, I cut five or six inches off the bottom of the breeches and used that.

Seeing how poorly provided we were, the captain let the mate give us some oil and we treated our oilskins to a coat of it to try and make them watertight.

Every time we painted, I managed to give my tarpaulin a coat of it until there was as much paint as hat. When I left New York I had a pair of duck breeches. I had worn them in the hold when I was working cargo, and they had become covered with oils and grease and had been patched so many times that I threw them aside. But now I hauled them out from under the bunk where they had been tossed and put patches of number one sailcloth on the knees. I had to put a patch about two feet long on each knee and one on the seat. They were of such stiff canvas that the breeches could almost stand alone, and when the knees got bent from kneeling, they stayed bent and gave me an appearance that was grotesque if not stylish.

Our pots and pans had also been lost with our clothes, so the cook gave us the empty soup and billie tins, which we cut down and used the bottoms for pans. For pots, we saved the condensed-milk cans as we emptied them, for I had given each man a can, along with some of the sugar I had bought.

They were rather small and had a tendency to grow hot with the coffee or tea and burned our fingers to handle them, but they were far better than nothing.

Some of our watch used the pans of the other watch, but that was more than I cared to do. I tried it once, but hungry as I was, the sight of that black, grimy pan with grease—from pea soup, cracker-hash, and meat—so thick you could cut it off with your knife, sickened me. It had not been cleaned since we left New York; as soon as its owner had scooped up its contents after each meal, he tossed it into the shelf or at the foot of his bunk and all the grease grew stale and hard in it. I always kept my panniken clean, either by wiping it out with a handful of shakings or by saving the crusts of my bread and so getting the benefit of all the soup as well as cleaning the pan by wiping it with the crusts. It was the same with my bunk. Very often I took out all my bedding, and while it was airing out in the sun and wind, I gave my bunk a good swabbing out. Some of the others, however, had made up their bunk at the beginning of the voyage and never touched it to clean it until ten months or a year later, when they packed up to leave the ship.

We found the winds variable after leaving the coast, and when the month of March came around we were beating our way south, tacking ship nearly every day and sometimes several times a day. This may not sound like much, but it is a job disliked by sailors. In a schooner it would only be necessary to haul the headsails and shift over the boom tackles, but in a square-rigger it is a more complicated job. As a rule, the officers waited until eight bells, when both watches were on deck and our captain, a strapping six-footer from Down East with a voice like a bull, seemed to delight in this maneuver. Taking his position on the poop, he'd tell the man at the wheel to "keep her away a point" while the mate was on the fo'c'sle head with two men to haul over the jibs and the second mate at the lee fore braces stood ready to let them swing around when the bark came head to the wind. Then the captain sang out "Tops'l haul! Let go and haul!"

All the lee braces had previously been "flaked down," as the process of coiling them down is called, each "flake" or turn being kept clear of the other. By a quick jerk, the second mate threw the braces off the pins and jumped back to escape the snakelike coils of the braces that buzzed through the blocks as the yards, with all their gear, creaked and swung around. Sometimes, when there was much sea, they swung around violently, clear up against the backstays, and started to swing back again before we, hauling in the braces hand over hand, could rally in the slack. Then the second mate and all hands tallied on to the fore brace and sweated it up against the backstay. Meanwhile the cook was hauling in the wet and dripping fore sheet that now trailed overboard and Lawrence, the cabin boy, was bracing round the to'gansel and royal, whose braces led up on the poop deck.

"Ya ha! Yo ho! Hi yah! Ho! Sweat 'em up!" sang out the second mate as the last pulls were given. Then, when the brace was stiff as an iron rod, came the order to "Belay all!" and the line of men swung in to the rail so the end man could make it fast on the pin. The strain on this brace is something enormous. Once or twice when I was twisting the rope around the pin, the fellows let it go, thinking it was belayed. Like a vise, the brace tightened and cut a piece clean out of my finger. Of course I swore as others did when they got pinched, and the finger was painful for weeks afterward. But without a second thought for the man who got pinched, the others hauled in the other braces and belayed them. At the same time, the mate was hauling over the jibs forward with his two men, and the captain was jumping up and down aft and shouting to lay aft to the main braces. So aft we ran helter skelter, crowding up the narrow poop ladder or vaulting up to the deck above, and ran to where the lee braces were made fast near the quarter. It was hot work running about in that manner and a man would get kind of short of wind.

"Haul away!" came the order as the mate or captain let go the braces and encouraged us by shouting, "Hand over hand now, rattle 'em in boys!" We all did our best, the Dutchman trying to outdo the Swede, the Swede the Yankee, and so on. As soon as the topsail braces were fast, some of us scattered about to the different halyards and hoisted up the gaff topsail and staysails that had been let go before we tacked, while the others braced the gansels and royals. Then the mate sang out "Relieve the wheel!" and if it was our watch on deck, the man whose trick it was relieved the man at the wheel, who followed the rest of the watch forward to the fo'c'sle, where we proceeded to coil down the fathoms upon fathoms of ropes that lay in confusion about the decks.

One day Hansen and I were sent up to double up the buntlines on the fore lower topsail. To reach the leeward one, we had to trim in the foot of the sail to the rigging. We had just taken a turn to hold it there while we cast off the buntline when the second mate sang out for us to "lay down" to the deck.

Hansen started down the rigging, leaving me to cast off the line that held the sail.

"Lay down," shouted Mr. Stevens again.

"Aye! Aye! Sir!" I answered and hastened to let the line go, but the strain of the sail jammed it hard and while I was getting it clear he again shouted.

"Lay down here, damn you! We're going about."

"Aye! Aye!" I answered and forgot to add "Sir."

"Aye! Aye!" he retorted, stopping on his way aft to shake his fist at me. "Aye! Aye! ___ ___ ___ ___ I'll aye, aye you! Lay down!" He was always proud of his ability to swear and let it out whenever he got the chance. But he was so absurd in this instance and kept raising his voice until at the last he was screeching in that high falsetto voice a woman uses, and I could not help laughing at him. They could not tack ship with the topsail lashed fast to the rigging, so I cut it adrift and came down. I thought he was going to sail into me when I reached the deck, but he took it all out in jawing.

Sometimes we caught a heavy slant of wind and had to handle the to'gansels and at other times it was a flat calm all night.

When there was no wind at night and it was our watch on deck, we sometimes lay down and took a quiet snooze on the spare spars, with a coil of rope for a pillow. A word from the mate put us on our feet in an instant and we grew so confident of our ability to awaken at the first call that we more often trusted ourselves to the extent of closing our eyes in sleep.

Sampson, who had taken Old Bill's place, and I were peacefully sleeping on the spars one night when a squall made its appearance to windward and the mate sang out to clew up the fore royal.

We both slept peacefully on, though he sang out three times, and then Joe, who was on lookout, came down off the fo'c'sle head and shook us. But the mate had suspected something and he also came down on the main deck, where the darkness was so profound he couldn't distinguish a man from a coil of gear. When he found we had lain stretched out right under his nose, he was so mad he swore that from then on one of us would walk the poop with him.

He kept his word and after that there were no more quiet snoozes. One of us had to keep walking fore and aft along the lee side of the poop, while he walked to windward, that he might know at least one of us was awake.

I was there one night, my pea jacket buttoned up close, with the collar turned up, and my hands buried deep in my breeches pockets to keep them warm. It was a breezy place up there, with no high bulwarks to protect you, and the wind swept under the foot of the mizzen staysail strong enough to lift me off the deck. It was getting close on to twelve o'clock that black and windy night, and the *Wright* had a homeward-bound cant on her with a band of white suds racing past a good eight knots an hour.

Suddenly, I stopped short in my walk to watch a shooting star. It went from astern clear across the heavens and then it burst off the lee bow with a bright bluish glare that lit up the bark like an electric light.

For an instant everything was bright as day, and then all was dark. For a minute or so I could see nothing. While I was blinking, like an owl in the sunlight, the mate came over and stuck his face close to mine with a look of amazement stamped on his features.

"Did you see that? What was it? Where'd it come from? Was it lightning?" He rattled these questions faster than I could reply and from his excited looks and actions, I judged he must have been pretty nearly asleep himself when the meteor, or whatever it was, exploded.

It was a weird kind of a scene; the bark roaring ahead into darkness, with a half-gale booming into the hollows of her canvas and singing among the gear, combined with the ghostly blue light. It gave me such a start that sleep did not bother my eyelids the rest of that night.

Something similar happened a few nights later. I was again on the poop when there was a sharp report followed by a sudden flash of lightning. Before the light had faded, the mate was roaring out for us to clew up sail. "Clew up your fore and main royals! Haul down the flying jib! Let go your main topmast staysail halyards!"

You'd think he had a man-of-war's crew at his command instead of three sleepy merchant sailors. He let go the staysail himself, and its hanks came rattling down the stay while we let go the flying jib and hauled it down on the jib boom. Then, one at a time, we clewed up the royals and ran aloft to furl them while Joe stowed the flying jib.

It was a good deal of sail to take off for a flash of lightning, but subsequent events proved the mate's judgment correct and the breeze that came sweeping down on the bark caused us to also furl the fore to'gansel and clew down the gaff topsail.

We were allowed a little more fresh water on the homeward voyage to wash our clothes with, but we had nothing to wash, except in warm weather, when we'd take off the only suit of clothes we had and go without them until they dried. I had got an empty firkin from the cook and this I kept for my washtub, filling it with rainwater whenever I got the chance and so had water for washing. I was but a poor hand at the washtub; once when we lay at anchor in Valparaiso, I sat on the fore hatch washing my clothes and had nearly finished when Scotty came along drawing solid comfort out of a stump of a clay pipe, and watched me, for it was a Sunday morning and there was nothing to do.

"What have you got there?" he asked pointing to the cake of soap in back of me.

"Good gosh! I've done all my washing and never touched it," said I. So he showed me how to soap my clothes before washing them and gave me some practical hints on this important part of bachelor housekeeping.

It was the custom of the mates to get someone in their watches to wash their clothes for them. Joe did it for Mr. Hill when it was his lookout and the cabin boy washed all the captain's clothes every Monday morning.

It made quite a homelike scene those days to see strings of clothes on lines stretched across the poop, the sacred deck, with real clothespins holding the shirts and sheets to the line. While Lawrence, in the scuppers, was deep into a washtub scrubbing like a washwoman.

Across the fo'c'sle head or on top of the forward house would be a string of coarse shirts, dungaree suits, etc., that made up a fo'c'sle hand's outfit; but instead of clothespins, each piece was seized on with a rope yarn, and maybe the jib boom back ropes would be decorated with a blanket or two or a string of socks seized to, it fluttering in the wind like a row of blackbirds.

Each Sunday, in order that one man should not have the same hours on watch each week, it was the custom to shift the watch by standing only a two-hour trick in the afternoon watch instead of the usual four hours.

When I went to the wheel at two o'clock on Sunday, March 12th, I found the bark was heading southeast by east and the course was "full and bye," I knew the bark was heading south and I hoped, as I took the wheel from Joe, that it would be my luck to bring her up to her course, but no, the wind backed more and more, until at four o'clock she was heading due east, a course for the South American shore.

When Captain Freeman came on deck, he looked at the compass first thing and, turning to me, said, "You're a bloody Jonah!"

I was comfortably dressed, it being Sunday, and I hoped to get below before there was any handling of sails to be done. But just at eight bells a squall came down on us and the captain sang out, "Mr. Hill! Let Davis go up and make the fore royal fast." And as I started forward he added, "Let him smell the wind a bit."

Now, it is not customary, at sea, to make a man go aloft and stow sails after he has stood his trick at the wheel. This job should have been given to one of the starboard watch and our watch allowed to go below, and but for the captain's interference, I would have been rolling into my bunk instead of scrambling up the weather rigging while the watch on deck clewed up the sail. I had just got the sail half furled when down came a squall of bitter cold rain and hail, and I got soaked to the skin.

We'd had headwinds ever since leaving the coast, but two days after this squall we got a fair slant. It came in the morning watch when we were below. I was awakened by the watch running past the house and the call "Yo ho! Square him!" as they squared in the yards. The splattering sound of the head sea gave way to steady seething as the bark began to race through the water.

The wind increased to a moderate gale in our watch that afternoon, and at night the bark ran along ten knots an hour by the log. For a ship laden as deep as she was, this was very good time, although she beat it off the Horn, which we rounded about a week later, going eleven knots before a whole gale under reefed topsails.

The nights were getting cold and heavy dew made sleeping on deck impossible. Rain squalls wet down the decks so often that we knocked off washing down in the mornings and were glad to see a dry spot occasionally.

I cheered myself up during the long lookout on the fo'c'sle head at nights by taking a can of condensed milk with me and eating it, a spoonful at a time. They lasted me until nearly to the Horn and my heart grew heavy as I emptied my last can and realized I had a couple of months yet before me to the Delaware, where we were bound.

One day during dinnertime, as our watch sat eating and smoking, the conversation turned to whales. We had seen several during the forenoon, spouting their fountains of spray high in the air, and in some way the conversation led up to the way they were captured.

Lawson, the new man, insisted that the ships had a cannon on their fo'c'sle head and sailed up to the whale and shot the harpoon into them.

"Vat!" said Joe, "the bloody ship couldn't get vid-in a bloomin' mile of dem!"

"Why couldn't it?" asked Lawson.

"Cause it couldn't, de vales vould go hoff like a bloomin' streak hif de ship come near dem."

"How do they catch them, then?" Lawson asked.

"Vye, in boats of course," answered Joe and Hansen both in the same breath, for, like politics, each man had his side and argued for it.

"Boats!" said Lawson. "How are they going to catch a whale eighty feet long in a boat? Tell me that." And he settled himself back against the bunk, with his empty pan still on his knees, and started to fill his pipe.

I had crawled into my bunk and lay listening to the fun, but when he spoke of whales eighty feet long, I chipped in and said I thought that was pretty big for a whale. "Fifty or sixty feet is as big as they run," said I.

"Well, even sixty feet then. How can they catch a sixty-foot whale with a rowboat?"

Here Hansen got his say in ahead of Joe and he told how the boats put out from the ship when a whale was sighted and crept cautiously upon him, how the harpooner stood up in the bow and hurled the harpoon into the whale; but when he said there was a line made fast to the harpoon and that the whale sometimes towed the boat at railroad speed miles away from the ship, Lawson interrupted him and refused to believe it.

"Well, how do they do it?" asked Hansen.

"Why there is a line made fast, as you say, to the harpoon, but the harpoon is shot from a cannon in the ship's bow."

"What becomes of this line if the whale dives?" Hanse asked him.

"There is a hawser made fast to the harpoon and the whale often tows the ships," he answered.

"A hawser," said Hansen laughing at the idea. "How would they ever haul in the hawser with a whale on the end of it."

"Say!" exclaimed Joe. "Vat do they do mid the vale ven dey kill him?"

Lawson's answer to this question was awaited with interest by the rest of us, but his reply was more than ridiculous and showed he knew nothing whatever about whaling.

"They hoist the whale aboard and cut him up and put him into barrels," he said.

Hansen and Joe laughed outright and Hansen said, "I supposed they lay him across from rail to rail?"

"Yes," said Lawson, "they do."

And so they kept arguing. Hansen told him how the ship sailed up to the whale when it was killed and how the blubber was cut off and hoisted aboard to be dried out, but Lawson would not be convinced and they were still arguing it in their bunks, between puffs at their pipes, when I fell asleep.

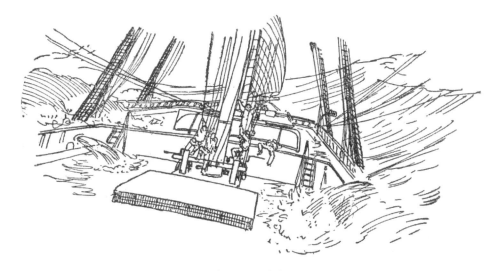

Chapter 20

Eleven knots before a full-fledged gale off the Horn—Water on deck—A sea breaks over the bark—Big seas—Pumping ship—The mate gets my diary and refuses to return it—The captain's poem—The mate's ugly temper—We pass a large iron ship.

On the seventeenth it started in to blow a living gale and we shortened sail to a reefed main upper topsail, lower topsails, and fore course; for four days the bark drove along smothered in the white suds of her own making and an occasional sea that would break aboard over one rail and go out over the other.

It was a good thing we were not bound to the westward. If so, we'd have been hove to; for the wind was screeching aloft something deafening and it took two men at the wheel to keep the bark running true before the mountains of water that came towering up astern, so high it took the breath out of a man to look at them.

Although it was bitter cold weather, when I was at the wheel, the perspiration ran in streams down my face and body as I and another man labored to keep the bark from broaching to.

It got so bad the last few days that the captain let only the strongest men in the watches take the wheel, and he himself and the mate often took a trick to relieve the men.

There was nothing to be done those four days after the sails had been furled but to hang on and pray the bark didn't get pooped.

It was enough to make one giddy to see the racing of white suds going past at the rate of eleven knots, to feel the bark, as she tore along before the gale, rolling so at times it was all we could do to hang on.

We spent all our spare time on watch huddled up in the lee of the cabin on the poop and left the main deck to the mercy of the sea. It was a grand sight, if it did not have such a deadly significance to it, to watch those solid green seas tumble over the rail onto the deck with a shock that could be felt from bow to stern and change in an instant into a boiling, flying, seething mass of white spume.

Back and forth it raced across the deck as the bark swung her spars quickly from side to side until the water was beaten, as by an eggbeater, into foam.

One night about midnight, when Hansen, Joe, and I were jammed up in a bunch by the coach-house door, trying to keep warm by the united heat of our bodies, I saw a sea come over the port rail and break clear over the other rail into the sea. It completely flooded the forward part of the bark. When the water had rolled partly off the decks, I noticed something black floating across from side to side amid the white suds and, watching my chance when the water drained off to about knee deep, I jumped in and grabbed it. As I dragged it forward where the rise of the decks made the water shoaler and the forward house formed a lee, I saw it was the cover off the hatch in the top of the galley. So, climbing up between the two boats stowed there, I crawled aft to the black square that marked the open hatch and looked down into it. And such a sight; the galley was half full of water and pots and pans were washing about promiscuously.

I thought of Lawrence as I looked in, for he slept in the top bunk of the galley and was locked in each night by the cook, who slept aft with the mates and captain.

He was awake, and as my eyes got accustomed to the gloom, I saw two white eyes looking up at me and the poor coon whimpered. "Wha's e matter, Massa Davis?" for he recognized my voice as I called his name to make sure that he was not drowned; for every time the bark rolled, the water washed up into his bunk.

"Everything's all right, Lawrence, only the hatch washed off." And I clapped it on and lashed it down.

It was some time before I could get aft, owing to the seas that broke aboard and flooded the waist of the ship, rail deep. But finally the chance came and I floundered aft to find the mate very much excited, asking the other two of my watch where I was. He thought I had been swept overboard. I told him about the hatch, but he ordered me to stay aft and not risk myself on the main deck again. "We need every man we've got," he said as he walked aft to stand by the men at the wheel.

It would be impossible to convince a man, who thinks he has seen some high seas, of the enormous height a Cape Horn swell rises to. When I look at ships now, as they lie alongside the docks, and see the tons after tons of cargo that go into them, and run my eye along their mammoth hulls, and look aloft at the tremendous height of their spars, it doesn't seem possible that such a large craft could be hurled about like a toy. You'd never suspect that a sea could sweep the full length of such a ship and pour off over the stern or break clean over them. If you could imagine how such a craft would look plunging half under and rising with tons of green water pouring off her decks, think of the condition the men must be in who are unfortunate enough to have to follow the sea for a living or, as in my case, fools enough to do it for pleasure. What chance has such a mite of humanity, with his feeble strength, on the deck of such a vessel when the seas are smashing everything they hit into kindling wood.

No wonder, then, that the watch huddled together in the lee of the cabin and clung to whatever came to hand to escape going over the rail and into the sea. No wonder we dreaded the time when the mate came forward just before it was time to call the other watch and told us to get ready to pump her out. We'd look to our oilskins to see they were lashed tightly to our sea boots and tie each other's coats at the wrists with rope yarns to keep the water out.

When the other sleepy watch came aft, we watched our chance and all hands got on the pump brakes and sent the heavy flywheels round to the clank, clank of the iron valve as the water gushed up black and dirty from the hold, to stain the milk-white foam on deck.

It was enough to awe any man to hear, above the clanking of the pumps and slopping and rushing of water all about, the ever-constant howl of the wind in the sails and gear aloft.

The mate, encased in his oilers, looked on from the poop above us and warned us whenever a sea threatened to break aboard. But he didn't always sing out in time and occasionally a sea came over the rail and knocked every mother's son of us sprawling, cursing and spluttering into the lee scuppers, soaked to the skin in the water.

By the time the mate was satisfied there was no more water to pump out, we were glad enough to be relieved and waded forward to the warm little box of a fo'c'sle.

The last day of the gale, the fore lower topsail sheet parted and the heavy clew-iron slapped a hole through the sail and split it from head to foot. We unbent it and sent it down on deck that same morning and Old Jim and the mate set to work, patching and sewing it up.

A queer thing happened to me the next day, when the wind had moderated and we were setting sail. We sent up and rebent the topsail and then hoisted the to'gansels and royals and kept the old wagon rolling along the best part of ten knots. Little Hansen and I were sent up to put a patch on the fore to'gansel. While we were laying over the yard sewing it on, the foot of the royal above us knocked my cap off and away it sailed, overboard for sure, I thought. Down it went, clean over the bow, but as it got in the lee of the topsails it dropped straight down and the bark shoved her bow forward just in time to have it land neatly on the fo'c'sle head. This was a piece of luck I never expected.

The wind held strong for several days as we passed the Horn, and held on to the eastward for some time to run down our longitude where the degrees were short, before we headed north.

One day the mate, who knew I was keeping a diary of the voyage, said to me, "What day was it we filled the water cask in Caleta Buena?"

"I got it in my book," I replied.

"Well go get it," he answered. So I brought it to him in the carpenter shop and he and the second mate looked it over. He didn't want to read it, he said, but just look over it to see the date of the day we took in our fresh water.

So I went on deck for a few minutes and when I returned I heard the second mate saying, "That will sell like hot cakes when they see the headings in big letters: 'Run away,' 'In hiding,' 'On the pampas,' etc."

At dinnertime I asked the mate for the book, but his reply was, "You don't get that book back. Those few pages in it will send Charlie and the rest of his gang to prison. I've been trying to get hold of that book for a long time and been forward looking for it."

He was referring to the part where I had written about deserting the ship and who it was that had helped us. None of the officers aft knew just how it had been done until then. I asked him for it again that night, but his reply was, "The captain's reading it. You'll get it back."

The next day, after dinner, I saw the captain on the poop and went aft and asked him for my diary. "I want to do some writing in it," I said.

"Do you?" he retorted. "Well I want to do some writing in that book myself." And then, seeing I was still waiting, he exclaimed, "Go on now, get out of this; I haven't got your book."

As I was passing the coach house at the head of the cabin stairs, the mate came out and I said to him, "Can I have my book now, sir? I want to do some writing in it."

"I haven't got your book. I sent it forward by a man."

I knew this was a lie, so I said, "That's too thin, if I don't get that book I'll raise a row," meaning to make him pay for it when I got ashore. "That's my personal property and you've got no right to keep it." I was mad clear through at his bulldozing and he knew it.

"Go on forward where you belong," he ordered.

The cook was looking out of his galley, listening to our argument as I came forward.

"Well, you'll pay for it, that's all," I said as I stepped in the fo'c'sle and shut the door.

Joe and the rest wanted to know what was the matter and I was just telling them about my book when the mate opened the door and shouted, "So you're going to raise a row, are you? Come out here if you want a row. I'll lick the whole lot of you. I'll give you all the row you want!"

His threats made the rest of the watch mad and we paused in our undressing as Joe sung out to him, "You come in here ef you vant a row and you'll get it." But the mate wisely stayed on deck and stormed away aft, muttering threats at us.

Soon after we had turned in, the captain looked in the partly opened fo'c'sle door and said, "See here, Davis." So I went into the carpenter shop with him, where he handed me my diary opened to a page in the back where he had written something and told me to read it. It was a poem and ran as follows:

The Sailor's Resolve

A sailor on the topsail yard,
While reefing softly sings,
"I'd rather pick some cherries here
    Than pull on these 'ere strings.

"I'd sooner of a kicking mule
    Be the undisputed boss,
Than haul this weather ear-ring out
    On this 'ere Flemish hoss.

"I'd rather steer my Betsy Jane
    Up to the alter rail,
Than be aloft on this 'ere night,
    A reefin' this 'ere sail.

> "I swear that when I get ashore
>   I'll splice that lovely lass,
> Buy that aforesaid mule as kicks,
>   And peddle garden sass."

I could not help smiling at such a comical poem and have no doubt he sought to smooth over matters by writing it in my book and returning it.

"Keep it out of sight and don't let the mate get hold of it," he said as he went aft. And I turned into my bunk and resumed my sleep.

Mr. Hill, the mate, was grumpy and sour as an old bull the next morning. Before it was daylight he sent me up to the fore royal to look for land. I knew we were passing Cape Horn, but also knew I could not see land at that time of day. However, it was play now for me to run aloft, after eight or nine months of that kind of work, so I was soon astride of the royal yard, holding on to the tie and counting the ships in sight. There were four in all, two outward-bounders, one on each bow coming along with a fair wind, and two going like ourselves, close hauled on the port tack. The latter were off our lee quarter, hull down.

When the mate called me down, for I would have stayed up there until he did, he made Joe, Lawson, and me wash down the poop without his aid, for he usually helped us; but little we cared, we scrubbed and splashed and joked away in spite of him.

Then he sang out to clew up the to'gansels, so we clewed up the fore and came aft to the main, well knowing this was only the beginning of the mate's spite. Just as we started to haul on the clewline, he mumbled out some order. Joe looked at me and I at Lawson, but none of us understood what he said. He had his back toward us and as we waited to hear what he said, he muttered again unintelligibly.

Finally we told him we couldn't hear.

"____ ____ your souls, open your ears, then!" he shouted and worked himself up into a furious rage. We were standing just at the edge of the poop, as the clewline was made fast to a pin in the rail up there, and when he saw us he flung his hat down on deck, threw his coat on the booby hatch, and came at us on a run.

"Get off of here," he shouted. "Get down on the main deck! Get down there!" and giving Joe and Lawson a shove, he sent both of them off the poop to the deck below while I jumped back against the rail.

Seizing the clewline, he gave it two or three fearful yanks and then let it go and went back to the hatch and put on his hat and coat. He never said another word until we had the sail clewed up and asked him if we should furl it.

"Yes, damn you! Yes!" he shouted and resumed his walk back and forth along the weather side of the poop, without so much as looking at us.

We spent the rest of our watch making sennite by the booby hatch and I kept my eye on a large, black, iron ship on our weather beam. She had a low square look, with stubby poles and flat trucks that pronounced her English. Her royals and spanker were stowed and with the weather clew of her mainsail lifted, she came edging down on us, now hull down in the hollow between the seas and then hove up on the crest until the red of her bottom stood out like a flash of fire against the white foam that swept aft as the hull passed through it.

The mate had called the old man up, as it was evident the ship intended to pass close under our stern, and together they hoisted the flags that, in the signal code, made out the *Wright*'s number.

It was a perfect day; the sun shone clear over the entire ocean with a hard blue sky overhead, dotted with piles of fluffy vapor and an occasional strip of mackerel sky that resembled the wake of a paddlewheel steamer.

It was something unusual for ships to pass as close as we were with this "Lime Juicer," as English ships are called. We could almost distinguish the features of her people as they paused in their work to hang over the rail and look at us. The red shirts of some of the sailors by the fore rigging caught my eye first and then the white apron on the cook as he stood half in and half out of his galley, looking at us.

Aft on the poop stood two figures, evidently the skipper and mate, eyeing us through a long telescope, and near them at the wheel stood the helmsman, dividing his time between watching the ship's course and us.

She did not appear to be going very fast and yet, as she drew away to leeward, it seemed but a few minutes before she was miles away, sinking her hull below the long, flat swells. It was not an everyday occurrence to speak to a ship and it made me feel a little as if we still belonged to that far-distant earth where the busy city of New York and all my friends belonged. It made me feel as if the solid earth still existed and had not sunk into oblivion when we left it.

Chapter 21

*Discard boots for shoes—Tobey and the sea—The cook loses his potatoes—
On lookout—Joe and Hansen have an argument—A sudden chill—
Icebergs ahead—Tack ship—The fóc'sle washed out again—Another gale—
A rainbow—The mate gets a ducking—Cleaning ship—Tarring down—
I spill some varnish from the fore royal yard.*

Far away on the northern horizon were four ships in sight and there they hung all our watch, and were still in sight when the sun went around the western edge of the earth and left us navigating in the dark.

During the night a breeze came up and the bark, with every stitch set, began to log ten knots an hour and kept it up all the next day, Sunday.

She was romping along at this rate during the forenoon and I was exercising my legs, walking up and down the deck from the fo'c'sle head to the break of the half deck. We had been heading up a couple of points north and east lately and the degrees of latitude we had crossed through began to show in the weather. It was still cold enough for heavy jackets, but the decks were no longer flooded with the seas.

On this particular day the decks had even shown patches where the planks had actually dried, and I ventured forth wearing only my low shoes instead of the rubber boots I had worn for the month past.

Tobey, the little puppy we had brought aboard in Valparaiso, was contentedly trotting along behind me, turning when I turned, but always maintaining a distance of about six feet behind me. He had learned this trick by following the men as they paced back and forth in their lonely watches at night and was now a regular sailor's dog and a favorite with everyone on board, except perhaps Lawrence, whose duty it was to keep the cabin clean.

The cook sat in the galley door on his stool, peeling potatoes for the coming Sunday dinner, and the mate continued his nervous trotting along the weather side of the poop. We were just going by the corner of the galley one trip when a lump of sea spouted over the weather rail and hit poor little Tobey square in the side and sent him rolling across the deck to leeward, yelping for all he was worth, half drowned and frightened to death.

I was shaking with laughter at the comical sight, and had just reached the lee of the main mast, when there was a shock to windward and a green sea broke over the rail and flooded the main deck. It was a good thing I was behind the mast, for the sea would have knocked me into a cocked hat it hit so hard. I escaped most of it by jumping into the network of buntlines and sheets that were around the mast and climbing up above the water until it had drained off.

The unexpected onslaught of the sea took the cook unawares. It nearly washed out the galley, soaked him to the skin, and sent his potatoes all over the deck, while the last I saw of Tobey he was going up under the bow as fast as he could leg it, with the water close behind him. I scurried around and saved the potatoes as soon as the water drained off, for the loss of them meant the loss of our dinner, or part of it at least. Tobey followed the water as it drained off and took his revenge by barking furiously at it.

As we were nearing warmer latitudes, the mates started us at cleaning and scraping preparatory to painting later on. All our watch we were picking and scraping the rust off the windlass with our sheath knives and running to the grindstone every little while to sharpen them. It was a monotonous job and I was glad enough when nighttime came around and the decks had been swept down, for the night watches gave us rest, there was nothing to be done except pace up and down and keep awake.

The weather we were having was rather sharp at night but, with a big full moon making daylight along the decks, it was the most enjoyable part of the twenty-four hours. I like being on lookout on such nights and paced back and forth from side to side, humming the airs of the songs that were popular when I left the States, or leaned with my elbows on the capstan, looking ahead but seeing scenes that had transpired at home, thinking over the good times I had had cruising on the yacht and the good food that I had not really missed until now. Hour after hour I stood thus, occasionally glancing aloft where the rounded bosoms of the sleeping sails caught the milky whiteness of the moon and gradually shaded down into shadow as the sail rounded in at the foot. The decks lay like ivory at my feet and were thrown into squares of blackness when the sails rolled between them and the moon.

Aft on the poop, the black figure of the mate came and went, while the captain occasionally poked his head up the after companionway or came and stood on deck by the rail puffing a new clay pipe. Lawson stood at the wheel and the other two of the watch, finding it too chilly to lie down on deck and take a nap, kept pacing back and forth, spinning yarns and laughing once in a while, for we were homeward bound now.

On the morning of March 30 there was a decidedly sharp chill in the air that made washing down rather disagreeable. After pumping ship, the mate sent me aft to sweep the water off the poop so it would dry quickly. While I was doing this, Lawrence, who was on his way aft to the cabin with dishes, called my attention to something ahead on the horizon.

It looked like a flat-topped island rising abruptly from the sea at its northern end and gradually sloping down to its southern end in a series of flat plains like steps to the sea.

"That's land," said Lawrence, pointing to it.

I knew there was no land in this part of the ocean, but thought possibly it was some cloud formation on the horizon; for more than once I have been astonished to see how much the clouds resembled mountains and islands. Sometimes I have seen what I could almost swear was a low, flat country with white mountain ranges towering beyond, but, as the sun mounted in the heavens, they melted away into the tossing sea line, leaving a clear horizon and as it was now early in the morning I thought this island ahead was another fake.

"No, that's a cloud," I replied.

The mate had seen us looking ahead, so he looked over the rail and when he saw what we were looking at he went down and called the captain.

"Boo!" exclaimed the captain as he stepped out on deck and shrugged up his shoulders. "That's an iceberg!"

Word soon spread to the watch below that there were icebergs in sight and as it was near breakfast time they turned out to have a look.

Down to leeward was a full rigged ship, hull down, heading for the ice just as we were. Just before eight bells she came about and, as the wind had been heading us, we met the ship *Webster* around eight bells, when all hands were on deck.

By that time we were close up to the berg and could see four other icebergs from the deck, while from aloft I could see fields and fields of broken ice forming a regular ice floe miles and miles in area; in fact, as far as I could see it was nothing but ice.

Now that the sun was up and we were close to the berg, we could see all its beauties; pinnacles of ice hung all about it like gigantic icicles with all the colors of the rainbow flashing through them. The waves at its base broke in masses of white spray that spouted through caverns and crevices of their own making. On top it was as smooth as a table, and from what I had read of icebergs I imagined that might once have been the bottom instead of the top. In places the sea had worn it into arches and caves that were festooned and decorated with all sorts of grotesque forms. It was a berg of considerable size, too, for its top was far above our mast-heads and I tried to imagine about how deep its bottom part must go. They say only about one-sixth of a berg stands above the water. It was certainly a cold neighbor and we were glad enough to see it sinking astern as we made the best of our way away from it.

That night the barometer went down with a drop and we were thankful we were clear of the ice. We furled both upper topsails, fore, and main course and set the storm spanker. The wind came along about nine P.M. and made things howl in great shape. We had taken out all the wooden shutters that protected the glass in the skylight some days ago, but had to put them back again in a hurry. A wicked sea kicked up all about us and hove the bark on her beam ends with every wave.

The old man didn't dare run off before it, for under our lee lay the ice, so with the best helmsmen at the wheel, she went floundering along, smashing in a door or a window once in a while, knocking us off our feet, or rolling an empty flour barrel out from under the fo'c'sle head and smashing it into staves before we could secure it.

In the fo'c'sle it was impossible to sleep, she jumped and rolled so. I stuck a short piece of a board on end at the edge of my bunk to keep from being thrown out and then had to spread my arms and legs apart to hold myself still.

We all spent a sleepless watch, drawing a little comfort and warmth through our pipes. Just when we were about to go on deck at eight bells, all bundled up and warm in our heavy clothes, a sea washed the lee door off and flooded the fo'c'sle. Joe, who was nearest the door, was knocked off his feet and sent across the floor, soaked to the skin. The rest of us hung on to the top bunks until the water ran out the open doorway again. Then we went on deck and relieved the second-mate's watch, letting them screw the hinges on the door again and bail out the fo'c'sle.

The gale lasted for three days; the last day, April 1, it gradually softened down until we had the main to'gansel on her and the log was doing a great business recording the miles of water the bark was getting over in a day. Every mile was so much nearer home; the bark was being driven and in the right direction. I was at the wheel at noon and overheard the captain giving the mate our position: latitude forty-five south, longitude fifty west. We were still farther south than I imagined. Forty-five was quite a ways south, but as Cape Horn lay in fifty-eight, we had covered thirteen degrees of latitude already.

The hard gray scud broke away during the morning and the blue sky smiled down on us between banks of fleecy white clouds. A few parting rain squalls came chasing after us, but they were only clearing-up showers. As one shower came up astern I noticed a beautiful double rainbow arching over with both ends on the water; it came directly for the bark, one end on each side, and must have passed over our mastheads, although I lost sight of it just when it was at the stern. I don't know why, but it gave me a very cheerful feeling. It seemed a token of good luck to have the beautiful arch go over the ship.

It amused me sometimes to watch the mate make his way along the decks when they were being washed by the seas tumbling aboard. He had on his low shoes one day, having discarded his hip boots, and from the after house he jumped to the booby hatch, from this to the capstan, and so onto the yawl boat stowed across the forward end of the half deck.

From here he jumped to the bitts around the main mast and so over the main hatch to the galley and forward. But this time he got caught nicely; he'd made his way to the bitts and was holding on to some of the many ropes that came down to it, watching for a chance to jump and run across the main hatch. Finally, when the mate thought the right moment had come, he jumped, but no sooner had he done so than he knew a sea was coming. He just turned and got hold of a rope when the main deck went out of sight under an immense sea that broke aboard and nearly drowned him. He pulled himself up on the bitts, a sorry-looking mess with water running in streams off of him. For about five minutes he was isolated on the bitts with the water waist deep all about him and pouring off the break of the poop in a waterfall. When he got the chance, he bolted aft and changed his clothes for oilers and seaboots.

We had good strong winds after this blow and made such good time north that the mate started us scraping down, in preparation for that homeward-bound job of painting ship.

When a ship nears land after a voyage, it is customary to paint and clean her from end to end. The ships that one sees alongside the docks in our seaports are not as ships are at sea; there they have been chafing for weeks alongside the wharves, their gear is all unwove or hanging loose, sails unbent or clumsily rolled up by men who took no pride in doing the job, and their decks are littered from end to end with dirt and dunnage from shore, the paintwork is all black and grimy and the decks unwashed.

But a ship at sea, especially a "homeward bounder," is another craft altogether. Every rope is in its proper place and kept hauled taut. The decks are scrubbed with brooms each morning until clean as a tabletop, and the paintwork is carefully washed off with ashes and water or, if the paint is fresh, swabbed off with a soft rag.

It was the job of scraping and varnishing, tarring down, painting and holystoning that we were now started on, regular housecleaning at sea.

Every watch, morning, noon, and evening, it was scrape, scrape, scrape until our knives were worn almost to nothing with resharpening and a watch below was eagerly looked forward to.

Everything that had varnish on it was scraped clean and revarnished afresh: royal masts, to'gallant mast, topmast, jibboom, spanker boom, mizzen mast, capstan bars, belaying pins, and stanchions all were treated in turn and either reslushed or varnished.

All the standing rigging was tarred down or blackened with black paint put on with a rag instead of a paintbrush. I used to delight in swinging aloft in a bos'n's chair made fast to a gauntline that was rove through a tail block on the masthead. From here the deck of the bark looked a mile below me; the heads and shoulders of the people moving about were all I could see, the bellying breasts of the sails bulged out hard and round with the trade winds blowing into them. With my legs twisted around the stay to keep from swinging away as the bark rolled, I daubed away, lowering myself down as I blackened the stay.

We put on the oldest suit of clothes we had for this work, for no matter how careful a man was, the constant tumbling and rolling of the bark was sure to swing him against the fresh paint. Sometimes it was all we could do to hang onto the stay, the mast heads swung so far from side to side that first we were under one side of the stay and then hanging under the other. It took one hand to hang on and the other to paint, while the paint pot, made fast to one side of the bos'n's chair, had to take care of itself. The paint was too thick to spill easily or else there was many a time, when the bark gave a sudden roll, when the paint would have been spilled onto the sails and deck below.

One day the bark was rolling along at seven or eight knots through the strong southeast trades. All her running gear was racked off and made fast up in the rigging while the rail and stanchion irons were being painted. The mate gave me an open-top, tin pail half-full of varnish and told me to varnish down the fore royal mast. Varnish was much more apt to spill, being thinner than the paint, and it was customary for the mate to tie a piece of canvas over the top of the can with a small hole in it to get the brush through. But when I asked him to put some canvas over it, his reply was, "Shut your mouth and do as you're told."

So up I started, the can hanging from a rope yarn in one hand and climbing with the other. I got over the foretop all right, then up the topmast rigging and as high as the to'gallant yard. From here up there were no ratlines to climb. The royal mast was a round, smooth pole some fifteen or twenty feet in length. The only rigging was two backstays, one on each side, and the halyard tie of the royal yard along the mast. Twisting my legs around the backstay, I went up sailor fashion and never spilled a drop of varnish, but just as I swung myself up on top of the royal yard, the can caught on the foot rope and spilled about half the varnish.

I looked for the mate, but could not see him, so I felt sure he had not seen me. The varnish sprayed out like rain and sprinkled the lee yardarms of the two topsails and two fellows who were at work there, tarring down the brace pennant; and as I started in to work, I heard some strong language come my way.

Chapter 22

Tobey is missing—The mystery is cleared—In the trade winds—Off the island of Trinidad—Down in the hold—Burning saltpeter—Bugs in the fo'c'sle—I spill black paint—Cranky Jim—Holystoning—I nearly have a fight with the mate—All hands at work.

Noontime one day when our watch came on deck, the other fellows asked us if we had seen Tobey. He had not been seen all their watch, nor did he appear again on deck. All day, as we worked, we looked for him. We searched the carpenter shop, the fo'c'sle, and every little nook and corner up under the fo'c'sle head where he used to run and hide out of the way of the water, but saw not a sign of him.

Then the second mate said someone in the crew had thrown him overboard. We all resented this; for although Tobey was a regular little thief and often ran off with a man's shoe or mitten, he was so cunning and playful that we all liked him. At mealtimes he sat on the deck outside the fo'c'sle door and had a way of shivering and whining that made him appear so pitiful that we tossed him bits of meat from our pans.

I knew there was not a man aboard who would think of drowning Tobey. Hour after hour at night he shortened a lonely watch by following us up and down the deck or endeavored to help us pull by getting hold of the end of the rope and dragging it along the deck, making us laugh so. Then when he tumbled over another rope, we could hardly pull our weight, we laughed so hard.

No, I was sure it was someone aft who had done the deed. I suspected the cook, for several times I had seen him chase Tobey out of the galley, and once Tobey ran up under the fo'c'sle head with half a ham from the galley and the cook at his heels. He got a thrashing that time. The cook took off the leather belt he wore and licked him good with it. So I knew there was no love lost between those two.

The second day after his disappearance, Albert came into the fo'c'sle and cleared up the mystery. It seems Tobey, who had the run of the bark from the captain's cabin to the fo'c'sle, had gone down into the saloon and vomited upon the polished hardwood floor. Lawrence was so mad at him for doing it, he tied the dog's forelegs together and dropped him overboard. Albert was at the wheel at the time and said he saw Tobey struggling along in the bark's wake as long as he was in sight. The crew was very mad when it learned the truth of the matter, and said things to the effect of "That dog was better than the nig."

Tobey certainly helped pass away many a pleasant hour that would otherwise have been lonely; whereas the cook and cabin boy, both from Barbados, were very stingy. The cook would not even give a man a drink of water in hot weather, nor a cup of hot water to dress his boils with in bad weather, and even when the captain ordered him to do so, he gave as little as possible.

Once, when the mate caught several bonito, he said if we cleaned them the cook would cook them for us. So all hands turned to and cleaned eleven of them, but the fish hung up forward until they rotted and had to be thrown over the side. The cook wouldn't dirty his pans to cook them, even though we were half-starved at the time. So I thought the men were right when they said the dog was better than Lawrence.

We had one more gale that was short and sweet and made us reef down. Once more the decks were flooded fore and aft, and oilers and seaboots came into demand. But it only lasted a day and a night, and on the tenth of April we picked up the first of the southeast trades.

The water had that clear transparent blue that is reflected from the clear blue trade-wind sky overhead, across the face of which went thousands of little balls of fleecy white clouds like rolls of cotton. Close hauled on the starboard tack, the *Wright* went forging through the ruffled sea as Joe said, "Like a bloomin' Vestern Hocean liner," heading northeast by north and gradually hauling more to the north as the skipper found by getting our position from the sun each noon, that we were pulling clear of the Brazil coast.

As soon as it was certain that we were in the trades, both watches were kept on deck in the afternoon and tarring down was the job. One day we got out all the old sails from the sail locker, sent down the new, strong sails we had bent for Cape Horn weather, and bent on the old patched ones in their place. And they were old sails; nearly every morning, when it got light enough to see aloft, a royal, to'gansel, or topsail was sure to be seen split from head to foot, while you could see the sun through the spanker.

Working aloft so much, we kept losing our caps overboard. As there were no more in the slop chest, we had to make the best shift we could. Joe lost two in one day and Albert had to wear his old so'wester all the time.

On April 12 we raised the island of Trinidad and had it in sight nearly all afternoon. It was a grim, barren-looking pile of rocks, but enough to give us crew members the bark's position. Charlie had a small geography book in his bunk and in it we found a map of South America and saw the island of Trinidad at twenty-three degrees, thirty minutes south latitude. So we knew just about where we were. Of course, the captain and mates knew well enough our position, but never gave it to any of us men. I used to keep account, as near as I could, of the number of miles we sailed each day and the course, and then reckon up, as near as possible, our position; but I always ran ahead of the ship.

After we passed Trinidad, we headed more to the north'ard and inside of three days were hauling to north-northwest. The trade winds held true day and night for over a week and by that time we had all the standing rigging tarred and blackened, and had started cleaning up the paintwork around the decks.

We were using wood ashes and water, but the mate hit upon a better plan for making a strong lye. He sent me down the fore hatch with a deck bucket and told me to fill it with saltpeter.

It was dark down there with everything on deck battened down to keep the water out. I could see no broken bags around the open fore hatch, so I crawled aft along the side of the ship in the 'tween decks, where there was a space left between the bags and the skin of the ship. I couldn't help thinking, as I crawled along like a rat, what my fate would be if the bark were to sink. I guess everyone has had the same feeling. It was just such a sensation as I felt once when I was a boy and crawled on hands and knees into a dark cave.

There was a ray of light shining down the main hatch, for the mate had thrown the tarpaulins off, and by its light I could see some white saltpeter lying there. I had to crawl on my stomach to get to it and in this position I filled the bucket. I was glad enough to get out of the fore hatch and into the sunlight again.

I didn't know what the mate was going to do with it until he got the cook's shovel from the coal box, filled it with saltpeter, and made me hold it over a barrel full of water. Then he took some hot coals from the galley stove and added them to the shovel.

I found out then though, for the stuff bubbled and smoked and then exploded with a bang that sent everyone present scurrying around the house. I let go of that shovel in a hurry and moved down out of the way of the hot ashes.

Saltpeter, or niter, is one of the ingredients used in the manufacture of gunpowder, but by the way it kept bursting on the shovel it seemed dangerous enough without adding anything to it. Parts of it seemed to be full of sulfur and thick, yellow smoke came off it, nearly choking us.

I held onto the tip end of the shovel while the mate kept putting the niter into it. Once he was just sprinkling some in when the whole business went up with a bang like a small cannon. I sat down plump on deck and nursed several small burns where the stuff spattered on me. The mate got a burn on his face and several on his hands that were quite painful. For several minutes the air was blue with sulfur fumes and strong English.

We dumped the ashes into the barrel of water until we had a strong alkali that would eat the dirt off anything. We scrubbed every bit of white paint with this wash to clean it of grease and dirt so the fresh coat of paint would stick.

The two boats stowed fore and aft on top of the fo'c'sle were also scrubbed, and then one day we rigged tackles aloft and hoisted them both off the house and onto the deck abaft the galley. This was done so the mate could put a new canvas cover on the roof of the forward house, the old one being torn and leaky. For three days we cut, tacked on, and then tarred the new canvas. During that time the boats lay side by side over the main hatch and took up nearly all of the deck thereabouts.

The nights were quite mild again and I took advantage of the time, when not at the wheel or on lookout, to get a little sleep. One night I crawled under one of the boats on the hatch and fell asleep. It was warm and nice under there and I slept as soundly as though I were in the fo'c'sle. In fact, I slept better than in my bunk, for now that we were up in hot weather again, the bugs came out of the wood until there was no sleeping in the fo'c'sle with them at all.

Many a time I lay in my bunk and amused myself watching the Croton bugs that filled the cracks of the bunk boards above me. I would take a match and start the line a-going at one end and watch them crowd by each other, like people on Broadway at noontime. They were packed like sardines, so if one moved he had to move those next to him. It was comical to see their two long feelers constantly waving to and fro like a line of sedge grass waving in the breeze.

They were harmless enough, but when one of them would drop on me, as they sometimes did, they gave me quite a start. Although they did not bite us, they got into our oilskins and ate the oil off them. The first time I noticed it, I thought I had scratched my suit on a nail or some other sharp thing, but when I showed them to Joe he said, "Vye dem's de Croton bugs."

Sometimes when we put on our oil coats, the bugs fell out by the dozens. Hansen nearly had a fit once when he pulled on his coat without shaking it to rid it of them. The bugs got down his back and tickled him so that the rest of us roared with laughter at his grimaces.

One time, when it was our watch below, I turned in with the crowd; but I hadn't been in my bunk more than half an hour when I decided to give it up to the bugs. I took my blanket out on deck and slept there. When I awoke at the sound of one bell, which was always struck ten minutes before eight bells to allow the watch time to dress, I jumped up thinking, as I was on deck, that it was our watch's turn to go below. But when I saw Joe, Hansen, and Lawson step out of the fo'c'sle, I was taken all aback and had to toss my blanket into my bunk and hurry aft with them. The constant changing of watches every four hours sometimes mixed me all up. I was not the only one, for at one time or other during the voyage, each one of us had been caught the same way.

As we neared the line, we ran into occasional rain squalls, but beyond clewing up a royal once in a while very little work of that sort was done. Once, I believe, we had to get the braces down from up in the rigging where they were stowed and haul the yards around. Lawson had thrown his old shoes over the lee rail and Fred had followed them with his rubber boots, a sure sign of a fair wind. Sure enough, the wind hauled almost dead astern and, with yards squared in and wind on the starboard quarter, the *Wright* crept north at the rate of three or four miles an hour.

Nearly all the dirty work, such as tarring down, was finished. One morning I was doing the last job of this kind, blackening the topsail sheets, when I met with an accident. The topsail sheets are of chain and lead under the fore and main yards and down at the front of the mast to the deck, where they are made fast around the heavy bitts. I was in a bos'ns chair with a can of black paint hanging clear under me, rubbing black paint on the links of chain with a piece of old flannel. The mate himself tended the gauntline I was on and lowered me down as I sang out, "Lower away," and I gradually came nearer and nearer to the deck. Below me were the main bitts with its many sheets and buntlines made fast to the pins. At the forward end of the bitts was a winch, which the mate had just scraped, cleaned, and painted a bright red.

I worked away wiping the outside of the links, running the flannel through each one to blacken it all and leave no holidays. The mate had eyes like a hawk and could see a bare spot if it were no bigger than a button. I never noticed that the second mate had made his clothesline fast from the galley to the mast just below me. The mate didn't see it either, until, just as he lowered me down a little more, the bark gave a roll and over I swung. The can caught on the clothesline and tipped over, dumping all the black paint down onto the red winch and the deck. The mate started to swear, but what he said I didn't hear, for he let go of the gauntline and down I came; saving myself from an ugly fall by grabbing hold of the chain.

Of course I got a dressing down for it. The spill was all my fault, I should have seen the line, where were my eyes? etc. As my watch was just going below to dinner, I had to get some kerosene and clean up the mess before I could go forward. But Mr. Hill was not as bad as the second mate, who sent two men in his watch up aloft and made them do some tarring down after six o'clock at night. This is something not usually expected of a sailor, but the second mate liked to show what a "hard case" he was and took such means as this, and swearing, to show it. But I noticed it was crazy Fred or poor little Hansen he gave these kinds of jobs to. Charlie and Jim were the buckoes of that watch and Old Jim got so mad at me when he couldn't make the fellows in our watch domineer over me that several times he pranced about, wanting to fight me or anyone else. But he was too old for us younger men to pitch into, so we just laughed at him and it became a byword with the mates to say, "Look out or Old Jim will get after you."

He was very easily irritated, being sick nearly all the homeward passage and constantly doctored by the captain.

On April 24 we crossed the line again on our way north, After the usual baffling calms in the doldrums under the equator, we caught the steady northeast trades and went bowling along, as if all the girls in Delaware had hold of our towline. We never touched a rope or went once into the rigging for more than two weeks.

But how we worked about the decks those days! The mate got out the holystones from the carpenter shop and put us to work one day, holystoning the varnish off the top of the after house and the half deck. Talk about work, I had often heard of holystoning decks and knew, from the descriptions I had read, that it was an arduous job, but the holystoning we did beat all I ever heard of. There wasn't a speck of sand aboard for scrubbing, and the stones we had were hard as flint and not the regular sandstone that is used.

First we wet the deck down all over and then, getting down on our knees in a row, we each took our "bible," or large stone, in our two hands and scrubbed back and forth across the grain of the planks until we had worn the wood bare. If we'd had sand to take hold and cut, it would have been easier, but without sand it sure made a man sweat to bear his weight and grind one of those stones back and forth all day. Our knees got so stiff and lame we had to fold our oilskins into a pad and kneel on them. When noontime came, only a small patch of deck was scrubbed bare, and all hands cursed at such work all during the meal.

It was my wheel when we turned to, and I was thankful for it. The two hours I stood steering the bark was a grateful rest. I watched the others scrub and dreaded to see the hands of the clock getting around to two o'clock. But they did and Joe was only too glad to drop his "prayer book" and take the wheel from me.

The stone he had been using was a small one and much softer than any of the others. It took hold and ground the wood down like sandpaper. The mate came around and watched us every little while, sometimes throwing a bucketful of water to wash away the pulp that the grindings formed under the stones. When he saw how the stone I was using ground the plank, he said, "Where's your big stone, Davis?"

"There it is," I answered, pointing to the block of stone the size of a paving block behind me. I did not use it because it was so hard to hold, it did not grind the deck at all, but slid back and forth over the wet planks. It was so heavy, I couldn't put my weight on it as I scrubbed and if I did it was so high it tipped and rolled over on my knuckles.

"Use the big stone," he ordered.

He watched me reluctantly take it and start rubbing with it and noticed that it did not grind any. He thought I was taking it easy, so he took hold of it and, gripping it low down, gave it three or four vicious grinds and said, "Grind so!"

"Oh! Yes!" I replied, meaning that it was easy enough to hold the stone that way for three or four grinds, but impossible for a man to keep it up, as we had to, all day. A man had to nurse his strength a little to keep up such work. I knew what the matter was well enough. The mates each had to holystone the floors of their staterooms, and as the stone I had was the best one in the ship, he wanted to save it for his own use, and so it proved later, but when I said, "Oh! Yes!" he flew into a rage.

"Oh! Yes!" he echoed. "You ___ ____ ____ __ _ ____ ! If you don't shut up, I'll break this stone over your head!" and he picked up a small holystone that one of the other men was using, as if to bring it down on my head.

That was one of the few times I found I had a temper. I was on my hands and knees, so he had an advantage over me. But the hard work I had been doing had given me muscles like a cat and I was ready to dodge and jump at him. As I waited for him to make a motion toward hitting me, I grew hot all over; I felt my blood go prickling into my fingertips and could hardly hold back my rising temper. I remember thinking at the time that if he didn't lay me out with the first blow, I'd lay him out for good. The work alone had made me mad, but to have him come around and bulldoze me was too much. I looked him square in the eyes and waited; but he didn't attempt to hit me, so I resumed my scrubbing.

For four days we were kept at this tiresome job, and at the end we had holy-stoned the cabin top and half deck. Then we started in cleaning all the white paint-work fore and aft with the soogy-moogy the mate had made with the burnt salt-peter. Charlie was kept at work sandpapering and then varnishing the poop, while Old Jim was made sail maker and sewed up the sails as we unbent and sent them down on deck. Two days in succession we sent the fore royal down after it split during the night. Once the gaff topsail split its full length, and so they kept going, now a jib and now a square sail as the rotten fabrics gave way to the fresh puffs of wind that increased the bark's speed at night.

Sometimes during the afternoons the old man himself stood at the wheel so that all hands might turn to and hurry along the cleaning up, for the bark was fast traveling north. When all the paint had been scrubbed, each man was given a pot of white paint and set at work laying on a fresh coat of white as fast as he could.

The mates kept going the rounds to see that each man was hard at work. Once the mate came along by the rail where Joe and Hansen were on their knees painting the inside of the bulwarks and stanchions, having a quiet chat as they worked. I was given the special job of painting the window sash red, and from where I sat I saw the mate go up to Joe and listen.

"Shut up that yaw-yawing!" he shouted and made the two separate so they could not speak to each other.

Chapter 23

Off Barbados—Gulfweed—Rats come on deck—A rat hunt—A rat in the fo'c'sle—Painting ship—Fred goes in swimming—A heavy sea and no wind—The bark gets pooped and the mate is soaked—We get a sounding—Nearing land—Tacking ship—Coasters in sight—The pilot schooner—A tug gets hold of us—Stowing sail—Off the Delaware Breakwater—The doctor examines us—Up the Delaware—A wreck—Our tug leaves us—A fair wind up the river—The man-of-war New York passes us—Pigeon Point, and at anchor—Good resolutions—Land sharks appear—Persuasions.

One day we passed a small brig, which the steward informed me was bound to Barbados, his native island.

"How far west is it, steward?" I asked him, for he was pretty well informed as to the ship's position and I wanted to find out how far north we were.

"About four hundred miles, due west," he answered.

Looking this up in Charlie's geography book, I saw we were in that betwixt and between latitude that lies just north of the equatorial current and south of the Gulf Stream. That's where the gulfweed floats along, sometimes in small patches and sometimes in fields miles in extent. To look at it, you would never think the bark could push her way through; but she did and left a long, open lane of water behind her like a canal. Portions of the grass, getting afoul of the bobstays, trailed along yards long under the stem, until some extra-deep plunge of the bow dislodged it.

The weather was delightful, rather hot during the middle of the day but balmy and warm at night. No one thought of going into the fo'c'sle to sleep, but stretched out instead on deck. I lay near the fore bitts one night, with Joe and the other two on the fore hatch. About midnight I was awakened by feeling something crawl up on my bare feet and come up my leg. I was so sleepy I thought it was Tobey, forgetting that he was overboard, so made no movement to scare him off. Up it came over my shoulder and I heard it sniffing at my neck and felt its whiskers tickling my ear; then I made a grab for it. Instead of Tobey, a large rat went across the deck and disappeared under the fo'c'sle head.

After that we saw several and all hands began to watch for them and chase them. One day one of the men, who happened to be up under the fo'c'sle head, saw a big brown rat come up through the chain pipe. It went scurrying aft with the man hot after it. It happened to be in the dogwatch, when we were below and, when we heard the noise, we jumped out on deck and joined in the rat hunt.

Such a time as we had for half an hour or so we never had before. All discipline was forgotten and the captain, mates, cook, and all hands went pell-mell fore and aft after that poor scared rat. Sometimes it went up on top of the forward house among the boats and booms stowed there, then down it jumped into the midst of us and nearly scared Hansen into fits when it used his neck and shoulders to land on. Hansen was on his hands and knees peering under the water cask when the rat landed on his neck, and the yell he let out sent it aft, flying between the old man's legs and onto the half deck with a volley of sticks and belaying pins at its heels. Even Old Jim, sour as he usually was, was roaring with laughter at the wheel, as the rat went down into the cabin with two men, the cook, cabin boy, captain, and mates all after it. But it went right through the cabin and came up the after companionway.

"Here he is! Here he is!" yelled Old Jim, letting go of the wheel to make a kick at the rat as it went around the wheel box, then forward over the house as we chased it. Sometimes it ran the whole length of the bark along the rail, at other times it dodged back and forth as each man made a whack at it with a rope or stick. Lawrence finally laid it out with a sweep of his broom handle, which caught Mr. Rat square on the nose.

Everybody was warm and excited after the chase, but it afforded a new topic of discussion and broke in upon our monotonous everyday life.

A few nights later our watch lay in our bunks, smoking our pipes and getting a little rest during the two hours we had below in the second dogwatch. I lay with my eyes vacantly fixed on the doorsill, thinking how much longer it would be before we reached the Delaware, when a little brown head with beadlike eyes and twitching, inquisitive nose appeared over the sill. I never moved, but waited until, attracted by the smell of food in the men's pans, the rat jumped into the fo'c'sle and ran under a bunk. Then out I jumped and slammed the door to.

"Vat de davel's de matter vid you?" demanded Joe, who lay in his bunk reading a book and who was startled by the sudden banging to of the door.

Albert and Lawson both lay with their necks craned out of the bunks, waiting to see what caused my sudden move. It was hard to see with the door shut, so I lit the lamp and said, "There's a rat in the fo'c'sle."

"Where?" asked Lawson as he jumped up and got hold of his boot. The rat, as if in answer to his question, shot across the floor and under another bunk.

We kept him on the go, now under one bunk, now another. Sometimes he jumped up into an upper bunk, eluding us for a time, but we turned over everything until out he jumped, scampering to another place. He knew well enough where he had come in, and every little while he jumped on the raised doorsill. Finding the door shut, up he went, sometimes as high as the roof and then off like a streak to some hiding place.

I had the broom and Lawson a couple of boots. Joe and Albert lay laughing in their bunks, watching us, for there was hardly room for the two of us to work, the place was so small.

We pulled out all the boxes, chests, and bags from under the lower bunks to give him no place to hide, but finally we lost him completely. We hunted high and low, but found no rat; we knew we had hit him once or twice and lamed him. Finally Lawson pulled out the old water barrel and there was the rat in a corner of the closet. I jabbed him with the broom and held him with just his nose sticking out, while Lawson held a lit match to it and so killed him. We proudly exhibited him at the main hatch to the mate and cook, and then hove him over the rail.

We soon had the painting all done except the white about the waterways near the lee scuppers. She was loaded so deep that the least sea washed in on deck. We plugged up all the scuppers, but even then the water came over the rail so we had to wait until we struck a calm one night, and then Joe went along with a lantern while I swabbed up the water and the mate slapped on some paint. The rail had been given a glossy black coat and the masts painted a wood color. All the little fittings sparkled under their new coat of paint and all the brass shown like gold, so that every little while you'd hear someone say, "My eyes! Don't she shine!"

Even the bright red stripes and names on the small boats had been touched up, all the deadeyes were scraped and oiled, and the stanchions along the to'gallant and fly rails were scraped and varnished. One afternoon, when the painting was nearly done, I was painting the gammon iron and bell standard black when Fred, of the other watch, came up on the bows, dressed only in a shirt and holding a long piece of old rope in his hand.

"Lower me down, Davis, will you?" he asked as he made a bowline fast around under his arms and fastened the other end on the bow.

"What are you going to do?" I asked, for I knew if the mate saw him he wouldn't let him go over the side.

"I'm going to take a swim."

"You can't swim as fast as that," I said, pointing down to the bubbles of foam going past about four miles an hour.

"Yes I can. You lower me down," and he put his legs over the bow. "Lower away!" he added, so I slacked away on the line until I heard him sing out "Ho!"

Then I took a turn and looked over to see how he was making out. He was striking out bravely enough, but the wash of the water swept him back against the bow and every time he kicked, his feet struck the planks. He paddled away, getting a good ducking every time a swell came along, until I thought he'd get drowned.

"Slack away! Slack away!" he shouted.

I paid out the line until he had all of it, but he was still shouting to slack away when I looked over to see where he was. Clear aft, under the cathead, he was floundering along, bumping against the side, unable to swim ahead of the bark. Then the line began to cut him and he shouted for me to haul him in. He weighed about a hundred and seventy pounds and I was not equal to the task of hauling him aboard. He made such a noise over the side that the cook and both mates came running forward to see what was the matter.

Together we hauled him aboard and the mate laughed so hard at the sight Fred presented that he couldn't give him the laying out he intended to. But Fred never tried to swim off the bow again.

We had variable weather after getting north of Barbados; as a rule it was fine, fair, summer weather, but occasionally we caught a heavy sea through which the bark went, plunging fo'c'sle head under. We sighted schooners and steamers every day and every day some sail aloft would burst and a couple of us were sent up with palm, needle, and twine to sew it up.

May 13 found us in latitude thirty-six north, longitude seventy-three west, rolling and tossing about in a high, short sea that threatened to roll the masts out and sent the topsails back against the mast with a slap that echoed up aloft like a thunder clap. All the light sails and courses had been furled to save them and when I took the wheel in the first dogwatch, I found her heading southwest with no steerage way on.

The seas were something fearful, evidently the result of some recent gale. They kept breaking aboard over the rail and flooding the decks; sometimes catching the bark a slap under the stern that shook her from end to end and smashed the water into foam for yards around. The bows would then be buried up to the foremast in a sea, and so the watch wore along.

The mate came aft with a brace and bit, chisel, and a hammer, and sat on deck in front of the binnacle box to fix one of the legs that had been knocked off. All of a sudden there came a rush of water behind me, the stern settled into the hollow and a sea came knee-deep over the rail. I jumped and got out of it, but it took the mate unawares. Sitting down as he was, the water came up to his neck and washed him, tools and all, across the deck. The look on his face was such a comical one that I laughed outright at him; just his head stuck out of the water, his mouth and eyes wide open, aghast.

When the water drained away and left him sitting on the deck, he turned to me and said, "What the devil you laughing at? I don't see anything funny to laugh at." But I did and burst out again as he picked himself up and went below to change out of his wet clothes.

We ran out of that heavy sea sometime during the night when our watch was below and all the next day we tacked ship against a headwind, with a cloudy sky overhead and thunder and lightning on the southern horizon, while inshore of us were three schooners, a barkentine, and a steamer, a sure sign that we were near the coast.

When the morning of the fifteenth dawned, we found there was nothing left of the flying jib but a mess of streaming rags flapping along the bolt rope, and the fore to'gansel had split almost three feet down the middle. Lawson and I went out and furled the rags of the jib; then, after we had washed down, Joe was sent out to unbend it and send in the rags while the mate and I sewed up the to'gansel.

The old man was on deck when we came down and ordered us to take a sounding. So we backed the main yards but got no bottom with the deep-sea lead at sixty fathoms. When we had filled away again and coiled down the braces, we got out another flying jib from the sail locker and had it bent by eight o'clock, when the other watch relieved us and we went below to get our breakfast.

That night a bounteous layout filled the mess pans and there was actually more than we could eat, which was as sure a sign as any that we were near land. While we were snoring away the forenoon in our bunks, the other fellows sent up and rove off the fish tackle and got the plugs out of the hawse pipes. All hands were kept up in the afternoon to shackle the cable to the anchors and hoist them over onto the rail, ready to let go at the stroke of a top maul.

Twice that afternoon we tacked ship and at suppertime we saw a steamer and a pilot schooner ahead and inshore of us. We had our flag for a pilot flying in the fore royal rigging, and in answer to it the schooner bore down toward us wing and wing.

Just before sunset we had the pilot close aboard, coming down on our weather bow before the long easy swells, so we backed our main yards to wait for him. Needless to say, all hands kept their eyes on that little schooner with a large black figure three on her mainsail. When she jibbed under our stern and came fore-reaching under our lee, I thought I had never seen a prettier sight in my life. She was a neat little craft, painted black and red, with a beautifully modeled hull that seemed to spring and curtsy to the long swells like a thing of life. She couldn't have been more than eighty feet long, a mere toy amid that broad expanse of ocean, yet her movements were enough to charm the eye of a sailor. Her low rail enabled us to see how they dumped the white yawl boat over the side and as soon as our pilot, who had jumped below for his valise, came up out of her small companionway, he dropped into the waiting yawl and came spinning toward us.

There was not more than a hundred yards between the two craft and, in a twinkling, the yawl was alongside and the pilot came up the side ladder we had dropped over for him.

The schooner lay stationary like ourselves, riding lightly on the swells. The pilot informed us she was the *Henry Edwards,* number three of the Delaware fleet. So, filling away our main yards, we left the *Edwards* ratcheting to windward, looking for more incoming vessels. We kept on making short boards until midnight, when the wind hauled fair and we laid our course for the Delaware under charge of the pilot who stood aft, talking to the old man and smoking a cigar.

We had just turned in at four A.M. after having been on deck since midnight, when Fred came into the fo'c'sle and said there was a tug alongside and for us to turn out. Of course I was tired, but the excitement of making land was so strong in me that I couldn't sleep. Stepping out on deck, I found it was still night. Close under our lee, a puffing, snorting, little tug was trying to keep pace with us. Its red light stared at us and the light from her pilot house and engine room reflected on our sails,

It was a windy night. The little tug jumped and splashed so that the old man and the tug captain had to shout to hear each other. When they had come to terms, the tug passed us her towing line, which we made fast to our bitts, and away she went ahead, with a shower of sparks pouring from her funnel.

At five o'clock the port watch was given its pot of coffee and, considering the fact that we had been on deck since midnight, we felt we should be given some, too. The steward wouldn't give us a drop, yet we had to stay up with the others and work after being up all night.

As it grew light enough to see, we started to clew up and furl the light sails, but held on to our topsails. About seven o'clock we were off the Delaware Breakwater and backed our main yards to wait for the quarantine steamer to come alongside.

This was my first view of the breakwater, so naturally I was interested in the long gray wall of rock that formed a shelter for the large fleet of vessels anchored beyond it.

A little white steamer came off and made fast alongside us and several men boarded us from her. For a few minutes they did nothing but ask and answer questions, while we in the crew looked awkwardly on from forward. Then the mate called all hands aft. We lined up along the port rail, cook, cabin boy, and all, while the doctor, with only one good eye, ran his gaze along the line, looking each one of us in the eyes.

"That'll do," he said, and I was astonished to find the examination, to see if there was any disease aboard, was over. Our looks certainly told for themselves that there was nothing the matter with us, for we were a hearty-looking lot of men after the hard work we had been trained to do.

As soon as the government tug left us, our tug started ahead again and the *Wright,* with her jibboom pointing up the muddy Delaware River, went plowing along as fast as steam and sail could drive her. We had not gone far before a drizzling rain set in and a stiff southeast wind drove the bark up on her towrope until we had to furl the fore upper topsail.

As we neared Brandywine Lighthouse we saw the masts of a recently sunken schooner sticking out of the water close. Our tug let go of us to steam over to the lighthouse and pick up the schooner's crew, who had saved themselves in their small boat.

On went the bark before the furious blasts of wind and rain that came driving along behind her, her topsails as hard as iron and a roll of foam at the bow, while tug and lighthouse both disappeared astern around a bend in the river.

All morning long there was no sign of the tug and all hands stood about the deck, encased in oilers keeping out of the driving rain in the lee of the house, or sometimes stepping into the fo'c'sle for a smoke and a yarn. When the tug appeared as a dot of steam astern, we clewed up and furled the main upper topsail to let her catch us. When she had us in tow again, we took in the two remaining sails and waited, doing nothing until we reached Pigeon Point, where we were to anchor.

It stopped raining about one o'clock and we stood on the fo'c'sle head, a group of wet but happy men. As we watched the welcome sight of green trees slipping by on either hand, something appeared ahead that puzzled the best of us. It looked like a dirty brown factory coming down the river, but as it grew larger and larger we saw it was a steamer, a new man-of-war, the *New York,* just leaving Cramp's shipyard for sea trials. As she passed close alongside, I drank in with amazement the tall stacks and the short masts, each with three turrets, one above the other. She had not yet been given her final coat of paint and much of her deck fittings were unfinished, but she went by us like a streak and our little bark gave one dip and curtsy as she rode through the *New York*'s wash, while that vessel disappeared down the river.

Nearing a point of land on our port bow, the mate came forward with a top maul to let go the anchor and told us that was Pigeon Point ahead. At the dock there we saw an old Cape Horn friend of ours, the *Coromandel,* unloading saltpeter.

We let go the tug's hawser and our pilot steered the *Wright* to about midstream opposite the point, where he gave the signal to anchor. With a heavy plunge, our starboard anchor went to the bottom and I was heartily glad to hear the roar of the cable as it went grinding through the iron hawse pipe.

When the tug started ahead, after hauling in her towing line, her propeller caught in the painter of the boat belonging to the shipwrecked schooner's crew—who stood huddled together with their chests and bags, watching us. The tug completely wrecked the small boat, cutting the bottom all out, so they cut her adrift and let her go floating away with the tide.

By the time we knocked off for supper, we had the bark pretty well stripped about the decks and found a very bounteous supper awaiting us; there was no excuse now for husbanding the stores as the voyage was practically ended.

All hands ate together and many were the schemes and plans laid out by the men to save their hard-earned money. Fred was going to pack up and go somewhere back in Maryland, where he had some relations. Joe was going to take a steamer direct for Holland to go back and see his mother, whom he had not seen since the day he ran away to sea from the sugar refinery where he worked six years ago. Once he got as far toward home as the village and stopped in the saloon to get a drink. But he never got any farther toward home; one drink led to another and when he sobered up he was at sea.

Hansen was going to start a tobacco shop and keep clear of the land sharks; they weren't going to get any of his payday. Lawson's mind was made up to keep clear of the rum shops. His last experience in the States had cost him dearly. He came ashore one night after a nine-month voyage with over a hundred dollars, got drunk, and woke up the next day to find himself on an outward-bound vessel with no money left.

After supper we lit our pipes and stood about, discussing our future plans, when a steamer came downstream towing a rowboat with two men in it.

"Ah! Here they come!" said Jim "Now let's see how long you remember your promises." For Jim was an old-timer and knew only too well the weak side of a sailor's nature.

Sure enough, when opposite us, they cast off from the steamer and rowed toward us.

"It don't take dem fellers long to smell a homeward bounder," said Joe.

"No, the bloody sharks know where the money is," replied Hansen.

And as the two men made their boat fast and came forward, all smiles, with their pleasant "Hello! Boys!" we all stepped into the fo'c'sle, our sea parlor, to receive them and their persuasions, which we knew would be advanced to get us to go to the boarding house they were the runners for.

Each house, or sailors' home as many of them are termed, has one man, called the runner, who does nothing but watch for incoming vessels, go aboard them, and try and get the sailors to come to his house. These two had probably heard from the tug that had towed us in and hurried down to be the first among us; for where we lay at anchor was some twelve or fourteen miles below Philadelphia.

They started in very gently, asking us what kind of ship the bark was, what kind of voyage we'd had, how long we had been out, and many other questions. I lay in my bunk, as did the others, while the runners came and stood by the side of us. I was amused to see how easily these men worked themselves into the good graces of my shipmates. One of them knew, or said he knew, a friend of Hansen's located somewhere in Philadelphia and that knowledge made him Hansen's fast friend.

One of the first persuasions they offered were a couple of well-filled whisky flasks. Another thing I noticed was how, when we said the ship was a poor home, they chimed in and denounced captains and ship owners louder than any of us.

One of them was the runner for Harry Grant's house and the other for Brown's boarding house. The former had a more earnest, persuasive way about him and got most of the men to say they would come to his house.

Charlie, the Prussian, and I had made up our minds to hire a room and not let any boarding master have the handling of our hard-earned money. Four years ago

Charlie had some friends, countrymen of his, living here. They kept a cigar store and he proposed going to them and taking a room. At first I was wary of such a proposition. I didn't know just what he meant by taking me among his friends and I didn't like to trust too much. But subsequent events made me ashamed of myself for thinking he'd had any other than honest motives in asking me to go with him. So when the runners offered me the bottle, I refused and said I was not going to any house. They thought I was only making excuses to go to some other place and insisted that I take a drink.

"Take a drink anyway," one of them urged, "whether you go with me or not." And then he added, "It's all right, good stuff!"

I tried to convince him that I never drank, but he wouldn't believe me, nor do I blame him, considering my surroundings. Old Jim finally told him it was no use arguing with me to take a drink, that I never touched liquor. Then he left me alone, but I knew he considered me as won because I said if I went to any sailors' boarding house, I'd go to his. It was nearly midnight before they left us and pocketed their empty bottles and rowed away.

Chapter 24

Rotten sails—Stripping the bark—I get impatient to go ashore—
We knock off—I borrow money from the captain—The runners try to
take my clothes bag—A haircut—The mates row us ashore—On our
way to Philadelphia in the train—I go with Charlie to his friend's to
board—We meet our shipmates—A gold watch—A temperance saloon—
We go down to Wilmington and get paid off—I buy a new suit of
clothes and arrive home that night—The end.

That night we stood anchor watches of one hour each. At six o'clock the next morning we washed down the decks and let all the sails loose to dry, for the sun had risen in a clear blue sky.

The sails by this time were rotten as punk. Many of them tore when we hauled on them, too rotten to bear their own weight. In fact, the fore upper topsail blew all to pieces with the gentle breeze that swelled the loose cloths.

Just before breakfast, a tug came alongside and the custom-house officers came aboard and examined our hatches to see that they had not yet been opened; then all hands were lined up on the poop again and our names were called off to see if all were there. We never did find out what became of Old Bill, who we had left on the mountainside behind Caleta Buena.

After a hearty breakfast we turned to unbending and sending down the sails that were now dry, rolling them up and stowing them away down in the sail locker. After that we spent the remainder of the day stripping off the chafing mats from the rigging and the rounding on the stays, racking off the halyards and all the running gear, except what we unrove and coiled away below. We quit work at seven o'clock that evening and I was mad with impatience to get ashore and go home.

"How much longer are they going to keep us lying here anchored in midstream?" I asked myself. And I lay awake a long time that night, thinking over what I would do when I got home and wondering what health I would find my folks in. For all I knew they might have died while I was away and I might find an empty home. Such thoughts as these kept passing through my mind and I longed to get ashore and get some news from home.

Next morning, May 18, after washing decks and doing a few small jobs such as putting the yawl on its davits, etc., we were told to "Knock off now!" and went scampering into the fo'c'sle like a lot of schoolboys just let out.

Clothes bags were hauled out and stuffed full of clothes, shoes, and bedding. When the runners arrived with a larger rowboat, nearly everybody piled into her, bag and baggage, glad to leave the bark.

I nearly had to fight with one of the runners to prevent him from taking my clothes bag into the boat. He insisted that I'd said I would go with him, but I got him to understand differently and got the cook to let me stow my bag in the galley while I went aft to ask the old man to lend me money enough to keep me until we were paid off.

I found him in a very good-natured frame of mind; he laughed and joked, promising to give me five dollars and set Charlie and me ashore at the dock. He told me there was a train that ran up to Wilmington every night with the workmen from the dock, and that we would be able to go up in that train.

Then I went forward and told Charlie it was all right, that I would go with him, so the runners put off with the rest of my mates and disappeared up the river.

During the afternoon, Charlie cut off some of my hair, for it was so long and curly it touched my shoulders and made me look like a wild man. When five o'-clock came around, we were rigged in our best shift, ready to depart. The old man came to the coach-house door and ordered the two mates to row us ashore. I could see they didn't like the job, the idea of a man, who had lorded it high-handed all the voyage, now rowing two ordinary sailors ashore. But it was the captain's orders and they had to obey. When all was ready, the mate suddenly remembered he had left his tobacco in his room and went back to get it, and again for his knife, until the captain came up on deck and told him to hurry up and put us ashore before the train left, or else we'd have to walk about five miles to Wilmington with our heavy clothes bags. This seemed to be just what the mate was trying to have happen, for he got the boat broadside on against the spiles of the dock, where the tide held her fast.

We shinned up on the dock and hauled the bags up after us, then we left the mates without so much as saying goodbye. We got on the train, which was filled with Negro workmen, and went up to the depot at Wilmington. Here we bought our tickets for Philadelphia and, while waiting for the train to come along, I sent a telegram to my mother, saying I would be home in a few days.

The sensations I felt sitting in the railroad car, watching the flying scenery along the line, are hard to describe. It seemed to me, as I looked down at my faded and worn blue suit and clumsy, convict-made shoes, as if I was looking out through some other person's eyes. The other passengers in the car were all respectable, well-dressed people and it warmed my heart to see my native countrymen once more and feel the refinement a woman's presence causes among men. The children prattling away seemed music to my ears, which for nine months or so had heard nothing but the coarse talk of men, hardened to the world by the rough usage it gave them.

When I remembered how I was dressed, I felt my cheeks grow hot and I couldn't blame the passengers for looking at us with curious glances, for our make-up was certainly grotesque. The only head covering I had was a small round sort of cloth jockey's cap that had shrunk with the washing I had given it until it just encircled the back of my head, while from under it my hair protruded in shocking disorder. It refused all attempts of the brush to make it lie smooth, and twisted and curled in every direction. The high-back seats hid a good part of me, so only the shoulders of my serge suit could be seen. Charlie, in the seat behind me, was a giant in stature. He had on the remains of a brown derby that somehow or other he had kept stowed away all the voyage. The rest of his clothes were, like mine, sadly the worse for wear.

But we were glad enough to be ashore again, no matter how we looked, and the first thing we did as we stepped out of the depot in Philadelphia was to hunt up a barber shop and get a shave and a haircut.

We had some difficulty finding the street car that would take us out to where Charlie's friends lived, but by making inquiries we got aboard the right one, which took us to Richmond, as the northern section of Philadelphia is called.

Charlie had not been here in four years and, as we stood on a corner under a gas lamp trying to remember where his friends lived, a man came by and glanced at us. "Hello!" he shouted. "Is that you Charlie?" and who should it be but an old acquaintance of Charlie's.

He told us where the cigar store was, and as we went down a side street I saw a high fence ahead, at the end of the street, with a large gate.

"What's that, Charlie?" I asked.

"That's Cramp's Shipyard," he replied. And I looked for the first time at the famous yard where many of our men-of-war are built.

Charlie's friends were located on a corner, where they kept the store and a boarding house. They were a thrifty old couple and received us with warm hearts as though we were their sons. But all the conversation was carried on in Prussian, of which I understood not one word. So while Charlie and all hands, including many friends who dropped in upon hearing that he was back, kept up an animated conversation, I sat waiting for the time when we should be shown our room, for I was tired and sleepy.

Charlie translated the drift of the conversation to me as we were undressing before turning in for the night. The bed had real sheets in it, a luxury indeed. It seems there were about five thousand workmen at Cramp's yard and they padded by the boarding house on their way to and from the yard. Charlie's friends had been trying for a long time to get a license to sell liquor, but another man on the next corner had got the license and was making money hand over fist.

The next morning, Friday, Charlie and I went back into Philadelphia to try and find out when and where we were to be paid off, for the captain couldn't tell us when we left whether it would be in Wilmington or Philadelphia.

At Harry Grant's we found Fred and Hansen together, out in brand new suits of clothes, new shoes, new hats, and I couldn't suppress a smile when they tugged at heavy watch chains, which they impressed upon me were solid gold. I looked closely at Hansen's and he, thinking I doubted his statement, settled the question by proudly informing me, "I know it's solid gold because de man said as it was." That, of course, was a clincher, so I said no more, but thought of that quotation "When ignorance is bliss, 'tis folly to be wise."

There were several men sitting around taking it easy, and up in the far corner, on a bench running around the wall of the room, I saw Old Jim, drunk as a lord. I couldn't help noticing how the sailor instinct showed itself in these men. There was a comfortable sitting room, with rockers and soft-bottomed chairs, adjoining this little room, which was really the entryway to the street, but not a soul was in there; while on the plain board seat in this bare room six of them were smoking and lounging about as if it was a dog watch in the fo'c'sle.

Charlie roused Old Jim and asked him where the others were.

"Let's go get them," suggested Fred; so we all started to leave, but not before Fred and Hansen swapped hats. There was a mirror in the room and in picking up their hats each tried on the others and Hansen asked me, "How do I look in this derby?"

"Better than you do in that sombrero," I replied.

"Will you swap, Fred?" asked Hansen.

"I'll go you," was Fred's reply, and they marched off with hats that a moment before were each other's, and never gave it a second thought. But to me it showed the depth of a sailor's thinking.

The five of us had a drink, then we got hold of Joe and Albert and stood about the corners, talking. Joe got me to one side and called my attention to his new suit of clothes, a loud black-and-brown check with squares like a checkerboard, and he also showed me his watch.

"Ve 'ave been to de te-ater," he added. "Had a bully good supper and all de drink ve vanted."

"Yes," I said, "and how much money have you got left?"

He made such a comical appearance as he laid one finger alongside his nose and looked at me, that I nearly laughed in his face.

"To tell you de troot, I ain't got over ten dollars coming to me," he answered.

"I thought you were going home?" I asked, reminding him of his good resolutions.

"Ah! Vell! Fot's de difference!" And turning to the others, he said, "Come on boys, let's have a drink."

As we walked up the block to a favorite saloon of theirs, I asked Joe where Lawson was.

"Vye! De bloody fool vent and got cut by a dago."

"Cut!" I repeated. "How was that? When did that happen?"

"Last night," he replied. "Ven ve come from de te-ater. I bought dis vatch for five dollars and Lawson he vanted von just like it for von dollar; de dago wouldn't give it to him for dot, so he started to go off vit it. Den dey got in a muss and Lawson got stuck in de neck. But it serves him right," he added as we stepped into the saloon.

Jim had partly sobered up by this time and all hands had a drink. I called for a glass of milk and expected to receive a sneer or a disgusted look from the bartender, as I was used to getting when I called for milk, but to my astonishment he looked at me and said, "That's right, young fellow, you stick to that and you'll be all right."

"Heavens," I thought, "what is this I've struck?" I made inquiries and found that there was a religious society that kept saloons, and in this way got hold of drunkards, suggesting to them when they called for a strong drink that they take something soft. There was also a law forbidding the sale of intoxicating liquors to men who showed that they were getting under the influence of it. Old Jim tried to start a row when the bartender refused him any more whiskey, but we bundled him out into the street and took him back to his boarding house.

Here we met the second mate of the ship *Thomas R. Dana,* which had lain astern of us in Valparaiso. His eyes were red, cheeks sunken, and he looked a living skeleton. He told us the *Dana* got around to New York all right, but from the time they left the coast until they reached New York they never left the pumps. Four men were chosen as quartermasters and they not only steered the ship, but scraped, cleaned, painted, and tarred her down while the others kept the pumps going day and night, stopping only when necessary to brace the yards or take in sail. I believed him, for as she lay at anchor in Valparaiso she was leaking badly, and all her crew had left, refusing to come around in her.

Charlie and I returned to our room for supper that night without having found out where we were to get our money.

But the next morning, the first thing we heard was the runner across the street shouting "Go down at once to Wilmington, the others have just gone." So we took the first train and found our way to the Deputy Collector's office, where we met the rest of the crowd waiting in the hallway as the office had not yet opened.

About noontime Captain Freeman and the Deputy Collector arrived with another man, whom the fellows said was the owner of the bark. In a few minutes I was called into the office, where behind desks sat the collector, captain, and owner. My name was read off, the date I had shipped, and the date we knocked off. After signing my name, my pay was counted out in bills and silver to the amount of $75.07, and I was given my discharge paper as an able seaman, which ended my career as a deepwater man.

One at a time the others were called in and paid off. Those who had not run away, nor taken much from the slop chest, got as much as a hundred and twenty or thirty dollars; but I was glad enough to get back home again at any cost, for I could earn as much here in a month as I received for ten month's work at sea. But the training and experience I had was certainly worth a great deal to me. My eyes were entirely cured of their weakness and I felt strong enough to knock over a bull.

That morning at the Wilmington train depot, Lawson got so drunk the runners had to lift him into the baggage car, taking care of him and his money, especially the latter.

As for me, I went at once to a clothing store and bought myself a complete new outfit and took the first train for New York.

About ten o'clock that night I rang the doorbell of my father's house in South Brooklyn, and . . . well you can imagine the reception I got.

The End